Cotton was King

Indian Farms to Lauderdale County Plantations

Alabama Plantation Series

Rickey Butch Walker & William L. McDonald

Bluewater Publication
Killen, AL 35645
Bluewaterpublications.com

Copyright 2018 © Bluewater Publications

First Edition

All rights reserved under International and Pan-American Copyright Convention. No part of this publication may be reproduced or transmitted in any form or by any means, electronic or mechanical, including photocopying, recording, or by any information storage and retrieval system, without prior written permission from the Publisher.

Published in the United States by Bluewater Publications.
Printed in the United States of America.

This work is based on the authors' personal interpretation of research.

Acknowledgements

Colonel William Lindsey McDonald and his family are credited for "Cotton was King." With emphasis on Lauderdale County, Alabama, the book was especially enhanced by Mrs. Dot McDonald allowing me to use some of the stories that had been written by her late husband. Angela Broyles of Bluewater Publishing had developed an agreement for me to use some of Mr. McDonald's writings in completion of the book with the permission of his family. Without the cooperation of the William Lindsey McDonald family and Angela Broyles, the contents of this book would be greatly diminished. Since I was an admiring fan of Colonel William L. McDonald's writings, I was very much honored to co-author the book. I greatly appreciate the opportunity that I was given to write and co-author this book.

Yoland Morgan Smith, a local historian, was also very helpful in the completion of this book. She provided family information on many of the cotton planters of Lauderdale County. Her work was very valuable in the development of "Cotton was King."

Dr. David Curott was very helpful in editing the book, "Cotton was King." He was kind enough to convert my series of 1830-1860 tables of cotton planters and the number of their slaves into a single document. Dr. Curott also provided some historic markers and did the book review to which I am very grateful.

**Bluewater Publications
books by
Rickey Butch Walker**

Appalachian Indians of the Warrior Mountains: History and Culture, ISBN 978-1-934610-72-5, $19.95

Appalachian Indian Trails of the Chickamauga: Lower Cherokee Settlements, ISBN 978-1-934610-91-6, $19.95

Celtic Indian Boy of Appalachia: A Scots Irish Cherokee Childhood, ISBN 978-1-934610-75-6, $19.95

Chickasaw Chief George Colbert: His Family and His Country, ISBN 978-1-934610-71-8, $19.95

Doublehead: Last Chickamauga Cherokee Chief, ISBN 978-1-934610-67-1, $19.95

Hiking Sipsey: A Family's Fight for Eastern Wilderness, ISBN 978-1-934610-93-0, $19.95

Soldier's Wife: Cotton Fields to Berlin and Tripoli, ISBN-978-1-934610-12-1, $19.95

Warrior Mountains Folklore: American Indian and Celtic History in the Southeast, ISBN 978-1-934610-65-7, $24.95

Warrior Mountains Indian Heritage-Teacher's Edition, ISBN 978-1-934610-27-5, $39.95

Warrior Mountains Indian Heritage-Student Edition, ISBN 978-1-934610-66-4, $24.95

Table of Contents

CHAPTER 1-INDIAN FARMERS 2

Doublehead's Reservation 2

Doublehead's Trading Post 12

Doublehead's Bluewater Home 14

Doublehead's Slaves 17

Doublehead's Assassination 23

George Colbert's Reservation 28

CHAPTER 2-LAUDERDALE SETTLEMENT 40

Captain John D. Chisholm of Tennessee 42

John Donelson's Muscle Shoals 56

Lauderdale County 62

Early Cotton Mills of Lauderdale County 65

Cotton Planters and the Number of Slaves 68

CHAPTER 3-COTTON PLANTERS OF LAUDERDALE 74

Armistead, Peter Fontaine I 75

Bailey, Jonathan-Bailey Springs 80

Baker, Elijah Adam 84

Barbee, Alfred Asbury 87

Beckwith, Jonathan 90

Binford, Hugh 95

Boddie, Nathan 99

Casey, Elisabeth Duckett 104

Coffee, John R.-Hickory Hills Plantation 106

Collier, Wyatt-The Oaks Plantation 116

Coulter, George-Mapleton 121

Foster, Thomas Jefferson-Malone House 126

Hannah, Alex John William 129

Hough, Joseph 133

Houston, David Ross-Wildwood Plantation 138

Ingram, Benjamin 146

Jackson, James III- The Sinks Plantation 150

Jackson, James-Forks of Cypress Plantation 154

Kernachan, Abraham and Robert 165

Key, William Henry-Buck Key Plantation 172

McDonald, James T.-Glenco Plantation 177

McVay, Hugh-Mars Hill Plantation 180

Nichols, John Martin-Nichols Hill 184

Noel, James Alexander 186

Patton, Robert Miller-Sweetwater Plantation 187

Peters, John 200

Rapier, Richard-Merchant Prince of Cotton 202

Rowell, Neal-Alba Wood Plantation 204

Simpson, John 206

Smith, Henry D. 210

Thompson, Joseph 212

Waits, James-Grandfather of T. S. Stribling 213

Weakley, James H. 217

Wood, Alexander Hamilton 220

Resources: 223

Index 226

Cotton was King

Indian Farms
to
Lauderdale County Plantations

During the early 1800's, Chickamauga Cherokee Chief Doublehead and Chickasaw Chief George Colbert were two of the largest land owning Indian cotton planters and black slave holders in the area of Lauderdale County, Alabama. Doublehead owned Doublehead's Reserve in the southeastern portion of Lauderdale County, and Gorge Colbert owned Colbert's Reserve in the southwestern portion of Lauderdale County.

The eastern and western boundaries of Doublehead's Reserve extended some ten miles north of the Tennessee River up the streams of Elk River to the east and Cypress Creek to the west. The northern boundary run some 40 miles parallel to the north shore of the river between Elk River and Cypress Creek. Doublehead's Reserve was some 400 square miles consisting of some 250,000 acres. In combination with his Irish brother-in-law John Melton, they owned 100 black slaves that they were using to farm cotton along the Elk River Shoals and Big Muscle Shoals.

George Colbert's Reserve extended some four miles north of the Tennessee River with the northern boundary running some 12 miles parallel to the north river bank. George Colbert's Reserve was some 48 square miles consisting of about 31,000 acres in the southwestern portion of Lauderdale County, Alabama. Colbert's Reserve was somewhat centered on the north landing of Colbert's Ferry crossing of Natchez Trace. By the time George Colbert was removed west of the Mississippi River, he owned some 150 black slaves who raised cotton on his plantation at Tupelo, Mississippi, and later in the Fort Towson area near the Red River in Oklahoma.

Chapter 1-Indian Farmers

Chickasaw Chief George Colbert was Doublehead's double son-in-law by his marriage to two of Doublehead's daughters Tuskiahooto and Saleechie. While living in northwest Alabama, Doublehead was actually living on land at the Muscle Shoals which was recognized as Chickasaw Territory by the Chickasaw Boundary Treaty of January 10, 1786. George Colbert stated that Doublehead was living and occupying the Muscle Shoals by his permission.

On April 26, 1805, General James Robertson of Nashville, Tennessee, sent a letter which states, "Since I saw you I have had a copy of the parchment given the Chickasaws by President Washington to thare clame of land North of Tennessee, and I have seen George Colbert and another Chickasaw chief who gave me the grounds for their clame, which I now think much better and stronger than I formerly had vewed it I will give you a sketch of thare clame… that from those repeated wars they the Cherokees had fell back and encroached on the lands of the Chickasaws. George Colbert asserts that Doublehead settled at the Shoals by his permition."

Doublehead's Reservation

During the 1770's, the Chickamauga faction of Lower Cherokees under the leadership of Doublehead planted villages along the Muscle Shoals area of the Tennessee River in the last quarter of the eighteenth century. There was Mouse Town at the mouth of Fox's Creek, Doublehead's Town at Browns Ferry, Melton's Bluff in present-day Lawrence County, Rogers' Ville west of Elk River in Lauderdale County, the large Lower Cherokee settlement of Shoal Town at "the mouth of Town Creek, extending a mile along the river and far up the creek" (Leftwich, 1935), Coldwater near Big Spring in present-day Tuscumbia, and Doublehead's Village north of present-day Cherokee in Colbert County. Other smaller Indian villages and Cherokee farms lay scattered between the larger Chickamauga settlements.

Doublehead-Chickamauga Warrior

Doublehead's terrible atrocities certainly added up to a significant sum especially in the Cumberland Settlements. In the early 1800's, Judge Haywood said he had more blood on his hands than anyone at that time in history. During the Chickamauga War from 1775 to 1795, Doublehead's reign of terror and raids on white settlers lasted 20 years and is well documented, even to the point of cannibalism. Chickamauga refers to the southeastern tribes, mainly Lower Cherokees and Upper Creeks, who were being supplied British arms and ammunitions by John McDonald who lived on Chickamauga Creek not far south of Chattanooga, Tennessee.

In June 1794, Doublehead led a Cherokee delegation to Philadelphia to meet with President George Washington. Doublehead became the center of attention of the president and other dignitaries. On June 26, 1794, Doublehead negotiated with President Washington and other government officials after which he signed for lasting peace with the whites in the Treaty of Philadelphia. He was assured $5,000.00 per year for his Cherokee people; however, his raids did not end until 1795.

Doublehead-Chickamauga Warrior

Doublehead's last major assault on the Cumberland settlers was against Valentine Sevier, the brother of Colonel John Sevier. John Sevier's army had been responsible for killing Pumpkin Boy, Standing Turkey, and Old Tassel, who were Doublehead's brothers, in addition to other relatives. Some four months after signing the Treaty of Philadelphia, Doublehead and some 15 of his fellow warriors were said to have viciously attacked the settlement of Valentine Sevier. "Valentine's Station near

Clarksville, Tennessee, was attacked by Chief Doublehead on November 11, 1794. The old frontiersman stood off the Chickamauga, but his daughter and her husband, Charles Snyder, and his son, Joseph Sevier, were killed in Snyder's cabin. His daughter Rebecca was wounded and scalped, but she eventually recovered. A frontiersman, who came to their assistance from Clarksville, reported that there were twelve or fifteen Indians. The Colonel prevented the savage band from entering his house, but they cruelly slaughtered all around him" (Brown, 1938).

Even though Doublehead had signed a peace treaty with President George Washington in June 1794, he ended his bloody war about one year later. Doublehead was not known to participate in another raid or battle after June 1795. After the end of his warpath, Doublehead became a changed man and sought peace with the white settlers. It would be the last twelve years of his life that Doublehead would become a peace seeking warrior. Doublehead would become dedicated to his business interests, and he would eventually lease portions of his reserve in present-day Lauderdale County to white settlers.

Doublehead-Cotton Planter

Within a year after signing the peace treaty, Doublehead turned his attention from war to his farming of cotton and his trading post at the mouth of Bluewater Creek. He quickly became very successful as owner of the large tract of land known as Doublehead's Reservation. Prior to his death, Doublehead became a very wealthy cotton planter and owner of some 40 black slaves. Together with his white brother-in-law Irishman John Melton, they owned 100 black slaves; John had married Doublehead's youngest sister Ocuma. Doublehead negotiated with the government for a cotton gin to be placed at Melton's Bluff.

Though he began to mimic the ways of the whites, Doublehead's change of heart was characteristic of other Cherokees during this time, many of whom adopted the manners and customs of the white settlers. Doublehead built a large house near Bluewater Creek in Lauderdale County, Alabama, but he continued to defend the Cherokees land rights. However, in various treaties, he accepted bribes which eventually led to his death. Doublehead with the help of Captain

John D. Chisholm formed the Doublehead Company that leased up to 1,000 acres in Doublehead's Reserve to more than 50 white settlers between the Elk River and Cypress Creek.

Legends have it that Doublehead was at other places at the Muscle Shoals from time to time. One site was near the home of his double son-in-law, George

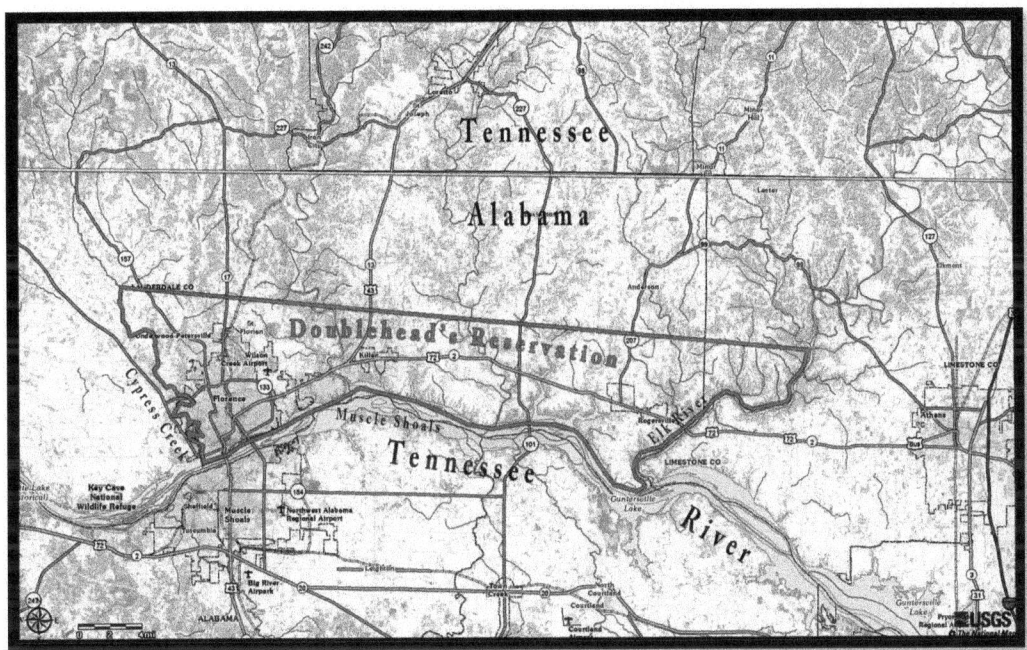

Colbert, north of Cherokee in present-day Colbert County, Alabama. The Chickamauga Cherokee Indian settlement near the Tennessee River in Colbert County was known as Doublehead's Village; this village site was located in the territory of the Chickasaw Nation. At that location, there is another nearby Doublehead Spring that is also shown on old maps at the site of Doublehead's Village. The other Doublehead's Spring is just west of the mouth of Bluewater Creek in Lauderdale County.

Old stories remembered by the family of James Jackson tell that Doublehead's son, Doublehead Doublehead, lived briefly on the knoll where the mansion at the Forks of Cypress once stood. In recent years, trade beads and other Indian artifacts were uncovered from the ruins of an early log house at this site. A few miles west of the Forks of Cypress was a cave where old-timers recalled seeing an Indian carving showing double heads at its entrance.

By treaty with the United States, Doublehead owned Doublehead's Reservation in the southeastern portion of Lauderdale County, Alabama. His reserve extended some 10 miles north of the Tennessee River from Elk River to Cypress Creek and ran some 40 miles parallel to the river. Doublehead's Reserve was recognized by the United States government as belonging to Doublehead and his heirs for 99 years renewable for 900 years; however, immediately after Doublehead's death, the government voided the treaty and did away with any claims to the area.

In 1798, federal efforts to assimilate the Cherokee economically and culturally began in earnest with the signing of the Tellico Block House Treaty. The United States government established gristmills and provided cottonseed, spinning wheels, and looms to the Cherokee. Federal agents were sent to teach farming techniques such as plowing and fence building. The "worm or angle" fences were zigzag fences made of split rails crossed at the ends.

Doublehead was instrumental in trading with the white folks passing through the territory he controlled; he also leased Cherokee lands to white farmers and settlers. By 1801 because of the increasing importance of trade with the whites, Doublehead was allowing white people to freely pass through his area at the Muscle Shoals. According to History of Alabama by Albert James Pickett (1851), "Dec. 1801: Emigrants flocked to the Mississippi Territory…constructing flat-boats at Knoxville, they floated down the river to the head of the Muscle Shoals, where they disembarked at the house of Double-Head, a Cherokee Chief…placing their effects upon the horses, which had been brought down by land from Knoxville, they departed on foot for the Bigby settlements." This migration by white settlers was after Doublehead's raids had ended, and he had accepted peace with the whites in June 1794.

On May 7, 1799, David Henley, Indian agent of War Department, wrote a letter to Doublehead praising improvement of the Indians in growing cotton and corn. Henley also acknowledges the Cherokees are spinning and weaving their cotton. On May 8, 1799, David Henley sent a letter by Doublehead and his letter of response to Secretary of War James McHenry to keep him informed.

After December 1801 or early 1802, Doublehead was living on the Tennessee River at Shoal Town and operating his trading post in present-day Lauderdale County, Alabama. By 1802, Doublehead had moved from the Lower Cherokee village of Doublehead's Town at Browns Ferry to Shoal Town which was located on Big Muscle Shoals of the Tennessee River between Big Nance's (Path Killer's) Creek, (Shoal) Town Creek, and Bluewater Creek.

As early as 1802, Doublehead requested from the United States government a keel to transport his cotton to New Orleans. After moving to Shoal Town, Doublehead continues his cotton farming operations and wants the transportation capability to send his cotton to the New Orleans market. According to a letter found in Henry Thompson Malone's book, "Cherokees of the Old South: A People in Transition" (1956), Doublehead sends a letter to Return Jonathan Meigs, Indian agent at Old Hiwassee Garrison near present-day Calhoun, Tennessee. On November 20, 1802, Doublehead requested a keel boat for transporting his produce.

"Sir:

When I saw you at the Green Corn Dance…you Desired me to come and see you and get some goods from you-My intention is to come and trade with you. But I am so Engaged Hunting and Gathering my beef cattle that I expect it will be a moone or two before I can come-I…have now one Request to ask of you-that is to have me a boat Built-I want a good Keal Boat some 30 to 35 feet in length and 7 feet wide-I want her for the purpose of Descending the River to Orlians & back I want her to be lite & well calculated to stem the Streem I am Determined to by the Produce of this place & the Return back by Water…I shall want two of your big guns to mount on the Boat-I am Determined for to see up the White & Red Rivers in my Route & open a trade with the western wild Indians-Let me here from you soon.

    I am Sir Your Reale
    Friend & Brother
    Doublehead
    Wrote by J. D. Chisholm
    Who presents his Compliments"

Doublehead wanted to expand his farm trade with people in New Orleans and the western wild Indians by keel boat. He offered a description for the boat he wants and expected the government to construct the boat. In 1803, Doublehead was promised a new boat for signing the treaty that authorized the Federal Road through Georgia. Bird Doublehead, the son of Doublehead, confirmed in an 1838 affidavit that his father sold some of his goods from his boat and stored the rest at his trading post; therefore, he did use his boat for trade as he had promised.

The government also agreed to build a spur of the Georgia Road to Doublehead's trading post at the mouth of Bluewater Creek on the Muscle Shoals. "After a complicated process of negotiations, an agreement was reached in October 1803 that defined terms for the Georgia Road. Doublehead, initially one of the strongest opponents of the road, was guaranteed operation of the ferry at Fort Southwest Point. The ferry was owned by the Cherokee Nation, but Doublehead was given control of the lucrative business. Doublehead further profited from the treaty by a provision guaranteeing that a spur of the Georgia Road would be built leading to his trading post miles away at Muscle Shoals" (McLoughlin, 1986). Doublehead's double son-in-law Samuel Riley ran the ferry at Southwest Point where the Clinch River runs into the Tennessee River. Samuel was married to Doublehead's daughters Nigodigeyu and Gulustiyu.

It is not certain that efforts were made to extend the road to Doublehead's trading post at the Muscle Shoals, but it is for certain he had a market with the government for his beef cattle as observed by Reverend Patrick Wilson in 1803. Wilson mentions that Tal Tsuske (Doublehead) supplied beef to a garrison on the Tennessee River below the Muscle Shoals. Wilson observed that the Chickamauga Cherokees controlled the Big Bend area all the way to the Natchez Trace crossing of the Tennessee River.

In 1803, Reverend Patrick Wilson traveled along the southern side to the Tennessee River and followed the South River Road. Today, the road is still known as the River Road in Morgan and Colbert Counties. The following excerpt describes the route, "The expedition continued on the Natchez Trace to present-day (Colbert County) Alabama, where Wilson observed land controlled by the Chickamauga Cherokee, who, although interested in European American material culture, were highly resistant to territorial encroachment in the Tennessee Valley.

Wilson is impressed with the Cherokee "advances in civilization" citing their ability to make and repair "accurately and strongly" laid fences. He draws particular attention to a cooperative work endeavor, which he compares to "an American frolic or barn raising."

At the Muscle Shoals, west of present-day Florence, Alabama, the Wilson's expedition left the Natchez Trace to follow (the River Road along) the south bank of the Tennessee River. Here the party rested in a Chickamauga Cherokee town (Doublehead's Town) administered by Tal Tsuska (Doublehead), a controversial and historically significant chief who controlled transportation routes, leased land to settlers, and led resistance against European American encroachment. Tal Tsuske and his followers controlled the Muscle Shoals area for many years" (Hathorn and Sabino, 2001).

By the time of Reverend Patrick Wilson's expedition and journey through Doublehead's territory in 1803, Doublehead had already moved from Doublehead's Town at Brown's Ferry to the Chickamauga Cherokee village known as Shoal Town. In early 1802, Doublehead made his move from the south side of the river in present-day Lawrence County, Alabama, to Shoal Town on the north side of the Tennessee River in present-day Lauderdale County, Alabama. He lived on the north side of the Tennessee River in Lauderdale County where he operated his large trading post, store, or stand at the mouth of Bluewater Creek.

Because Tal Tsuske's (Doublehead) house was located on the north side of the Shoals, Wilson's expedition party stayed with another Chickamauga chief, Skiowska. Patrick Wilson described the Cherokee home in a most detailed narrative, "Not only were Skiowska's wife's kitchen and household furniture in good order, but she also used plates, bowls, tea cups and saucers, a tea kettle and coffee pot, and churned butter in a churn with a proper dasher and lid to provide for her visitors. Wilson documents her use of the large Indian spoon, an artifact that even today has communal significance among southeastern tribes" (Hathorn and Sabino, 2001).

The rich bottomlands around Doublehead's Bluewater home at Shoal Town did not always produce an abundant harvest. A severe drought in 1804 brought an appeal for help. In an 1804 letter, Doublehead requested assistance from the UnitedStates Government because of the total failure of the corn crop. Doublehead was no stranger to the government when asking for help, money, or handouts. The Cherokee Agent at Hiwassee sent three hundred bushels of corn for which he billed Doublehead a total of $150.00 for this relief. However, records reveal that this amount was later returned to the village by the War Department.

The particular letter was sent from Doublehead at Shoal Town to Return J. Meigs, Indian agent at Hiwassee Garrison. The circumstances were recorded in Malone's (1956) book, "A scarcity of corn caused by a drought in the Cherokee Nation during the year 1804 was a crisis which Meigs faced in his typical fashion. The first request for food came from Doublehead and other Cherokees in the Muscle Shoals area on the Lower Tennessee River. The Agent immediately sent them three hundred bushels of corn, for which the Indians paid $110. Meigs, however, requested and received permission from the War Department to return the money; he thought it his duty 'to give the necessary relief- believing that humanity and interest combine to make it proper especially when interesting negotiations with them are now soon to be opened.' Meigs' policy pleased his government. Henry Dearborn sent him the President's congratulations, urging Meigs to continue helping needy Indians:

Colonel Return Jonathan Meigs
12/19/1740-1/28/1823

You will embrace so favorable an opportunity for impressing the minds of the Cherokees with the fatherly concern and attention of the President to the distresses of his red children."

Doublehead's Trading Post

By the Treaty of Philadelphia in 1794, Doublehead was granted a trading post on a large land reserve on the Tennessee River in the area of Bluewater Creek in present-day Lauderdale County, Alabama. The trading post was located at the Lower Chickamauga Cherokee village known as Shoal Town which was adjacent to Big Muscle Shoals.

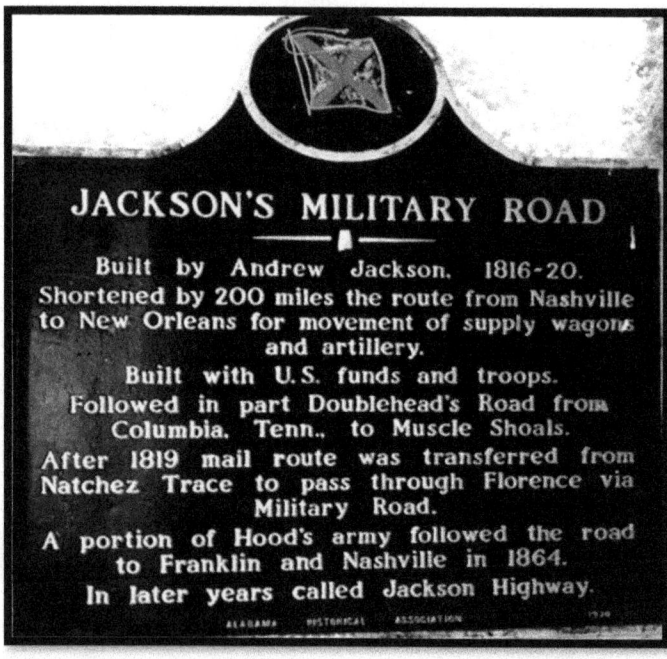

Early pioneers described Doublehead's trading post as being on the east bank of the Bluewater Creek. The trading post was at the mouth of Bluewater Creek where it runs into the Tennessee River at the point where Doublehead's Trace crossed the Tennessee River. The Trace crossed the river from Lauderdale County by an early Bluewater Ferry to Green Bluff between Big Nance's Creek and Town Creek in present-day Lawrence County, Alabama.

According to Return J. Meigs letter to Secretary of War dated December 1, 1809, Doublehead and his Lower Cherokee followers had built the 100 mile Doublehead Trace from Franklin, Tennessee, to the Muscle Shoals. According to the 1970 historic marker, notice that Jackson's Military Road followed Doublehead's Road from Columbia, Tennessee, to the Muscle Shoals. Doublehead's Trace forked at Loretta, Tennessee, with the east fork crossing at Shoal Town and the other fork crossing the Tennessee River at Bainbridge Ferry.

Doublehead's Trading Post was located where his road crossed the Tennessee River at the east mouth of Bluewater Creek to Green Bluff. Doublehead sold merchandise to the Chickasaws, Creeks, Shawnees, Cherokees, Yuchi, and white settlers leasing Doublehead's Reserve. Three affidavits given in 1838 by Caleb Starr, Catherine Spencer, and Bird Doublehead confirm Doublehead's trading post at the mouth of Bluewater Creek.

Caleb Starr

Caleb Starr tells about the different tribal people who traded at Doublehead's Trading Post. The following is part of the sworn testimony of Starr who gave his statements on August 11, 1838. "Affiant understands from everybody that Doublehead kept a dry goods Indian trading store at the reservation and it was a great place to trade, for it was near to the Creeks, near to the Chickasaws, and in the Cherokee Nation, and a good supply of goods at that place, such as the place and times _____ without _____ have been equal to all the stores now in this place and it was when goods were sold to Cherokees for money and skins and no auditing. Sworn to and subscribed before me, 11th of August 1838, James Liddel."

Bird Doublehead

Bird Doublehead in a sworn affidavit given on June 21, 1838, remembers the following about the store his father Doublehead owned. "Affiant remembers that…stock of goods, and after selling some of them in the boat, he put the balance in the store with the other goods and a white man called Phillips kept the store. Affiant thinks there could not have been less than $3000 worth of goods in the store. Affiant thinks the goods were not sold on a credit."

Catherine Spencer

In an affidavit on June 8, 1838, Catherine Spencer, daughter of Pumpkin Boy and niece of Doublehead, gave the following statement about Doublehead's Trading Post. "Affiant states that Doublehead had a store there and a white man named Phillips was the clerk…and the Cherokee people came there daily and bought goods for cash, and Phillips refused to sell goods on a credit to the Cherokees. It was commendable stock worth about two or three thousand dollars, and Doublehead told affiant just before he was killed that he had three thousand dollars in a trunk in the store room. Affiant says large quantities of money in Phillips hands but cannot state how much as she never counted it; affiant did not know of her uncle buying anything after that time and thinks there would have been as much as more than $3,000 cash on hand… Affiant states that as soon as the news came that Doublehead was killed Phillips shut up the store and kept it shut up and quit selling goods." Based on the testimony of Catherine Spencer, the Doublehead' Trading Post closed shortly after August 9, 1807; the date of Doublehead's assassination.

Doublehead's Bluewater Home

Approximately one fourth mile downstream from Doublehead's trading post on the west side of the mouth of Bluewater Creek is a high rock palisade along the north bank of the Tennessee River that appears on early maps as "Doublehead Bluff." In the same area there is "Doublehead's Spring" which is less than one quarter mile west of the mouth of Bluewater Creek.

Doublehead's Spring just west of Blue Water Creek-1823

Doublehead's final home was on the north side of the Tennessee River at Shoal Town between Center Star and Elgin in East Lauderdale County, Alabama. Doublehead lived at Shoal Town from 1802 until his death on August 9, 1807.

Around 1802, Doublehead built a large two story house overlooking the Bluewater Oldfields lying east of Bluewater Creek adjacent to the North River Road in Lauderdale County, Alabama. Doublehead's home was styled after some of the cotton plantation houses in the east that he had seen in his trips to Washington, D.C. Territorial records indicate that the house where Doublehead lived was commodious.

On one occasion, Doublehead wrote the Cherokee Agent requesting aid for two poor middle-aged women living at his place with large families composed entirely of girls. An east Tennessee paper reported that Doublehead's home may have operated as a house of entertainment. The description would lead one to think that it might have supported Doublehead by serving as one of the oldest female professions.

Doublehead's Home at Bluewater Oldfields

The house of Doublehead may have been used by the Samuel Adams family. In a letter dated July 20, 1802, Doublehead had requested permission for this family of sixteen people to enter his village "in the plan of promoting civilization amongst the Cherokees." Later that summer, Silas Dinsmoore, Choctaw Indian Agent, while travelling over the Natchez Trace, was surprised to find this family here. He called them "a pretty dismal group-lazy and shiftless."

In 1818, Daniel White purchased the Doublehead's home place and used the house as a stage stop known as Wayside Inn. Some think that White may have had a "claim" to Doublehead's house as early as 1812.

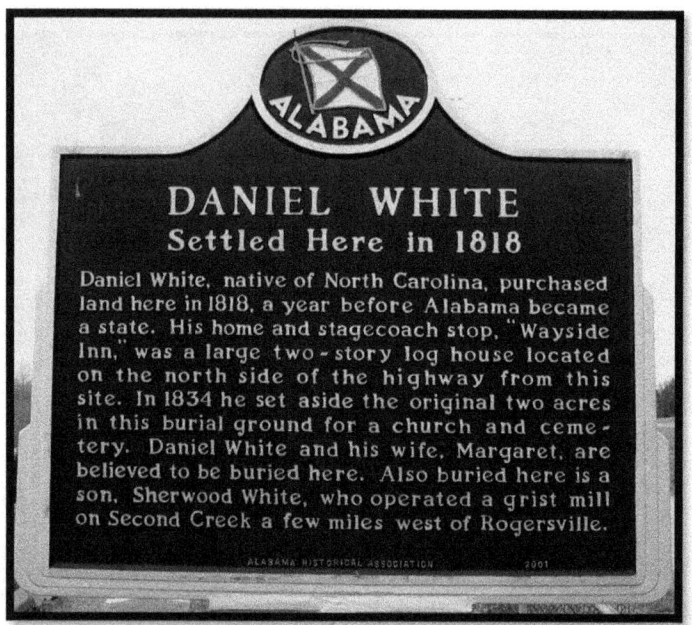

According to the 1809 census of Cherokee Indians by Return J. Meigs, there were nine white folks living in Shoal Town among some 214 Cherokees. Just to the east along the North River Road, six white settlers were living in Rogers' Ville among thirty Cherokee Indians. Therefore, it is well documented that white people were living with the Cherokees in the area prior to the first legal white land acquisition in 1818. It is quite possible that Daniel White could have been one of those whites as early as 1812 living among the Cherokees in Doublehead's house. Doublehead's home was destroyed in 1962 during the construction of making four lanes of Highway 72 from Athens to Florence, Alabama.

Cherokee Chief Doublehead left indelible footprints in the history of the Muscle Shoals. He looms among North Alabama's legendary figures as one whose personality seems to have matched his name. Doublehead suddenly changed to become a friend of the white settlers who first arrived at the Muscle Shoals around 1806 at his invitation to lease Cherokee lands. Even though he partnered with some white traders, he originally opposed a lot of white people coming and settling on Cherokee lands. Later, he invited whites with offers of long-term leases on the land along the Muscle Shoals.

Doublehead's Slaves

Doublehead owned some 40 black slaves and raised cotton, corn, horses, hogs, and beef cattle which he sold to the government. His brother-in-law, John Melton, had some 60 black slaves; together, they were heavily involved in farming cotton, corn, and other agricultural activities. Doublehead had a cotton gin placed at Melton's Bluff for cleaning their cotton; Anne Royall described the cotton gin during her visit to Melton's Bluff in 1818.

By January 7, 1806, Doublehead signed the Cotton Gin Treaty which placed a cotton cleaning machine at Melton's Bluff. In 1838, three people gave sworn affidavits describing Doublehead's estate which included information on his black slaves who worked his cotton plantation at the Muscle Shoals in the first years of the early 1800's.

Catherine Spencer's Affidavit

Catherine Spencer, daughter of Pumpkin Boy and niece of Doublehead, gave an affidavit on June 8, 1838, concerning Doublehead's black slaves. "Came Catherine Spencer and makes oath that she lived at the house of Doublehead the Chief when he was killed which was many years ago, she thinks it was about 27 years ago, and that she lived in his family about 12 years. Applicant is the niece of Old Doublehead, and is the only daughter and child of Eyahchutlee (Pumpkin Boy), a brother of Doublehead, and Chaueukah is her mother, and was then a grown woman about 19 years old and affiant states that the following described property was there and belonged to Doublehead the Chief when he was killed to wit.

One Negro man named Andrew about 21 years old, very likely $1,000.00. One young Negro man named Joe a Race Rider, very smart $650.00. One mullatto boy named Ben, 16 years old $600.00. One brother of his named George, 14 years old $550.00. One Negro boy named Jacob about 15 years old $550.00=$2,350.00.

One Negro man named Riddle about 22 years old $800.00. One Negro woman named Phebe about 25 or 6 years old $500.00 and her four children, the oldest 10 and youngest 2 years old at $200.00 each on an average is $800.00. One Negro woman named Mary or Polly about 23 years old $500.00 with her two children---$350.00.

Austin, a man between thirty and 40 years old $600.00 and his wife Magon about 30 years old, a house woman, good cook, washer and ironer $600.00 with five children the oldest a boy 12 years old and ranging from him down to the youngest about 2 years old, all worth on an average $200.00 each, $1,000.00. This man and woman came by the death of the applicants father (Pumpkin Boy) to the Old Chief Doublehead with this affiant when she was moved to his quarters after the death of her father, and from this man and woman these five children were raised and all these seven Negroes were once the right of this applicant, but affiant does not know where it is now. Affiant declares most solemnly on her oath that she never sold them to anybody nor been paid one dollar for them.

All of the above described Negroes were there before the Georgia Negroes were brought there, and applicant states that a white man named (John D.) Chisholm was gone to Georgia to collect money due Old Doublehead when he was killed and shortly after that Chisholm returned with nine grown negroes from Georgia and left them there as a part of Doublehead's property and said he got those nine negroes in place of the money due unto Doublehead. Affiant and the other Cherokees evidently then took these nine negroes and put them in the negro cabins with the other negroes and provided for them as for the other negroes of Doublehead and they remained there as a part of his estate until taken off by the white men; five of these Georgia negroes were men worth $700.00 each--$3,500 and the other four women worth $500 each--$2,000.00 all stout able negroes and well grown, the names not recalled nor the ages.

There were 30 head of cows and calves worth $12.00 each--$360.00 and about 100 head of fine stock cattle, big and sturdy heifers all worth 5 to 8 dollars each $650.00 one fine stud horse at home worth as the people said $700.00 and one other stud horse at South West Point said by the people to be worth $1,000.00 and there were 8 other fine mares and geldings bought of Rik=e=ti=yah = John Christy's mother worth $100 each-$800.00 and nine other head of common draw horses and colts worth about 50 or 60 dollars each, say 55 on an average $495.00 and five good horses called first rate and worth $500.00 Doublehead paid a fine negro named Mary for the 8 bought of John Christy's mother with a view to increase his stock of horses, and that negro was not any of those housed here==this John Christy has gone to Sekausas.

50 head of sows and pigs and shoats and small stock hogs running about the house $3.00 each -- $150.00. One hundred head of large hogs running out in the woods worth $5.00 is--$500.00…One of the negroes named Andrew who could speak and understand both English and Cherokee stated to affiant that he understood what the white men said and he told this affiant that these white men were not meaning to save the negroes and the other property for the children of Doublehead and that they were meaning to get it all for their own use and fixing to steal it and that if the white men did act so with the property he, Andrew, would run away and come back to the nation again. The other negroes seemed to be concerned that these white men would take them where Bird Doublehead was and went cheerfully and the negroes assisted the white men in collecting the stock and loading up the wagon and one of the negroes drove off the team and the plantation was left without and human being on it but her aunts and Wah=hatihi. It was the understanding with all the Indians that the children were to have all this property at last. Wah=hatih got some Indians to (aprint hein) and they gathered the crops and put it away and no more white men came there to (couriett) for the goods of the heirs of Old Doublehead."

It is believed that the white men who came to Muscle Shoals to take Doublehead's black slaves and property were: Thomas Norris Clark, Samuel Riley, James Black, Joseph Phillips, and John D. Chisholm. It is believed that these men took most of Doublehead's slaves and possessions; of these white men, Samuel Riley's family would have been the only legal heirs to the estate of Doublehead.

Thomas Norris Clark, who lived at Southwest Point, was schooling Tassel and Bird Doublehead, Doublehead's sons. Samuel Riley was Doublehead's double son-in-law and operated Doublehead's Ferry at Southwest Point; his family were legal heirs of Doublehead. James Black was the school master that schooled Doublehead's daughters Alcy and Susannah near Hiwassee Garrison (Peggy was living with her mother in McMinn County, Tennessee). The white man by the name of Phillips (probably Joseph Phillips as mentioned in Caleb Starr's 1838 affidavit) ran Doublehead's trading post at the mouth of Bluewater Creek and was an acquaintance of Chisholm. Captain John D. Chisholm and Big Nance got into a legal confrontation and personal dispute over the ownership of some of Doublehead's black slaves; Big Nance, sister of Doublehead, claimed that she was a legal heir to three of the slaves taken by Chisholm. Two of Doublehead's brothers, Wau hatchy and Ulau hatchy, got one slave each.

Bird Doublehead's Affidavit

According to an affidavit given by the Bird Doublehead on June 21, 1838, his father Doublehead owned many slaves and considerable property. Portions of the affidavit are given as follows: "Sworn to oath inscribed before me this 21st June 1838, Testimony of Bird Doublehead re: Estate of Doublehead, Cherokee Agency East. Bird Doublehead, Son of Doublehead, a Cherokee Chief, makes that he had for some years previous to the time his father was killed as well as after and recalls its about 29 years ago he had been living at Thomas Norris Clark's at Kingston, Tennessee (South West Point) for the purpose of going to school and was living at Clark's at the time his father was killed. In the fall prior to his death affiant went home to his father's at the Muscle Shoals on the Tennessee River on a visit and remained at his father's house about three months, and again at the expiration of that time affiant returned to Clark's and continued to reside with him as affiant sometime in the year 1812 and was residing there at the time of his father's death…Affiant recollects well to have seen a considerable quantity of property belonging to his father. Consisting of a large stock of horses, he thinks 30 or 40 head, old and young. Among them one brown stud horse purchased by affiant's father from Old Peelin for the sum of $1000, one thousand dollars. This horse [mah] a stand at South West Point. Affiant's father was a stock raiser and had some fine breed mares and was trying to improve his stock of horses. There was also a large stock of cattle of which affiant's father had given affiant 20 head as part of the cattle belonging to affiants step mother the wife (Kateeyeah Wilson) of the Chief Doublehead which part affiant presumes Thomas Wilson her brother got at Doublehead's death, but Doublehead still owned a considerable stock of cattle besides. He had as affiant believes also a large stock of hogs he is unable to say how many. He also had a large quantity of valuable household and kitchen furniture worth as affiant believes at least $600. Affiant states there was a store there but affiant is unable to give any account of the quantity or value of the goods therein but thinks there was a pretty general apportionment.

    Affiant remembers that…Doublehead had also a considerable stock of Negroes besides those afterwards brought from Georgia…Those Negroes he had owned many years [torn part] of time before the recollection of affiant. Others were born there, and [Ms yellow boyz Bins oGimjyd] very likely were bought by Doublehead a few years before his death…The next fall after Doublehead was killed Clark went to the Muscle Shoals and to the late residence of affiant's father he did not inform affiant when he started what was his beliefs or where he was going. After an absence of some weeks Clark returned home to Kingston and brought with him 21, twenty one, Negroes and some horses. Phillips the store keeper also came back with Clark. Phillips informed affiant that Clark had got the Negroes and horses at the residence of affiant's father and that some other Negroes had also been taken that belonged to Doublehead [torn part] and had been by him delivered over to some other men, one of them to [Wau hatchy] one to [Ulau hatchy] his brother, two Cherokees, and one to (John D.) Chisholm a white man, and the balance to some person or persons who are not recalled at present. Affiant was confident Phillips statement in relation to the property was true from the fact that of the Negroes brought by Clark there were several affiant had himself known to have been in his father's family many years Jarrit, Austin, Magin, Andrew and Pheby and Peter Dempsy and some others which affiant understood had come from Georgia. Affiant understands that Clark has disposed of the property which he took of the estate of affiant's father and has applied the [proceeds] to his own use [some] of the property affiant knows he sold one Negro,

Peter, to Sam [Martin] and other portions of the property affiant is informed he sold of which is one negro, Dempsy, a [brother?] to [Crozing] of Knoxville."

Bird Doublehead describes considerable farm property of his father Doublehead of which was claimed by Thomas Norris Clark. Bird goes on to tell that all he got from Clark was one wore out saddle and a horse. Both affidavits of Catherine Spencer and Bird Doublehead indicate that Doublehead's property was taken without giving any to his heirs. In addition to their affidavits, Caleb Starr, who witnessed the death of Doublehead, also gave an affidavit concerning Doublehead's slaves.

Caleb Starr's Affidavit

According to Caleb Starr's affidavit given on August 11, 1838, "John D. Chisholm was going to Georgia to collect money due to Doublehead in Negroes. The number I do not remember. A man named Joseph Phillips, a small man and a keen land speculator come on with Chisholm and there was one other of the company came on besides Phillips and Phillips after told affiant that several Negroes had been sent on the shortest road to the Muscle Shoals to pay up for portions of the reservation, which was called and known as the Doublehead Reservation and the Negroes were called Doublehead's Negroes and all the _____ served to be in the name and for the benefit of Doublehead. Affiant knew Samuel Riley (Doublehead's double son-in-law) and knew he did not have more than two or three Negroes before Doublehead's death and did not know of his having any more afterwards."

According to the affidavits given in 1838 by Doublehead's niece Catherine Spencer, Bird Doublehead, and Caleb Starr, it appears that Doublehead had received some of the black slaves from Georgia in return for land in Doublehead's Reserve between Elk River and Cypress Creek. It was specifically noted that Thomas Norris Clark took 21 of Doublehead's black slaves and several of his horses to his home at Southwest Point at the mouth of the Clinch River where it runs into the Tennessee River. Both Catherine Spencer and Bird Doublehead testify that Clark stole the black slaves of Chief Doublehead after his death.

Doublehead's Reservation was given to him by a treaty with the United States Government; the reserve included all the lands ten miles north of the Tennessee River between the Cheewalee (Elk River) and Teekeetanoah (Cypress Creek). Through a treaty, Doublehead also secured a cotton gin or a cotton cleaning machine to be placed at Melton's Bluff in Lawrence County, Alabama. Doublehead was also given by treaty a section of land reserve at Southwest Point at the mouth of the Clinch River were it enters the Tennessee River. His double son-in-law Samuel Riley operated his ferry at Southwest Point. John Riley, Doublehead's grandson, and John D. Chisholm also got a section of land at Southwest Point during the 1806 treaty. Thomas Norris Clark also wound up getting the three sections of 1806 treaty lands at Southwest Point.

The cotton gin at Melton's Bluff was to encourage Doublehead and John Melton to become heavily involved in cotton farming; together they owned some one hundred black slaves. Some two years prior to his death on June 7, 1815, John Melton and his mixed Cherokee Scots Irish family moved their primary dwelling and farming operations at Melton's Bluff in present-day Lawrence County to Limestone County on the north side of the Tennessee River, east of Elk River, and south of Fort Hampton.

It was said that Melton feared attacks from the Creeks, but he probably feared assassination since he also benefitted from Doublehead having the cotton gin placed at Melton's Bluff. According to folklore, John Melton and probably his Cherokee wife Ocuma were buried in the McNutt Cemetery in Limestone County, Alabama; the cemetery was on the Limestone County farm of John Melton.

Doublehead's Assassination

Doublehead made shady deals with government officials to the benefit of his personal estate and to members of his family which was disliked by many of the other fellow Upper Cherokees. After his secret dealing with the government was exposed, Doublehead would realize a widespread decline in his respect among the Upper Cherokees. The loss of his feared Chickamauga warrior status would embolden his own people to carry out Doublehead's assassination on August 9, 1807.

There are those who write that the wily old Chief Doublehead was a wife beater, and that years prior to his assassination, his fierce attack on one of his wife resulted in her horrible death. Her brother-in-law half blood Cherokee James Vann was said to have been involved in a conspiracy that led to Doublehead's death on the Hiwassee River in the summer of 1807.

Wayne Gatlin at Doublehead's grave east of Bluewater Creek

Doublehead's murder by fellow tribal members Major Ridge and Alex Saunders including a white man by the name of John Rogers would lead to a second division of the Cherokee tribe. The first division was the result of the older Upper Cherokee leaders who signed for peace in the Cherokee Treaty of 1776, and the Lower Cherokees of the Chickamauga faction who continued to fight primarily under the leadership of Dragging Canoe, Doublehead, John Watts Jr., Bloody Fellow, Duwali, The Glass, Kattygisky, and others. The second division of the Cherokees came about because of the assassination of

Doublehead; those who left North Alabama in the summer of 1809 and 1810 became known as the Old Settlers or Cherokees West.

Doublehead's corpse was brought back to his home on Bluewater Creek in Lauderdale County for burial. There are colorful stories associated with his place of interment, which at one time overlooked his home, the Bluewater Oldfields, and the northern portion of the Cherokee village of Shoal Town that lay within Doublehead's Reservation. One of Doublehead's slaves said, "On stormy nights old Doublehead's spirit would rant and rave over the hills and hollows of Bluewater Creek."

After his assassination near Hiwassee Garrison, members of the Doublehead family transported his body back to his home in Lauderdale County, Alabama. He was buried on the hillside near his home by his family. Old legends persist that his grave is near the summit of the hill behind the house where he made his home on the east side of Bluewater Creek and just a few yards north of present-day Highway 72. Today, a historic marker for Doublehead is about ¼ mile east of Bluewater Creek on the south side of Highway 72. The old pile of rocks that mark his final resting place is on the rise north of the historic marker. The grave stones are the only original sign of the once great Chickamauga Cherokee Warrior who terrorized the Cumberland settlements around the Big Lick or French Lick which is present-day Nashville, Tennessee.

Cherokees West

After Doublehead was murdered by Major Ridge, Alex Saunders, and John Rogers, many of Doublehead's family and friends made arrangements with President Thomas Jefferson to leave the Muscle Shoals of the Tennessee River. Many followers and family members of Doublehead left the area of North Alabama for fear of the same fate as Doublehead.

In the summer of 1809, some 1,130 of Doublehead's people prepared to leave the Muscle Shoals of the Tennessee River for lands west of the Mississippi River. Most of the passports for Indian Territory west of the Mississippi River were approved by government officials in January and February of 1810.

The following is from "The Cherokees" by Grace Steele Woodard published in 1963 and found on page 131, "However, in 1808, the Compact 1802 was not needed to effect the removal of some 1,130 Chickamaugans to lands west of the Mississippi (today Dardanelle, Arkansas, in Pope County). Jefferson had merely to suggest to Tahlonteskee and other Chickamaugans that if they did not care to remain in the same country with their enemy countrymen, they could remove to Dardanelle Rock. Thus, in the spring of 1808, Tahlontuskee fearing assassination notified President Jefferson that his people were ready to migrate."

According to microcopy 208, roll 4, and number 2371, Colonel Return J. Meigs writes to the Secretary War and addresses the Chiefs of Cherokees assembled at Wills Town on November 2, 1809, "On 20 day July, Taluntuskee brought me the names of 386 men and 637 women and children who wished move over the Mississippi after that 107 more wanted to go making a total of 1130. Cherokees now own no land west of Mississippi those there are there by counting on the government." After Meigs speech on November 2, 1809, the passports for the removal to the west were approved and issued in January and February of 1810 to the Lower Cherokees of the Chickamauga faction who were family or loyal to Doublehead.

On December 1, 1809, Cherokee agent Return Jonathan Meigs completed a census of the Cherokee Nation and reported 6,116 Cherokee males and 6,279 Cherokee females for a total of 12,395 Cherokee Indians. In addition, he indicated that the Cherokees owned 383 black slaves. Meigs also enumerated 341 whites living among the Cherokees. Notice that there were more black slaves among the Cherokees than white people.

The December 1809 census figures were over two years after the assassination of Doublehead. Meigs may or may not have included all the Old Settlers or Cherokees West who left for the Indian Territory west of the Mississippi River earlier than 1809 and 1810.

Blood Law

Tahlonteeskee Benge, Doublehead's nephew, also lived near Bluewater Creek at Shoal Town in present-day Lauderdale County, Alabama. Tahlonteeskee moved to Bluewater Creek in Arkansas after the summer of 1809 following the assassination of Doublehead. Tahlonteeskee's group of Cherokees, known as the "Old Settlers" or "Cherokees West," moved west with permission of President Thomas Jefferson, but they did not abandon their ancient "Blood Law."

Major Ridge
1771-6/221839

Some 30 years after their migration, the Old Settlers carried out the Blood Law (eye for an eye) upon the arrival of their enemy countrymen. Shortly after Major Ridge and his followers arrived in Indian Territory west of the Mississippi in 1839, some 70 Cherokees were assassinated by Doublehead's family, friends, and followers according to the blood law of their ancestors.

Doublehead's son Bird Doublehead, some of his half-brothers, relatives, and some 40 other Cherokees were members of the assassination teams that killed Major Ridge, his family members, and friends a little over 30 years after Ridge murdered Doublehead. Major Ridge was shot five times and died on June 22, 1839. Ridge's son John Ridge and nephew Elias Boudinot were assassinated within a few hours on the same day as Major Ridge. Over 70 Cherokees were assassinated upon their arrival to Indian Territory west of the Mississippi River.

George Colbert's Reservation

George Colbert's Reserve was some 31,000 acres on the north side of the Tennessee River in Lauderdale County at the Natchez Trace Crossing. George Colbert operated Colbert's Ferry on the Natchez Trace between present-day Lauderdale County and Colbert County until about 1819. George Colbert, the double son-in-law of Doublehead, was the son of Scots Irishman James Logan Colbert and his Chickasaw wife.

James Logan Colbert

James Logan Colbert came to Chickasaw country with traders of the British. The hub of British trade was located in Olde Charles Town, South Carolina, where many pack horsemen would bring goods of English merchants along the High Town Path into North Alabama and northeastern Mississippi to trade with the Cherokees and Chickasaws. It was from this eastern colonial area that James Logan Colbert first came into the Chickasaw Nation of the southeastern Indian Territory at a young age.

According to James Adair, Colbert had lived among the Chickasaws from childhood. His contemporary, fellow trader James Adair wrote that Colbert "...lived among the Chikkasaw from his childhood, and speaks their language even with more propriety than the English. He married three Chickasaw wives and had nine children: seven sons and two daughters. He led his life as an Indian trader, interpreter, and leader of men during a time in history which was a turbulent struggle for land and new opportunity" (Adair, 1775).

James Logan Colbert was born at Plumbtree Island in North Carolina, in an area of Scots Irish Indian traders; he came to the Chickasaw Nation as an assistant to those Indian traders. According to Chickasaw interpreter Malcolm McGee from an interview with Lyman Draper in 1841, McGee stated that Colbert was, "a native of the Carolinas, probably South Carolina and came to the Chickasaw Nation prior to 1750." It is highly probably that James fell in love with the beautiful Chickasaw maidens and chose to stay among them.

At one time, James Logan Colbert stated, "I was born in the Carolinas and about 1740, moved to the Chickasaw Nation and married into the tribe." Apparently, in a letter dictated to Governor Harrison of Virginia on July 25, 1783, James Logan Colbert stated, "I wish to serve the country in which I live and was born."

On July 5, 1782, a declaration was made by Spanish merchant Silbestre Labadie who had been a captive of James Logan Colbert in the spring of 1782 when his boat and goods were captured at Chickasaw Bluff on the Mississippi River. Labadie stated that, "James Logan Colbert was about 60 years old, possessed of good health, and a strong constitution. An active man, despite his years, he had a violent temper, and was capable of enduring the greatest hardship. He had lived among the Chickasaws for 40 years and boasted that he was owner of a fine house and some hundred and fifty blacks. He said he had several sons by Chickasaw women, who were very important chiefs in that nation."

If the statement made by Silbestre Labadie in 1782 is correct on Colbert's age of 60, it appears that James Logan Colbert was born about 1722. If Labadie's statement of Colbert living with the Chickasaws for 40 years is correct, then James Logan Colbert had been living with the Chickasaws since 1742.

James Logan Colbert died on January 7, 1784, in Alabama at 62 years of age. After conducting some business in St. Augustine in 1783, he began his journey home. James Logan Colbert had stopped by his friend and advisor Creek Chief Alexander McGillivray's house for a short stay. He then left there about January 4, 1784. Three days later his horse threw and killed him or his black slave Cesar killed him.

George Colbert

George Colbert was the half Chickasaw and half Scots son of a Chickasaw woman named Sofa or Minta Hoye and a white man named James Logan Colbert. George was born on the west side of Bear Creek where it empties into the Tennessee River in the present-day northeastern most corner of Mississippi.

George Colbert, or Tootemastubbe, was perhaps the most well known and pleasing in appearance and manners of James Logan Colbert's sons. George was described as illiterate but had much influence, stood acceptably fair, and talked very common English. He was opposed to modern innovations and missions but tolerated missionaries. George Colbert was opposed to formal education and whiskey; however, it is documented that he sold whiskey to travelers.

Chickasaw Chief George Colbert
1744-11/7/1839

According to William Lindsey McDonald (2007), "Various accounts describing George Colbert's appearance and character present an interesting study of this leader among the Chickasaws. Cyrus Harris, Governor of the Chickasaw Nation after their removal, described him as 'Illiterate but had some influence and stood tolerably fair; talk common English.' A Methodist preacher called him a 'Very shrewd, talented man and, withal, very wicked.' Dr. Rush Nutt, a Natchez planter, said that he was the 'Greatest of the Chickasaws, displays genius and talent…but is an artful designing man.' Colonel Return J. Meigs, Cherokee Indian Agent, described him as, 'Extremely mercenary miscalculates his importance, and when not awed by the presence of the officers of the government takes upon himself great airs…'"

From The New York Missionary Magazine and Repository of Religious Intelligence by Cornelius Davis in 1800, missionaries visited the Chickasaw Nation and recorded daily religious activities they had with members of the Colbert family. The record provides a unique view of life among George Colbert's people and their religious beliefs and relationships prior to Indian removal.

The following extract from Reverend Joseph Bullen, a Presbyterian Missionary from New York, July 29, 1799, "George Colbert, a Chickasaw Chief, called in a decent dress, and lodged here. He informed me how he and his brother Levi had labored to further the pious and benevolent designs of the Society; that he, Levi, and a number of others, wish to learn good things: no get drunk, but work, make corn, cotton, cattle, hogs & c."

In December 1801, the United States Government agreed to build cabins for travelers, a store, stables, a large dwelling house, a new ferry boat, and other facilities for George Colbert. The ferry location was moved upstream from the mouth of Bear Creek because that area was subject to flooding. George Colbert agreed to operate the ferry where the Natchez Trace crosses the Tennessee River in present-day Lauderdale and Colbert Counties, Alabama. His home and other building were built on the Colbert County side of the river.

George Colbert was unwilling to allow individual traders to sell merchandise to the Chickasaws because it would diminish his profits. George Colbert organized trading activities to Tuscumbia and Florence, Alabama which were opened to white settlement in 1818. George was able to oversee trade in the Chickasaw Nation, and he did not allow outside traders unless he approved of the transactions. He would accompany large numbers of his people to stores in the white towns to make sure that the Chickasaws were treated fairly by the white merchants.

"James Simpson grew up across the river at Florence. As a boy of ten years, he was fascinated when George Colbert and other Indians came to town and bought supplies at his father's store. As an old man, Simpson wrote about these scenes of the past and gave an interesting description of George Colbert: He was tall and slender and handsome with straight black hair that he wore long, which came well down to his shoulders. His features were that of an Indian, but his skin was lighter than that of his tribe. He wore the dress of a white man of his day and always appeared neat and clean. He frequently ate dinner at my father's house in Florence, Alabama. The building now known as the Commercial Hotel was my father's store and he had reputation among the Indians as being an honest and just man and as a consequence of the Indian trade. George Colbert often crossed the river in canoes with thirty or fifty of his tribe to purchase goods in Florence. The Indians seemed to enjoy roaming over the store looking at everything. They wore buckskin clothes of their own making. Some of them wore feather head dress" (McDonald, 2007).

George Colbert and Doublehead

George Colbert's father-in-law Chickamauga Cherokee Chief Doublehead arrived in the Muscle Shoals area by 1770. Doublehead used marriage to strengthen his position and his iron clad grip on the Muscle Shoals area of North Alabama. The marriage of two of his daughters to George Colbert was a brilliant move that secured his position among the Chickasaws. When Doublehead's occupation of Muscle Shoals came into question, Chickasaw Chief George Colbert confirmed that Doublehead had his permission to live on Chickasaw lands. The agreement of George Colbert was probably greatly influenced by the fact that he had married Doublehead's oldest daughters.

After Doublehead's death on August 9, 1807, George Colbert and the Chickasaws demanded that the white settlers who had leased land from Doublehead and lived on Chickasaw land be removed. Therefore, the government established Fort Hampton in Limestone County, Alabama, to remove white squatters on Chickasaw lands. Later, George and William Colbert along with other Chickasaw and Cherokee warriors joined with General Andrew Jackson's Army to defeat the Creeks on March 27, 1814.

George married two daughters of Doublehead and Creat Priber: Saleechie Doublehead and Tuskiahooto Doublehead. Creat Priber was said to have died from severe abuse and beatings by Doublehead. Doublehead was known as a wife abuser and was known to kill another wife to whom he had a violent relationship; she was a sister to half blood Cherokee James Vann's wife. The beating death of James' sister-in-law was one of the reasons that he agreed to be the leader of the assassination group that would kill Doublehead.

George Colbert's two Cherokee wives were said to be among the most beautiful women in the region. Mail or post rider John Swaney had the route from Nashville to Natchez and told of George's pretty wives. He gave details about George Colbert and his Ferry as found in Jonathan Daniels' book, "The Devils Backbone" (1985).

According to Daniels, "The Indians were contrary the mail rider remembered in his old age. They would not come across the river for him if he failed to get to the landing before bedtime…The Colberts were more than contrary. They were shrewd, strong, and had a Midas Touch for making money... From the beginning, however, these Scotch Chickasaws were careful to avoid banditry... Certainly such charges were unjustified when Swaney crossed the river to spend the night with George Colbert…Whatever may have been its comforts or discomforts, Swaney always remembered the pretty half-breed-or even eighth breed-daughters of the household. So did others. Tired and dirty boatmen and well-accoutered gentlemen, too, stopped sometimes just to stare at girls who were described by turns as 'the prettiest woman in Mississippi' or even as 'the most beautiful woman on the continent.'"

Tuskiahooto

According to Colonel William Lindsey McDonald, "Tuskiahooto, Colbert's principal wife, reputed to be the fairest of all the Indian princesses, presided over George Colbert's household at the ferry. Old families of Colbert County recall with some amusement this rich Indian lady's refusal to ride in the elegant carriage provided according to her means. She followed this vehicle, which was driven by a slave, astride her favorite pony seated on a colorful blanket, and quite often she was barefoot. Washington socialites were likewise amused when she accompanied her husband (George Colbert) to a dinner at the White House dressed in the latest fashion and barefoot. It was a dark day for the Chief when Tuskiahooto died. He was never the same afterward."

According to an article by Richard Green (2009) in The Chickasaw Times, "On July 11, 1794, a group of Chickasaws, including Chiefs Piomingo and George Colbert, arrived at the President's House in Philadelphia for a welcoming ceremony hosted by President George Washington. Chief George Colbert, who had been with Piomingo and George Washington at the meetings in 1794, signed the land cession treaty as the Chickasaw's principal chief. John Quincy Adams was a member of the U.S. Senate, which ratified the treaty in 1807."

George's second marriage was to Tuskiahooto. She was born about 1760 in Tellico Plains, Tennessee, and was also the daughter of Chickamauga Cherokee Chief Doublehead and Creat (Drags Blanket) Priber, half German and half Cherokee. Tuskiahooto Doublehead Colbert's grandfather Christian G. Priber was a German genius; therefore, she was one-fourth German and three-fourths Cherokee.

Based on tradition, Tuskiahooto was considered one of the most beautiful women in the country and was the favorite wife of George Colbert. She was George's principal wife and lived at the Colbert's Ferry home until she died around 1817. Tuskiahooto died at her and George's home at Colbert's Ferry which was adjacent to the Natchez Trace in Colbert County, Alabama. George Colbert took her death very bad and it bothered him to his last days on earth.

In the treaty of 1834, George made sure to include his wife's burial site in the reserve that was set aside for his personal use. Therefore, the reserve was extended sixty yards south of his house at Colbert's Ferry to include the grave of Tuskiahooto. There is no record of George and Tuskiahooto having any children.

According to provisions of the treaty, "Also there is a fractional section, between the residence of George Colbert, and the Tennessee River, upon which he has a ferry, it is therefore consented, that said George Colbert, shall own and have so much of said fraction, as may be contained in the following lines, to wit.-

beginning near Smith's Ferry at the point where the base meridian line and the Tennessee river come in contact,-thence south so far as to pass the dwelling-house, (and sixty yards beyond it,) within which is interred the body of his wife (Tuskiahooto),-thence east of the river and down the same to the point of beginning. Also there shall be reserved to him an island, in said river, nearly opposite to this fraction, commonly called Colberts Island."

Saleechie

George lived with his wife Tuskiahooto at Colbert's Ferry in present-day Colbert County, Alabama. After the death of Tuskiahooto in 1817, he moved from Colbert's Ferry on the Tennessee River to Wolf Creek some four miles west of Tupelo, Mississippi. In Mississippi, George and Saleechie Doublehead Colbert operated a substantial cotton plantation with the assistance of black slaves. George had a very successful cotton farming operation, and prior to removal, he owned some 150 black slaves.

George and Saleechie (Standing Fern) had seven children who were one eighth German, three eighths Cherokee, one quarter Scots Irish, and one quarter Chickasaw. George fathered seven children by his wife Saleechie: Jane, Susan, George, Jr., Vicy, Vina, John, and Nancy. Pitman Colbert was adopted by George and Saleechie, and he had good education.

Saleechie (Shullachie or Salechie) Doublehead Colbert was born about 1762 in Monroe County, Tennessee; she was one-fourth German and three-fourths Cherokee. According to the 1818 census report, Saleechie was listed on the Chickasaw Roll as a resident of the Chickasaw Nation in Mississippi. On November 14, 1837, George Colbert and Saleechie were forced to the West as part of Indian Removal where George died two years later on November 7, 1839, at Fort Towson. Saleechie died February 1, 1846, in Indian Territory west of the Mississippi River.

George Colbert's Reserve

George Colbert's home at the ferry was the site of a significant conference between the Cherokees, Creeks, Choctaws, Chickasaws, and the United States

Government in September 1816. His home was designated for this meeting as the Chickasaw Council House. Representing the government were Andrew Jackson, David Meriwether, and Jesse Franklin. At this conference the Chickasaws ceded their land north of the Tennessee River, as well as some territory south of the river; however, certain tracts were reserved. George Colbert was given sixteen square miles on the north bank of the river, including his ferry landing, in what eventually became Lauderdale County, Alabama. George Colbert's Lauderdale

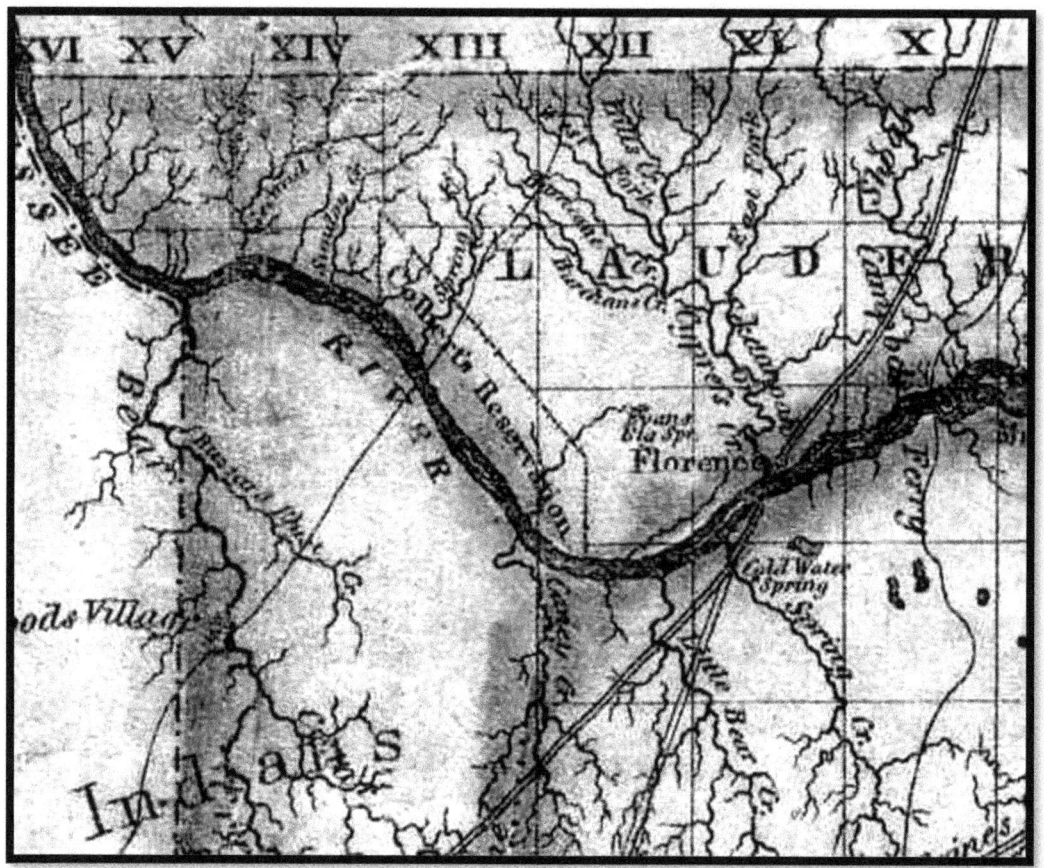

County land became known as "The Reserve."

George Colbert deeded this land back to the United States on May 15, 1819. However, prior to this time, he had sold certain parcels of land to white settlers; including a rather large farm to the Walston family that was located south of what was to become the Oakland Community. At one time a U.S. Post Office was located there with the designation as Reserve, Alabama (McDonald, 2007).

As seen in the John Melish Map of 1818, George Colbert was given a reservation of some 30,000 acres in Lauderdale County, Alabama. The reservation was to encourage the Colbert brothers to sign the Turkey Town Treaty of September 20, 1816. The treaty gave up Indian claims of the Chickasaw Nation to all their land north of the Tennessee River in present-day Lauderdale County, Alabama, except for Colbert's Reserve.

Colbert's Old Reservation was on the north side of the Tennessee River with the landing of Colbert's Ferry somewhat near the middle of the reserve. The area became known as Colbert's Reserve which extended some four miles from the north shore of the river and ran some 12 miles east and west parallel to the river. The reserve was in the bend where the Tennessee River turned north toward the State of Tennessee containing some of the most fertile and rich land in the area.

Colbert's Reserve is identified as follows in Article 4 of the Treaty with the Chickasaw on September 20, 1816. "The commissioners agree that the following tracts of land shall be reserved to the Chickasaw Nation:

1. One tract of land for the use of Colonel George Colbert and heirs, and which is thus described by said Colbert: "Beginning on the north bank of the Tennessee River, at a point that, running north four miles, will include a big spring, about half way between his ferry and the mouth of Cypress, it being a spring that a large cow-path crosses its branch near where a cypress tree is cut down; thence westwardly to a point, four miles from the Tennessee river, and standing due north of a point on the north bank of the river, three [four] miles below his ferry on the Tennessee River, and up the meanders of said river to the beginning point."

2. A tract of land two miles square on the north bank of 'the Tennessee River, and at its junction with Beach creek, for the use of Appassan Tubby and heirs.

3. A tract of land one mile square, on the north side of the Tennessee river, for the use of John McCleish and heirs, the said tract to be so run as to include the said McCleish's settlement and improvements on the north side of Buffalo Creek.

4. Two tracts of land, containing forty acres each, on the south side of the Tennessee River, and about two and a half miles below the Cotton Gin Port, on the Tombigby River, which tracts of land will be pointed out by Major Levi Colbert, and for the use of said Colbert and heirs.

It is stipulated that the above reservations shall appertain to the Chickasaw nation only so long as they shall be occupied, cultivated, or used, by the present proprietors or heirs and in the event of all or either of said tracts of land, so reserved, being abandoned by the present proprietors or heirs, each tract or tracts of land, so abandoned, shall revert to the United States as a portion of that territory ceded by the second article of this treaty."

The 1816 treaty also allowed the Chickasaws to retain their land claims on the south side of the Tennessee River in a portion of Franklin County from Cane Creek to the west. George Colbert and his relatives owned several tracts of land in the area west of Cane Creek. These Chickasaw lands in Franklin County were not released to the United States until their removal from the area in November 1837.

George Colbert was the recognized chief of the Chickasaw Nation at the time of removal and until his death on November 7, 1839. Since George Colbert was a veteran of the American Revolution serving under General George Washington, he was buried with honors at Fort Towson. George had been commissioned a major in the army and awarded a sword. He also served under General Jackson by whom he had been commissioned a colonel in the Seminole Wars. George died at 95 years old on November 7, 1839, at Fort Towson in the Choctaw Nation of Towson County, Indian Territory and his body was interred at Fort Towson.

Today, through Chief George Colbert's children, his siblings, and many relatives, a large number of people in northeast Mississippi and northwest

Alabama are related to the historic Colbert family. Many of the descendants of Chief Colbert are not recognized or tribally enrolled citizens of the Chickasaw Nation in Oklahoma, but that does not diminish their pride in their native roots and ancestry.

Chapter 2-Lauderdale Settlement

The first cotton farmed in Lauderdale County of North Alabama was grown primarily by Doublehead of the Chickamauga faction of the Lower Cherokees and George Colbert of the Chickasaws along Muscle Shoals of the Tennessee River. The shoals stretched from the vicinity of the mouth of Fox's Creek, on the present-day county line of Lawrence and Morgan Counties of North Alabama, westward to the Mississippi State line. Lauderdale County bordered the shoals on the north bank of the Tennessee River except the portion upstream from the mouth of Elk River. Beginning upstream, the Tennessee River shoals which bordered Lauderdale County, Alabama, included Elk River Shoals, Big Muscle Shoals, Little Muscle Shoals, Colbert Shoals, Bee Tree Shoals, and Waterloo Shoals. The Lower Cherokee and Chickasaw Indian people previously inhabiting the area referred to the Muscle Shoals as "Chake Thlocko" which means Great Crossing Place or Big Ford.

The northwest Alabama counties adjacent to the Muscle Shoals were opened to white settlement by the 1816 Turkey Town Treaty land cessions from the Chickasaws and Cherokees. The Chickasaws were paid $120,000.00 and the Cherokees were paid $60,000.00 for their land claims. The counties of North Alabama included Franklin, Lawrence, Lauderdale, Limestone, Morgan and the southwest half of Madison. White settlement began in Lauderdale County in early 1818; however, many white settlers had leased land in Lauderdale from Doublehead prior to the Turkey Town Treaty. The land claims under Doublehead were deemed void and those settlers had to re-enter their leases after the treaty was ratified and the government land sales begin in 1818.

The sale of Indian lands along the Muscle Shoals led to a mass migration of wealthy colonial planters and their black slaves into the Tennessee Valley of northwest Alabama. This great migration to cotton country was called "Alabama Fever." The cotton planters primarily from North Carolina and Virginia had depleted the nutrients in their soil and wanted the rich farm land of the great bend of the Tennessee River. They had been told of cotton growing higher than a man on the rich alluvial bottoms of the Tennessee River Valley.

Cotton planters organized as groups to make a wagon train trek across the Appalachians to obtain the rich fertile Indian lands along the Muscle Shoals for their farming activities. Some wagon trains consisting of forty to fifty families with their black slaves traveled over rough mountainous terrain to newly acquired Indian lands in order to purchase their cotton plantations. Some cotton planters were already established in the northeastern portion of the original Madison County which was formed about 1806 becoming the first county in North Alabama.

The cotton plantation system was readily transplanted from the overworked and nutrient depleted farm lands of North Carolina and Virginia to the rich alluvial river and creek bottoms adjacent to the Muscle Shoals of Lauderdale County, Alabama. The steady demand for cotton made the plantation product the nation's leading export prior to the Civil War, and it also made the slave owning plantation holders wealthy and powerful people. These large cotton planters controlled the political and economic status of northwest Alabama until the Civil War destroyed their enterprise.

According to an article titled "Lauderdale County, Alabama, History of the Shoals" and published in the Times Daily, Thursday, February 25, 1999, by Harry E. Wallace, "The largest slaveholder in Lauderdale was John Peters…Large plantations in Lauderdale ranged from a low of 1,250 acres owned by Lawrence Thompson to 12,000 acres owned by Henry D. Smith. The average plantation was 3,000 acres in 1860. The most commonly produced commercial crop was cotton.

Lauderdale plantations produced large quantities of corn and butter. Of the total, 23 produced wheat, wool, potatoes, sweet potatoes, and hay. Over half produced peas, beans, and rye. Peters was the largest producer of cotton, bringing in 681 bales in 1859. Other large planters of Lauderdale in 1860 were George Armistead, Nathan Boddie, Janet Collier, J. M. Cunningham, George W. Foster, James L. Holland, John M. Hood, Andrew J. Hutchings, Jane Irons, Sarah Jackson, Robert T. Kernachan Sr., William H. Key, Robert M. Patton, Sidney Posey, Neal Rowell, John Simpson, Joseph Thompson's estate, Robert H. Watkins, John S. Wilson, and Matthew Wilson."

Captain John D. Chisholm of Tennessee

Captain John D. Chisholm was born on August 8, 1738; his family migrated from Drum, Scotland, to South Carolina. For many years of his life, Chisholm lived in Knoxville, Tennessee, and he was known as John Chisholm of Tennessee. He went west about 1810, but in 1818 some ten years prior to his death, Captain John D. Chisholm moved back from Arkansas to the old Doublehead Reservation in Lauderdale County, Alabama. Chisholm entered land in the area in March 1818, and he remained at his farm until his death in 1828. He is buried in the Chisholm Family Cemetery on the Chisholm Road or Highway 17 about five miles north of Florence.

Some historians think that John D. Chisholm may have been born in Scotland, but others think he may have been born in South Carolina. Regardless of where he was born, John Chisholm was documented in the colonies by the early 1770's. In 1774 at the Battle of Point Pleasant, Virginia, John D. Chisholm was listed as a private on the roster of Captain William Nalle's company. In 1777, he was a justice in the Washington County District Court; on November 7, 1780, John D. Chisholm was the deputy surveyor of the county under the supervision of James Stewart. In 1784, he was a representative of Washington County with John Sevier; Chisholm became a strong supporter of Governor Sevier (White, 1930).

By the late 1780's, John D. Chisholm settled in east Tennessee near General James White's Fort or Station that became Knoxville. He became friends and an employee of William Blount (March 26, 1749-March 21, 1800) the first governor of Southwest Territory. Chisholm worked as an Indian agent and was referred to in government documents as Captain Chisholm. During the time Chisholm worked for Governor William Blount of the Southwest Territory as an Indian agent, he was paid compensation by the United States Department of War.

On December 8, 1796, Secretary of War James McHenry sent a letter concerning compensation for services rendered to Governor Blount by John Chisholm. The letter is as follows, "Sir, Mr. John Chisholm has presented at this office the following accounts for settlement. Account No. 1-Containing charges for expenses said to be incurred in the fulfillment of instructions herewith from Governor Blount under the date of the 6th November, 1795, including compensation for his said services from the 6th November 1795 to the 24th March 1796—amounting to 1697. Account No. 2-contains charges for _____ expenses on his carried over—1697."

While in Knoxville, John D. Chisholm built a tavern behind Governor Blount's mansion, and the first courthouse. The Chisholm Tavern was on the same block as the William Blount Mansion. Chisholm completed his home and tavern about 1792; after standing nearly 200 years, Chisholm's Tavern was demolished in the 1960's and a historic marker was put on the site.

John D. Chisholm's Tavern in Knoxville, Tennessee
Historic American Buildings Survey in 1934

  Captain John D. Chisholm was a very active Indian agent to the Southeastern tribes including Chickasaw, Choctaw, Creek, and Cherokee. He worked with Governor Blount and Governor John Sevier in negotiations with tribal leaders. In the spring of 1792, Chisholm worked for Governor Blount as an Indian agent and messenger to the Creek Chief Alexander McGillivray; he traveled to Florida and wound up in the Creek Indian country of Georgia. In July 1795, Chisholm conducted a delegation of Chickasaw and Choctaw Indians to Philadelphia to meet with President George Washington.

  John D. Chisholm was described as a large robust Scotsman with a fair complexion and had very red hair characteristic of Celtic people. In May 1797, he was described as follows, "John Chisholm was a large man, with very red hair, and was between fifty-five and sixty years of age when he sailed for England. He was pugnacious and cared little who was ruling so long as he was in exciting action, preferably a fight. Often he came to blows with friend or enemy alike, as court records show...." (White, 1930).

"Davy described Chisholm as he appeared in Philadelphia: He was a hardy, lusty, brawny, weather-beaten man .... While drinking some porter, he appeared sociable; said that he was a back country man; that he had long lived among the Indians, and was with them during the last war; that he was well known to the Spaniards; that his name was Captain Chisholm; that he had been an interpreter to the Indians last winter in this city" (White, 1930).

Captain John D. Chisholm became an advisor to the Cherokee Indians; thereby, he became friends with Chickamauga Cherokee Chief Doublehead. John D. Chisholm and Doublehead first met on July 2, 1791, at the signing of the Treaty of Holston. Both of their names are on the treaty as members of the signing party ratifying the terms of the agreement between the Cherokees and United States. Doublehead and Chisholm remained friends until Doublehead's death in 1807.

John D. Chisholm accompanied the Cherokees to Philadelphia to meet with President George Washington. Sometime after the Treaty of Philadelphia in June 1794, Chisholm left his wife and family in Knoxville, Tennessee, and moved to Doublehead's stronghold at the Muscle Shoals in North Alabama. Chisholm served as the personal legal advisor to Doublehead in his negotiations with the United States government officials and settlers leasing land from Doublehead.

The letter of December 26, 1796, from the United States Secretary of War concerning the expense reimbursement to John D. Chisholm verifies his trip with Indian representatives to Philadelphia to meet with President George Washington. The letter from Secretary William Simmons is as follows, "I certify that there is due to John Chisholm the sum of seven Dollars and 48/100 being a balance of his account of expenses for himself, two interpreters, and eight Indians from Philadelphia to New York and returning. Wm. Simmons"

> Accountant's Office
> Dec 26th 1796
>
> I Certify that there is due to John Chisholm the sum of seven Dollars & 48/100 being a balance of his account of expences for himself, two Interpreters & eight Indians from Philadelphia to New York & returning
>
> D. 7 48/100
>
> The Sec.y of War
>
> W. Simmons
> Acc.t

    Captain Chisholm became involved with Governor William Blount in the Blount Conspiracy that plotted with a British agent to take Florida from the Spanish and make a new colony. Governor Blount conspired with Great Britain to take lands from the Spanish and place him as governor. Eventually, Blount faced impeachment proceedings because of his shady and secret deal with the British.

    John Chisholm worked with Blount who devised the plan to become Governor of Florida after it was taken from the Spanish with the aid of Great Britain. Through a British agent and minister known as Liston, a deal between Blount and England was being developed. Chisholm planned to go to London with the paperwork and work out the secret details that Blount proposed for the British takeover of Florida from the Spanish. Captain John D. Chisholm left for England on March 20, 1797, and arrived on May 1, 1797. When he arrived, he was given a large sum of money. Chisholm was told that the deal had fell through and that he needed to return to America. Chisholm immediately boarded another ship and returned to the United States somewhat in disgrace (White, 1930).

Sometime prior to his trip to Great Britain, Chisholm had married a Cherokee Indian woman named Patsy Brown. While living at the Muscle Shoals, John D. Chisholm had fallen in love with Patsy Brown, the Cherokee daughter of Captain John Brown of the Brown's Ferry in Lawrence County, Alabama. The Brown's Ferry Road ran from Big Spring in present-day Huntsville and crossed the Tennessee River at Brown's Ferry adjacent to Doublehead's Town and then continued to Gourd's Settlement (Courtland) in Lawrence County, Alabama. The ferry had been named in honor of the Cherokee Indian family of half blood Captain John Brown and his three Cherokee wives. After leaving Brown's Ferry, Captain John Brown founded and settled at his village called Otali (present-day Attalla) on the Coosa River. Otali in Cherokee means end of mountain; the Lower Cherokee town was located at the end of Lookout Mountain.

Chisholm tried to get his brother-in-law Cherokee Colonel Richard Brown who lived at Brown's Village near Gunter's (present-day Guntersville) to accompany him; however, Richard Brown refused the request. Richard Brown fought with General Andrew Jackson at the Battle of Horse Shoe Bend during the Creek Indian War in March 1814. In a sworn testimony to the United States Senate, Governor William Blount stated, "Chisholm (the Captain) tried to get Brown, who is the brother of his Indian wife, to go with him to England."

Governor William Blount
3/26/1749-3/21/1800

After leaving London, Chisholm returned to Cherokee villages at the Muscle Shoals in North Alabama where he continued to work as an advisor to Chickamauga Cherokee Chief Doublehead. At the time, Colonel Return J. Meigs at Hiwassee Garrison was the government Indian agent for the Cherokees under the direction of the Governor of Tennessee. John D. Chisholm and Doublehead established a friendship that lasted until Doublehead's death on August 9, 1807.

Captain John D. Chisholm acted as Doublehead's attorney in his business affairs and wrote numerous letters for Doublehead. Chisholm eventually helped him establish Doublehead's Company and Reserve that leased land to many white settlers along the Muscle Shoals. Doublehead's Reserve was in present-day Lauderdale County, Alabama, and lay between Cypress Creek to the west and Elk River to the east; the reserve extended northward from the Tennessee River ten miles up both streams.

Chisholm Moves West

After Chickamauga Cherokee Chief Doublehead's assassination, John D. Chisholm was wounded, but survived; however, Chisholm continued to act as an advisor to Doublehead's nephew Tahlonteskee Benge. In 1810 for fear of his life, Chisholm went west of the Mississippi River to Arkansas with the Lower Cherokees under the authority of President Thomas Jefferson. The Cherokees who left North Alabama were relatives or friends of Doublehead, and many of them also feared being killed because of their association and support of Doublehead.

John D. Chisholm left North Alabama because of threats on his life from the Chickasaws, but before his death, he would return to own land in Lauderdale County, Alabama. The Chickasaws wanted the United States Government, not only to remove all the white settlers and intruders on Doublehead's Reserve, but also remove John D. Chisholm from their country.

The Chickasaws formal request for Chisholm's removal is found in microcopy 208, roll 4, and number 2130. The letter from King Henderson of the Chickasaw Nation is dated August 25, 1808, and is addressed to Henry Dearborn, United States Secretary of War.

"We are informed that the Cherokees in 1805 sold part of our country north of the Tennessee River opposite to Muscle Shoals to the United States. We went to Muscle Shoals to meet Doublehead and his friends but they were not there as Colonel Meigs had summoned Doublehead, John D. Chisholm, and all his friends to Highwassee.

Since Doublehead's death, Chisholm acts as [agent] for Doublehead-Meigs too. When Major Thomas Lewis was agent to Cherokees, John D. Chisholm was banished from the country and went to the Creeks, Colonel Hawkins moved him from thence and he come back to the Cherokees, he then found a friend in Doublehead and he supported him till his death.

We request as a particular favor, that you will be so good as to remove John D. Chisholm out of the Indian country. We have no doubt but government has been informed of Chisholm's character. If the government does not choose to make Chisholm quit the red peoples land, please to give us leave and we will take him out of it.

Relying on the Government of United States to remove bad white men from the red peoples country, we have not attempted to remove Chisholm, depending on the government to have done it for us-otherwise we should have done it long since."

Signed By
Chinnabbe King et, George, William, James Colbert, and 28 others

Evidently, John D. Chisholm got the message from the Chickasaws and planned his move along with Taluntuskee and some 1,130 Cherokees who received passports in January and February of 1810. In his letter to Colonel Return J. Meigs, Chisholm indicates that he will visit when his wound gets well. It is not certain how he was wounded and if it had a direct impact on his decision to move.

As found in microcopy 208, roll 4, and number 2246, John D. Chisholm's letter on March 18, 1809, requests from Indian agent Return J. Meigs the laws of the United States as follows, "I hope you will write me by the bearer what prospects from your late travel to the Federal City. I also beg the favor of the Colonel to send me the 4th volume of the laws of the United States also the volume that contains the treaties of Hopewell-I will bring them back with great care. I am preparing to move over the Mississippi this summer-All the Indians are preparing in this quarter for the same purpose-nothing will be done until I see you and have your council, pray sir, let me hear by the return of Joel Walker the prospects. Let know how the European Business is like to terminate-Don't fail to lend me Laws. They will be used to no bad purpose I will bring them up with me which will be as soon as Walker [the messenger] returns and my wound gets well."

John D. Chisholm

Within a week Meigs replies to Chisholm letting him know that some of the Cherokees in the lower towns have requested to move west of the Mississippi River as found in microcopy 208, roll 4, and number 2074. The following statement is from Colonel Return J. Meigs to John D. Chisholm and dated March 24, 1809, "Cherokees of the lower towns requests permission to remove West of Mississippi." Some seven months later, Meigs notifies the Secretary of War Henry Dearborn of the number of Cherokees willing to move west of the Mississippi River.

Because of his expertise in dealing with government officials, John D. Chisholm became one of the prominent leaders of the Cherokees West or Old Settlers. In 1814 after removing to the west of the Mississippi River, John D. Chisholm was selected by the Old Settlers to go to Washington D. C. Chisholm represented the western Cherokees for the purpose of making a legal claim to the Arkansas lands and the right to establish a separate government from the eastern Cherokee Nation.

Chisholm's Legal Problems

After John D. Chisholm removed west, he got into a legal confrontation because of a debt owned by his son Dennis. The court case confirms that even though Chisholm's ancestry was Scots, he was a prominent member of the Western Cherokees. Other important information concerning his life is found in the court case published by the University of Arkansas at Little Rock, William H. Bowen School of Law, Territorial Briefs and Records.

Portions of the record are as follows, "Robert Clary vs. John D. Chisholm, Abstract, 23 January 1811. Robert Clary acting through his attorney…filed suit against Dennis Chisholm, he also sued Dennis' father John D. Chisholm for a debt of $207.33 for whiskey, corn, pork, bacon, and flour…John D. Chisholm was born in Scotland and emigrated to America in the 1700's. He had several wives, and at one time married to a Cherokee woman…He lived for a while in Tennessee, where he and the Indian Chief Doublehead swindled settlers in fraudulent land deals in the Muscle Shoals area. He was a prominent member of the Western Cherokees, who migrated to and settled western Arkansas in the early 1800's. He would later represent the Cherokees at the Treaty of Cherokee Agency in 1817…Ignatius Chisholm was John D. Chisholm's son, and father to Jesse Chisholm, of Chisholm Trail fame…Robert Clary…complains…said John D. Chisholm on 13th day of September 1810 was justly indebted…in sum of two hundred and seven Dollars & 33 cents. Executed 8th March 1811."

Notice in the court case of 1811 that John D. Chisholm was reported as living in Tennessee. Later in 1818, he was also listed as being "John D. Chisholm of Tennessee" according the Old Land Records of Lauderdale County, Alabama. In addition, Captain Chisholm is listed as having several wives one of which was Cherokee; his Cherokee wife was Patsy Brown, the daughter of half blood Cherokee Captain John Brown and his Cherokee wife. John Chisholm was identified as a large red headed Scotsman who had migrated to America in the 1700's.

John D. Chisholm's Children

Captain John D. Chisholm was married several times; some of his wives included: Elizabeth "Patty" Sims Fauling; Martha Holmes, a mixed blood Cherokee; Patsy Brown, the Cherokee daughter of Captain John Brown; and Mary who is buried next to him in the Chisholm Cemetery north of Florence, Alabama. John and his wives had several children.

John D. Chisholm, Senior fathered the following children:
1) John D. Chisholm, Junior (1775-1847) is buried next to his father in Lauderdale County, Alabama;

2) Dennis Chisholm (1778-1828) caused a court case because of not paying a debt which got his father also sued;
3) Elizabeth Chisholm (1778-1818);
4) Ignatius Chisholm (1779-1838) married Old Tassel's daughter;
5) James Chisholm (1781-??) was arrested as an intruder by Captain Addison B. Armstead the day Doublehead was killed;
6) Elijah Chisholm (1784-??);
7) Deborah Chisholm (1786-1837);
8) Joseph D. Chisholm (1786-1827);
9) Isaac Chisholm;
10) Martha Chisholm;
11) George Chisholm,
12) Thomas Chisholm (1790-1834) became the third chief of western Cherokees; and,
13) Titus Ogdan Chisholm (1793-1831).

Possibly, two other Chisholm boys are sons or grandsons of John D. Chisholm since they entered land adjacent to him or where he had originally entered property. Joseph McHenry Chisholm and Benjamin F. Chisholm entered land on or adjacent to John D. Chisholm of Tennessee in present-day Lauderdale County, Alabama.

John D. Chisholm's son Ignatius married the daughter of Old Tassel, Doublehead's brother. Ignatius's son, Jesse Chisholm a half blood Cherokee, became important in history working with western tribes and for his namesake the Chisholm Trail. According to court records of 1811, John's son, Dennis was carried to court for not paying a debt; Dennis had followed his father to Indian Territory west of the Mississippi River.

John D. Chisholm Returns Home

For some eight years, John D. Chisholm served as the Western Cherokees representative to many meetings and treaties until 1817 when he returned to Lauderdale County, Alabama. After the Turkey Town Treaty of September 16-18, 1816, took the Indian lands and removed the Indians from the Muscle Shoals, Chisholm realized that as a white man he had the right to enter land in the area of

Doublehead's Reserve. Chisholm had learned to love the area during his years of living on the great Muscle Shoals of the Tennessee River in Lauderdale County, Alabama.

Sometime in late 1817 or early 1818, it appears that John D. Chisholm's family left Indian Territory west of the Mississippi River and returned to his old stomping grounds in Lauderdale County, Alabama. On March 5, 1818, John D. Chisholm of Tennessee first entered 164.06 acres of land in Lauderdale County, Alabama, in Section 18 of Township 2 South and Range 9 West (Cowart, 1996).

From March 5, 1818, through December 5, 1818, John D. Chisholm of Tennessee entered some 1,320 acres of land in Townships 1, 2, 3 South and Ranges 9, 11 West in Lauderdale County, Alabama. Approximately 920 acres were located north of Florence in Township 2 South and Range 11 West along the present-day Chisholm Road (Cowart, 1996).

Very likely, John enjoyed his new and independent old age away from the Chickamauga Cherokee people to whom he had devoted much of his life. Now on his own and not tied to a cause or struggle on behalf of tribal Indian people, he lived on his farm in peace and tranquility without being involved in conflicts or political situations. For some 10 years prior to his death in 1828, he lived on his own land in Lauderdale County, Alabama, where he probably enjoyed watching his children and grandchildren grow and prosper.

On April 26, 1830, John D. Chisholm, Junior entered 79.69 acres in the east ½ of the southwest ¼ adjacent to the 39.85 acre tract in the southwest ¼ of the southeast ¼ of Section 4 of Township1 South and Range 9 West in Lauderdale County, Alabama, that his father originally entered on November 21, 1818. On August 15, 1849, John D. Chisholm, Junior entered an adjacent tract of 39.85 acres in the southwest ¼ of the southwest ¼ of same section, township, and range.

On November 30, 1847, Joseph McHenry Chisholm entered 39.85 acres of land in the northwest ¼ of the southwest ¼ between the two tracts entered by John D. Chisholm, Junior. On September 14, 1854, Benjamin F. Chisholm was officially given the same 39.85 acres of land in Section 4 of Township1 South and

Range 9 West in Lauderdale County, Alabama, that was originally entered by John D. Chisholm, Senior of Tennessee on November 21, 1818 (Cowart, 1996). The land where the Chisholm boys entered their land was in the exact same area as John D. Chisholm, Senior of Tennessee had entered in 1818.

The younger John D. Chisholm, Junior is buried near John D. Chisholm, Senior in the Chisholm Cemetery north of Florence. In 1830, the young John Chisholm owned 13 black slaves that he probably inherited from this father. John Sr. and Nance, the sister of Doublehead, had a disagreement over some of Doublehead's slaves which John D. Chisholm claimed belonged to him.

Joseph McHenry Chisholm and Benjamin F. Chisholm entered land adjacent both senior and junior John D. Chisholm in Lauderdale County. The middle name "McHenry" probably came from the United States Secretary of War James McHenry who helped Captain John D. Chisholm receive compensation for work done for Governor William Blount. Both Joseph McHenry Chisholm and

Benjamin F. Chisholm are also probably the sons, the grandsons, or close relatives of Captain John D. Chisholm, Senior.

John Chisholm, Senior is buried in the Chisholm Cemetery about five miles north of Florence, Alabama, just a few yards west of the Chisholm Road. His wife Mary is buried next to his grave with the exact same kind of tombstone. His tombstone states, "In memory of John Chisholm, Senr. Born in the year 1738 on the day of August 8, died on 9th of October 1828" (Find a Grave Memorial Number 28901894).

Also buried near his father's grave are his son John Chisholm Jr. and other family members. John D. Chisholm, Jr. was born on November 22, 1775, and died on July 30, 1847. He was the son of John D. Chisholm, Sr. and Elizabeth "Patty" Sims Fauling Chisholm. John, Jr. became a preacher; he married Esther Lynn (1780-1852) on September 27, 1798; she is also buried in the Chisholm Cemetery.

The John D. Chisholm Family Cemetery is located north of Florence about five miles at Latitude 34.9025791 North and Longitude 87.6705778 West and is just a few yards to the west side of Highway 17. Today, Highway 17 still bears his family name and is known as the Chisholm Road which runs through the Florence area. In addition, the Chisholm Trail in the West is named in honor of his grandson Jesse Chisholm.

Today, some historians say that John D. Chisholm of Tennessee is buried somewhere in Arkansas, and that he died at Hot Springs in 1818 while visiting the springs for their healing powers. He would probably laugh and let them continue to think that way. The remains of the legal advisor, assistant, and partner of the Last Chickamauga Cherokee Chief Doublehead and Governor William Blount of Southwest Territory will forever rest in his land of Lauderdale County, Alabama, along with the remains of the old chief who lies on a hill just east of Bluewater Creek.

John Donelson's Muscle Shoals

In March 1780, Colonel John Donelson caught his first glimpse of the Muscle Shoals in North Alabama and fell in love with the area. Donelson began his historic voyage down the Tennessee almost forty years before his grandson-in-law General John Coffee and his surveyors laid out the towns of Florence and Tuscumbia; he was the grandfather of Coffee's wife Mary.

In spite of the dangers he faced at the moment he was passing through the Muscle Shoals, John Donelson resolved then and there to return as its owner and promoter. The hand of fate made no allowance for the older man's dreams, but later was to deal more favorably with his young kinsman, General John Coffee, his son-in-law General Andrew Jackson, and his grandson Captain John Donelson.

In 1779, John Donelson I, a Virginia surveyor, prepared to move his family from Fort Patrick Henry at present-day Kingsport, Tennessee, to the Big Salt Lick or French Lick at present-day Nashville, Tennessee. Traveling with Donelson was his daughter Rachel, who later married Andrew Jackson, and several other families.

Donelson began the four-month water trip journey down the Tennessee River, up the Ohio River, and then up the Cumberland to become one of the founders of Nashville. His flotilla consisted of thirty flatboats and canoes. They arrived at the head of the first rapids of Elk River Shoals on March 12, 1780, and, fortunately, found the Tennessee River extremely high. This, more than anything else, enabled their safe passage over these rapids and safe passage through all six of the shoals making up the Muscle Shoals. However, they did encounter gunfire from an Indian village-perhaps Melton's Bluff-as they were preparing to make their dangerous ride over the Muscle Shoals (Davidson, 1946).

Colonel John Donelson

Doublehead and the Lower Cherokee along the Tennessee River were firmly in control of the eastern and western ends of the Muscle Shoals, which consisted of a series of six sets of rapids covering some 35 miles of the river. On March 14, 1780, "When Colonel John Donelson and his company drifted down the Tennessee River, they encountered hostile Indians at both ends of the Muscle Shoals. At the lower end of the shoals, five of their party was wounded." This is one of the first confirmed conflicts with white settlers and the Chickamauga faction of Lower Cherokees at Doublehead's bastion of the Muscle Shoals. The Muscle Shoals stretched from just west Fox's Creek near present-day Decatur, Alabama, to Waterloo in western Lauderdale County, Alabama.

Donelson's first view of the Shoals was from his boat, "Adventurer," as he led his flotilla of frontier crafts in their terrifying passage over its treacherous rapids, rocks, and reefs of the Muscle Shoals. These perilous obstacles were not his only concern; he was fleeing from hostile Chickamauga Indians who were firing from the banks and cliffs along the way.

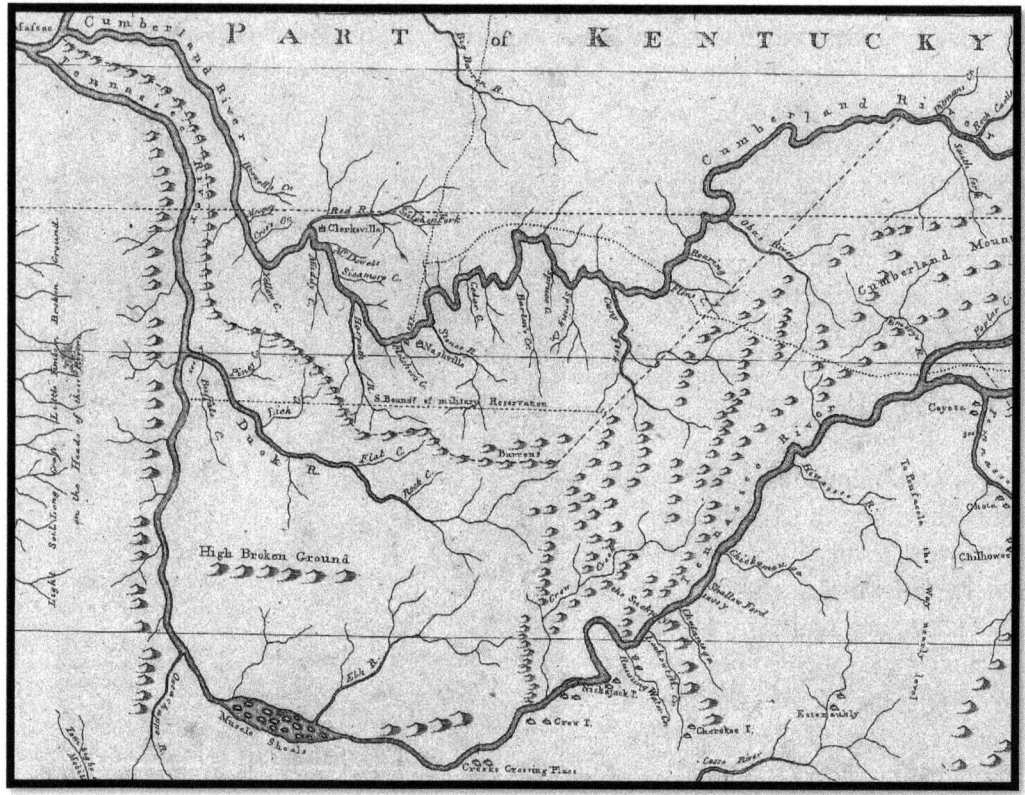

After the start of the Chickamauga War in 1775, Dragging Canoe, Bowl (Duwali), Glass (Tauquatehee), Cuttyatoy, and Doublehead had stopped earlier voyagers and white settlements along the Great Bend of the Tennessee River. Since their Chickamauga warriors controlled the southern portion of the river, they were likewise as determined to ravage the boats of Donelson and prevent the white settlement of their sacred buffalo hunting grounds along the Cumberland River to the north.

Colonel Donelson, with his crew of forty men along with one hundred and twenty women and children, left Fort Patrick Henry three days before Christmas on December 22, 1779. These were the families, of the first settlers at Nashville, who were to join the men who had made their way overland under General James Robertson.

The initial plans were to disembark at the Shoals and travel by land northward to Nashville. However, upon reaching the Shoals, Donelson searched in vain for a sign that Robertson was to have left. He had no other recourse than to proceed by water to the mouth of the Tennessee, up the Ohio, then up the Cumberland River to Nashville.

The Donelson fleet arrived at the Shoals on Sunday, March 12, 1780. He wrote in his Journal: "Set out, and after a few hours sailing we heard the crowing of cocks, and soon came within view of the town; here they fired on us again without doing injury. After running until about ten o'clock, we came in sight of the Muscle Shoals… When we approached them they had a dreadful appearance… The water being high made a terrible roaring… the current running in every possible direction. Here we did not know how soon we should be dashed to pieces, and all our troubles ended at once… But by the hand of Providence, we are not preserved from this danger also. I know not the length of the wonderful shoal; it had been represented to me to be twenty-five or thirty miles…"

Colonel John Donelson was not the average adventurer. Born April 7, 1725, in Somerset County, Maryland, his father was an importer and his maternal grandfather an Episcopal clergyman. His great-uncle was the first president of Princeton. As a young man, Donelson moved to Virginia and became a personal friend of George Washington. In his newly adopted state, he was elected vestryman for two parishes, appointed surveyor for two counties, and three times elected to the House of Burgesses. His military rank came about by being made a lieutenant colonel in the Virginia Militia.

John Donelson, as most successful men somehow manage to do, married well. She was Rachel Stockley of Accomack County, Virginia. Rachel was born in an old Hanoverian hip-roofed mansion built by her great-grandfather who was a member of the House of Burgesses. Eleven children had been born to the Donelsons when, in 1778, John's speculation in an iron industry swept away his accumulated wealth. Soon afterwards, he met General James Robertson and became a partner in the adventure that led him down the Tennessee and across the great Muscle Shoals.

After settling near Nashville, Donelson tried time and again to make good his dreams to own the Muscle Shoals. In July 1783, he and Joseph Martin, Cherokee Agent, bought for $5,000 in merchandise, the entire Muscle Shoals region. They dealt with twenty-two Indians whom they believed to be Chickamaugans: four chiefs, twelve young braves, and six women. They later learned that these Indians had no legitimate claim to the land.

Next, Donelson and friends acquired a grant of the entire Muscle Shoals district from Georgia. But that state's title to the Shoals was also disputed. Not only did the Donelson party not have a legal claim, they faced even greater problems with the enraged Chickasaws who were not about to allow white settlers in the area.

Donelson made three hazardous trips to the area during a four-year period that kept him away from Nashville most of the time. However, the Indians finally drove him from his Muscle Shoals, thus ending his dreams forever. The old colonel met his death April 11, 1786. It was reported that he had been killed by the Indians. However, his family maintained that he knew too well the ways of the Indians to have fallen at their hands. He surely must have been waylaid by white outlaws, they said.

One of the most interesting coincidences in the history of the Muscle Shoals, or maybe it is not coincidental, was that three of the prominent men in Donelson's family were later to be greatly involved in its development. General John Coffee, who was married to Donelson's granddaughter, Mary, became the key figure in the founding of Florence. Like John Donelson, the old patriarch of Mary's family, Coffee became so fascinated with the Muscle Shoals that he made it his home for the remaining days of his life. Coffee was aided and abetted by none other than Colonel John Donelson's son-in-law, General Andrew Jackson.

Colonel John Donelson's grandson, Captain John Donelson, eventually settled in Lauderdale County, Alabama. Captain John Donelson was born to John Donelson II (1755-1830) and Mary Purnell Donelson (1763-1848) in Davidson County, Tennessee, on April 23, 1787.

On November 6, 1823, John III married Eliza Eleanor Butler in Davidson County, Tennessee. Eliza was born on April 20, 1791; she was the daughter of Edward Butler, a Revolutionary War hero, and Isabella Fowler, daughter of a British officer. When their father died in Tennessee in 1803, Eliza and her siblings became the wards of Andrew and Rachel Jackson. Eliza died on November 4, 1850 (Find a Grave Memorial Number 87142558).

From March 11, 1818, through December 15, 1847, John Donelson entered 2,352 acres in Township 3 South and Ranges 9, 10, 12 West in

Lauderdale County, Alabama (Cowart, 1996). According to the 1850 Lauderdale County, Alabama, the estate of John Donelson owned 160 black slaves.

John Donelson III died on April 28, 1840 (Find a Grave Memorial Number 38635479). He is buried in the Coffee Cemetery which was located on

1823 Marriage Record of John and Eliza Donelson

John Coffee's Hickory Hill Plantation at Florence in Lauderdale County, Alabama.

No other family had a greater interest and a more abiding love for the beautiful Muscle Shoals than the family of Colonel John Donelson. They surely have left their mark in the legacy of Lauderdale County and the land of the Muscle Shoals where "Cotton was King."

Lauderdale County

Florence

Florence became the focal center of the cotton planters that migrated into Lauderdale County; the cotton gins and mills were usually located close to the town. Many of the more wealthy planters would have a residence in Florence, which was similar to Courtland in Lawrence County and Tuscumbia in Franklin County. Florence was the business and wealth center of the cotton industry of Lauderdale County, Alabama.

Before steamboats arrived at Florence on the Tennessee River, cotton and other goods were floated to the ports at New Orleans in cotton-boxes which were large flat bottomed boats sixty to eighty feet long. The cotton was also transported on pole or keel boats which were flat or decked boats usually with a single pole in the rear for steering. After reaching their destination, the cotton boxes were broken up and sold as lumber; however, the pole-boats were sometimes filled with supplies and pushed or paddled upstream to their origin.

The first steamboats on the lower Tennessee began operations after the Turkey Town Treaty of 1816. However, it was 1821 before the first steamboat reached Florence in Lauderdale County, Alabama. Small steamboats reached Florence and Waterloo, which were the main ports on the lower Tennessee River, only five or six months each year because of low water levels.

According to an article titled "Lauderdale County, Alabama, History of the Shoals," and published in the Times Daily, Thursday, February 25, 1999, by Harry E. Wallace, "The Civil War brought great destruction to the Counties of the Tennessee Valley. Almost all transportation, communication, and industry were destroyed. Education facilities ceased to operate and the 'cotton kingdom' was virtually destroyed. Post-war recovery would be long and painful."

Political Representatives of the County to Civil War Era

Most of the pre-Civil War political leaders of Florence and Lauderdale County were the wealthy slave owning cotton planters or their older children. Many of the sons of the first cotton barons became military officers in the Confederate Army.

The following political representatives of Lauderdale County, Alabama, are found in "Alabama Trails, History Of Lauderdale County, Alabama, Her Resources and History," by Willis Brewer in 1872: "Representatives 1819-Jacob Baylor and Thomas Garrard; 1820-Hugh McVay and Jonathan Bailey; 1821-G. Masterson and John Craig; 1822-James Jackson and Francis Durett; 1823-James Jackson and C. S. Manly; 1824-Jacob Baylor and J. P. Cunningham; 1825-Jonathan Bailey, William B. Martin, and George Coulter; 1826-Hugh McVay, Samuel Craig, and Henry Smith; 1827-Hugh McVay, Samuel Craig, and Francis Durett; 1828-J. L. D. Smith, Wm. George, and Francis Durett; 1829-John Pope, Samuel Craig, and Francis Durett; 1830-Hugh McVay, Wm. George, and J. P. Cunningham; 1831-Hugh McVay, Samuel Craig, and John McKinley; 1832-Cornelius Carmack, George S. Houston, and Samuel Young; 1833-Cornelius Carmack, James Jackson, and Samuel Harkins; 1834-C. Carmack, Jas. Jackson, S.

Young, and J. B. Womack; 1835-C. Carmack, S. 0. Posey. L. Garner, and E. Sheffield; 1836-C. Carmack, C. Posey, John McKinley, and H. M. Patton; 1837-C. Carmack, Geo. Simmons, J. M. Boston, and E. Sheffield; 1838-C. Carmack, J. Douglas, Jas. M. Boston, and B. R. Garner; 1839-Henry D. Smith, J. Douglas, and A. O. Horn; 1840-Henry D. Smith, J. Douglas, and J. R Alexander; 1841-Henry D. Smith, J. Kennedy, and J. K. Alexander; 1842-Henry D. Smith, J. Douglas, and John Kennedy; 1843-B. B. Barker. J. Douglas, and J. R. Alexander; 1844-H. D. Smith, W. Baugh, and J. R. Alexander; 1845-E. G. Young, B. B. Barker, and J. C. F. Wilson; 1847-L. P. Walker, John E. Moore, and J. S. Kennedy; 1849-L. P. Walker, R. M. Patten, and Joseph Hough; 1851-R. W. Walker, V. M. Bouham, and O. H. Oates; 1853-L. P. Walker and Wm. Rhodes; 1855-R. W. Walker and H. D. Smith; 1857-S. A. M. Wood and H. D. Smith; 1859-S. D. Harmon and H. D. Smith; 1861-S.C. Posey and J. H. Witherspoon; 1863-Alexander M. Alexander and T. L. Chisholm; 1865-Edward M. Alexander and B. E. Bourland; 1867-(No election); 1870-B. F. Taylor."

Land Grants

Many of the military veterans who served prior to the white settlement of Lauderdale County were given land grants. According to the "Alabama Land Grants and Land Patents Collection, 1810-1854, Box 4, Folder 6, Land Grants," the following individuals were given land in northwest Alabama: 1) Herman, Alexander, Lauderdale County 1836; 2) Herman, Robert, Lauderdale County 1836; 3) Hodges, Henry W., Lawrence County 1836; 4) Harris, Peter, Lauderdale County 1836; 5) Howell, Levi, Lauderdale County 1836; 6) Hunt, James, Lauderdale County 1836; 7) Hutchings, John (John Coffee, Executor), Lauderdale County 1837; 8) Hicks, Robert H., Lauderdale County 1836; 9) Henderson, Martha, Lawrence County 1836; 10) Harvey, James W., Lawrence County 1836; 11) Holland, Thomas, Lawrence County 1836; and 12) Hough, Joseph, Lawrence County 1839.

Early Cotton Mills of Lauderdale County

Globe Cotton Factory

In 1840, the Globe Cotton Factory was built on Cypress Creek. Eventually the cotton factory was expanded and three dams were built to support the additions. By 1857, the Cypress Creek water powered operation included three cotton mills, a flour mill, and two corn mills. The Globe Cotton Factory employed as many as 310 people by 1860; the employees included women and children who were paid an average of two dollars and fifty cents each week. The Union Army burned the facilities at the Globe Cotton Factory in May 1863. One factory called Cypress Mill, was rebuilt after the war, but its operation was never successful.

The following is an article titled "Assault on Lauderdale, History of the Shoals," and published in the Times Daily, Thursday, February 25, 1999, by Harry E. Wallace. "On May 26, 1863, a Federal force of 1,380 under the command of Col. Florence M. Cornyn left Corinth, Miss., determined to end the industrial productivity of Lauderdale County. At the time, Lauderdale was a leading producer of cotton and wool cloth, leather and food. Accompanying Cornyn was Capt. Risden Deford, son of a former Methodist circuit rider. McDonald said Deford knew the location of the mills, tan yards, and foundries and led Union forces against people who had earlier welcomed him and his father into their homes. Cornyn's force entered near Rawhide (Cloverdale) and after dividing his force, they burned the mills and tan yards along Big and

Little Cypress Creeks, Cowpen Creek, Shoals Creek, and Cox Creek. The 'Defender of Florence' was Brig. Gen. Sterling A. M. Wood, son of Florence's first mayor. Wood's forces met the Federals near Cox Creek on the Coffee Road (Cloverdale Road) and were quickly forced to fight a retreating movement back into the city. Wood's men held Florence most of the day as units of Cornyn's men burned the Globe Cotton Mills on Cypress Creek near the present site of the Florence Golf and Country Club. Local citizens recalled seeing the smoke from the center of the city. After forcing Wood to retreat, Cornyn ordered a block of homes and buildings burned to cover his withdrawal. Cornyn's raid devastated Florence and industry in the valley. In addition to the destruction of the Globe Mills, worth more than $1 million, Cornyn destroyed food and grain and stole horses, mules, cattle and slaves. William L. McDonald has said that Florence and the Shoals area did not recover industrially until the Tennessee Valley Authority came into the valley in 1933."

Eagle Cotton Factory

In 1846, William McKnight, Junior and his partners, Louvick and Wiley Park built the Eagle Cotton Factory. The old cotton mill was destroyed by the flood of 1902. At the time, the cotton factory employed seventy-five people. The late Ina Foutch recalled that her grandfather, William James Redding, mill supervisor, stayed up all night watching the dangerously rising water. After the mill washed away, Redding was not able to reach his home for two days because of the flooded creeks in the area.

Fortunately, the nearby mill village was on higher ground and survived the flood with very little damage. Yet, the jobs held by these workers had been washed down the creek with the mill. A number of these employees moved to Florence where they found work in the Cherry and Ashcraft Cotton Mills.

Remembered as the Freshet of 1902, the folks in Lauderdale County, Alabama, and the adjoining Tennessee Counties, talked about it as long as they lived. A number of weather watchers referred to it as the "hundred year flood."

Torrential rains had pounded the area "for days on end," and on Good Friday, March 28, 1902, the creek banks overflowed. In its April 4 edition, the

Florence Herald reported serious damages ranging from Second Creek at Waterloo to Bluewater Creek in East Lauderdale County. The foundation of the bridge in Waterloo was moved out two feet. The Huntsville Road Bridge in Bluewater Creek was washed away and the steel approaches to the Bluewater Creek Bridge at Hostler's Mill were wrecked.

The Gunwaleford Road Bridge and the Waterloo Road Bridge over Cypress Creek, west of Florence, were completely swept away. Big and Little Cypress creeks were six feet and five feet, respectively, above the highest flood mark every known. The floodwater had risen ten feet above the floor of the Waterloo Road Bridge before the structure broke loose. Parts of David Allen Sharp's Mill could be seen at various places in the rushing waters of Little Cypress Creek. It is believed that some deaths occurred, but details were not mentioned by The Herald.

The floodwater on Shoals Creek was especially damaging. The two Lauderdale County bridges, one at Happy Hollow and the other on the Huntsville Road, were destroyed.

One of the worst disasters occurred near the Horseshoe Bend on the Shoals Creek south of Lawrenceburg. The dam broke and washed away the remains of the Eagle Cotton Mill that had recently been damaged by a fire. The nearby cotton gin and gristmill also were victims of the 1902 freshet.

Before the building of Wilson, Wheeler, and Pickwick Dams, and the beginning of TVA's flood control system, there were annual swellings of the Shoals mainly because of heavy rainfalls plus the spring thaws among the mountains upstream. Generally, at least one flood occurred annually in the 652 mile stream of the Tennessee River. Records kept by the U. S. Corps of Engineers show that the greatest flood to inundate the Tennessee Valley prior to 1973 was in March 1867. Because of the variations in the riverbed, a rise of fifty feet in Chattanooga (a big flood) would register, perhaps only five feet above the normal river level at the Muscle Shoals. The highest record on the Tennessee River at the Muscle Shoals occurred in March 1897 when the construction site of the Riverton Canal and Lock System was inundated and heavily damaged. It was during this flood that a steamboat was said to have unloaded its passengers at the foot of South Court Street.

Cotton Planters and the Number of Slaves

According to the 1850 Lauderdale County Slave Schedule, 535 slave owning cotton planters in the county owned a little over 6,000 black slaves which made up about 35 percent of the total population living there in that time. Only 77 of these slave holders were women who owned some 800 black servants that they had basically inherited from their deceased husbands or fathers. However, only 21 white females owned over 20 black slaves; these ladies were Martha Armistead (22), Nancy Barnett (30), Elizabeth Beckwith (45). Matilda Bedford (46), Marry Coffee (61). Janet Collier (83), Julia Fuqua (30), Sarah Hannah (51), Mary J. Hood (48), Miss M. Houston (71), Sarah Ingram (21), Jane Irion (97), Sarah Jackson (81), Mary Key (20), Miss M. McIntyre (21), Nancy Pool (21), Catherine Probasco (30), Milly Tate (21), Nancy Vaughn (24), Mary and Lucy Westmoreland (28), and Priscillia Wilson (40).

The following tables give the 192 cotton planters in Lauderdale County, Alabama, who owned over 20 black slaves. The tables list slave owners and numbers of slaves from 1830 through 1860. These planters and slave numbers are found in the United States Census records and the slave schedules.

Lauderdale Planters	1830	1840	1850	1860
Allen, Lewes	43			
Anderson, Chapman			24	
Armistead, Peter Fontaine	30			
Armistead, George		103	114	133
Armistead, Mrs. M.			22	
Bailey, Richard A.				24
Baloo, George	45			
Barnett, Nancy				30
Barnett, Thomas			26	
Beckwith, Alexander				48
Beckwith, Elizabeth				45
Beckwith, Jonathan	29	29	66	
Bedford, John				28
Bedford, Matilda	46	25		
Beleu, George	42			
Benford, Hugh			20	
Benningfield, Charles				29
Binford, L. H.				28
Boddie, James				21
Boddie, Nathan			79	94
Brooks, Robert	50			
Bryan, Joseph	34			
Burton, William M.	21			
Carroll, Wilson				39
Chambers, Edward O.	34			
Chandler, Elijah				23
Cheatham, Christopher	49			
Cheatham, Kit		45		
Coburn, C.		92		
Coffee, John	83			
Coffee, Mary		75	61	20
Coffee, R. S.				20
Collier, Janet				83
Collier, Wyatt	26	40	64	
Cox, P.		21		
Craig, John	55			
Crittenden, Benjamin			22	
Crittenden, B. F.				31

Name				
Crittenden, William H.		29	23	E 25
Crow, Jno		20		
Cunningham, J.	22			
Cunningham, Jonathan			47	
Cunningham, J. M.				71
Dameron, S.		57		
Dillahunty, J. B.		30		
Dillahunty, Harvey		45		
Donahoo, John	22			
Donelson, John (Estate)			160	
Douglass, James				24
Douglass, Jonathan	63			
Duglis, James			21	
Ellis, A. G.				24
Foster, George W.			67	98
Fuqua, John			29	
Hannah, Sarah	51			
Haraway, P. L.				21
Hardin, Jno		32		
Hardin, Presley			61	
Harden, P. W.				70
Harkins, Martin			36	
Harkins, M. (Crow manager)				49
Harrison, D.T., Luke & John				47
Hawkins, Josiah			26	
Hawkins, Wiley T.				47
Hawn, Samuel	75			
Hayes, Jessee	32			
Herndon, George				E 25
Hightower, Hardy	43	56		
Hightower, John Oldham		36		
Holland, James			25	50
Hood, James	39			
Hood, John			64	82
Hood, Mary J.		48		
Hough, Joseph			28	47
Houston, David	36			
Houston, Miss M.			71	
Houston, H.		60		
Howell, A. W.				23
Hutchins, Andrew J.		92		156

Name				
Hutchens Estate			101	
Ingram, Benjamin		25		
Ingram, Henry			20	49
Ingram, Joseph & Benjamin				34
Ingram, George				32
Ingram, Sarah			21	
Irion, Jane				97
Irvine, James			82	
Irwin, James		48		
Isbell, lewis			21	
Jackson, James	73	86		
Jackson, Sarah			66	81
Jones, Dr. A. H.				22
Jones, Francis H.			22	
Jones, Thomas R.		21		
Jones, William E.			62	
Jones, William E. (*by J.Skipworth)				30
Jordon, George	46			
Jordon, William				E 25
Kennedy, Hiram		28	27	E 25
Kennedy, J.S., managerJ.Roberts				37
Kernachan, Abraham	46			
Kernachan, Robert		81	27	22
Kernachan, Robert T. Jr.			39	49
Key, John	29			
Key, Mary A. R.				20
Key, William H.			74	149
Kidd, William	20			
Koger, William			52	
Kroger, William, estate				57
Lansford, Thomas Adams		30		
Lassiter, Thomas W.		30		
Lee, Nathan	48			
Lorance, John		75		
Lovell, Charles	25			
Malone, Mitchell			32	43
Marks, Lewis L.			36	
McCally (McCully), P.		113		
McCartney, Robert		35		
McDonnell, Joseph	23			
McIntyre, Miss M.			21	

Name				
McVay, Hugh	24	35	42	
Moore, Lewis C.				29
Nance family				21
Nance, Sterling			23	
Nelson, Mayhaw	35			
Noel, Edmond			25	35
Noel, James		43	53	
Noland, William H.			21	
Noyer, Willi		46		
O'Neal, B.			28	
Paddy, N.		69		
Patton, Robert M.		24	73	117
Perkins, Harden			62	
Perkins, Thomas				50
Peters, Jack				29
Peters, John			198	313
Phillips, J.				20
Plucknett (Blackwell), D. F.		26		
Pool, Nancy				21
Pope, John	57			
Posey, Sidney C.			40	50
Price, James B.& Wm.H.				23
Probasco, Catherine			30	
Reed, James	36			
Reynolds, Hue				20
Rowell, Neal		27	72	89
Savage, Samuel	25			
Scrags (Savags), G. M.		80		
Shoulders, Ben, Wm., C., & Allen				28
Simon, George			21	
Simons, George				59
Simpson, John		83	99	117
Smith, Henry	105	120		91
Smith, Henry D.		105	137	98
Smith, Joseph L.	34			
Stewart, James W.			31	
Summerhill, Horace				23
Surrell, Charles	27			
Taler, Benjamin			37	
Tate, Milly			21	
Taylor, Benjamin				49

Name				
Taylor, S. F.		37		
Thompson, Joseph		41	E 87	106
Thompson, Lawrence	80	66	56	64
Thrasher, Hanson	51			
Tucker, William R. (A.)		33		
Underwood, L.		71		
Vaughn, Nancy				24
Vaughn, Samuel	75	24	46	
Waits, Joseph W.	81			
Walton, P.		92		
Walker, Richard, manager Josh.Paulk				39
Walston, John & James				41
Watkins, R. H.			85	
Watkins, R. W., manager R Hamlet				77
Westmoreland, Mary & Lucy				28
White, Moses				22
Whiteman, Moses		71		
Williams, David			40	
Williams, D. C.				40
Williams, Henry		34		
Williams, James J.			40	
Williams, James Paul		39		28
Williams, John		28	30	49
Williams, Jno. J.		42		
Williams, John S.			66	
Williams, Nelson	25			
Wilson, John S.				92
Wilson, Matthew		38	53	99
Wilson, Priscilla			40	
Witherspoon, James				36
Wood, Alexander's sons				27
		E:Estate		

Chapter 3-Cotton Planters of Lauderdale

The Tennessee River was used as early as 1764 as a water route by white settlers passing by Lauderdale County through the Muscle Shoals. They were headed for the Natchez District of West Florida which had been opened up for settlement by the 1763 proclamation. Most of the early emigrants from Virginia and North Carolina traveled by land to Southwest Point (present-day Kingston, Tennessee) at the junction of the Clinch River and Tennessee River. These white settlers floated down the Holston, Tennessee, Ohio, and the Mississippi Rivers to their new homes.

After the start of the Chickamauga War with the signing of the Treaty of Sycamore Shoals in 1775, the Natchez District migration slowed to a trickle. However, the flood gates of migration into Lauderdale County became wide open with the Turkey Town Treaty of September 16 and 18, 1816, ceding of Indian lands along the Muscle Shoals of northwest Alabama. The 1816 treaty was ratified by congress in July 1817, after which the federal government opened up these Indian lands for purchase starting in 1818.

After the Indians were removed, the federal sale of Cherokee and Chickasaw lands began in 1818, along the Muscle Shoals which led to a land rush called "Alabama Fever." Groups of slave owning cotton farmers organized wagon trains to make the hazardous trek across the Appalachians to obtain the rich fertile lands along the Muscle Shoals of Tennessee River Valley for their cotton farming activities. Some wagon trains consisting of forty to fifty families with their black slaves traveled over rough mountainous terrain to newly acquired Indian lands of Lauderdale County, Alabama, in order to purchase their cotton plantations. They were drawn to the Muscle Shoals of the Tennessee River Valley by stories of the rich soil where "Cotton was King."

The wealthy eastern planters coming to the Muscle Shoals area brought with them many black slaves to use in the labor of reaping the wealth through the planting, working, and picking the cotton. Their plantation system was readily transplanted from the poor lands of the eastern colonial states to the rich river bottom lands adjacent to the Muscle Shoals of northwest Alabama. The steady demand for cotton made this product the nation's leading export during the first half of the 1800's; it also made the slave owning plantation holders wealthy and powerful people with a sense of self-importance. Prior to the Civil War, the large slave holding planters enjoyed a time when cotton was king.

Before the end of the Civil War, the wealthy cotton planters of the Muscle Shoals that depended on slave labor experienced a disastrous decline in their money and power. Many of these slave owning planters lost everything during and after the Civil War.

A few of the very wealthy plantation and former slave owners were able to hold on to vast tracts of Turkey Town cession lands that were passed down to their future generations by placing their lands in a trust. Today within the Tennessee Valley of northwest Alabama, many early cotton planter families still enjoy these large land holdings that they were able to gain through the free labor of their black slaves.

The following are family profiles on some of the many cotton planters that called Lauderdale County home. From 1818 through the Civil War, there were so many planters that it is not possible to discuss all in this book or to find information on their plantations. The plantation and slave owners are listed in alphabetical order.

Armistead, Peter Fontaine I

Peter Fontaine Armistead I was born in Hanover County, Virginia in 1780. He was the second son of Bowles and Mary (Fontaine) Armistead. Peter F. Armistead I descended from Colonel John Armistead of Hesse in Gloucester County, Virginia. Peter I married Martha Henry Winston; she was born on July 7,

1784, in Culpepper County, Virginia. Peter I and Martha Winston Armistead were the descendants of wealthy aristocratic families of Virginia.

Martha Winston Armistead's paternal home near Brandy Station in Culpeper County, Virginia, was known as "Glen Ella." In her early life, Martha Henry (Winston) Armistead lived in the home that was built about 1799 by her father Doctor Isaac Winston. Martha was a cousin of both Patrick Henry and Dolly Madison and, like her husband, connected by blood to the agrarian cotton planters Virginia.

By early 1818, Peter and Martha were living in Lauderdale County of North Alabama. They put their Virginia property up for sale and migrated from Culpepper County, Virginia; however, the land records of Lauderdale County, Alabama, report that Peter was of Frankfort, Kentucky. Between 1819 and 1822, while living in Lauderdale County, Peter and Martha Winston Armistead sold their Virginia property. In 1821, George Thorn bought their plantation home in Culpepper County, Virginia.

Peter, Martha, and their children settled in the fertile, rolling countryside bordering Cypress Creek some five miles west of Florence, on the present-day Savannah Highway. Peter first entered 160 acres of land in Section 31 of Township 2 South and Range 11 West in Lauderdale County on March 7, 1818. By 1823, he had entered some 860 acres of land in Lauderdale County. From March 7, 1818, through October 20, 1823, Peter Armistead entered 864 acres in Townships 2, 3 South and Ranges 11, 12, 13 West in Lauderdale County, Alabama. The vast majority of the land he entered was 464 acres in Township 3 South and Range 13 West (Cowart, 1996).

According to Vicki Rice in the website Rootsweb, "A History of Trinity Episcopal Church 1824-1976, Florence, Alabama", Peter Fontaine Armistead I had a 600 acre land grant dated June 5, 1814, and settled there. The National Register of Historic Places states, "The Armistead house stands on land first purchased from the federal government on March 7, 1818, with the dwelling erected soon after the initial purchase, probably in the early 1820s."

As with many of the wealthy planters, the name of the head of the plantation was carried through several generations of their sons and such was the situation with Peter Fontaine Armistead. Peter I and Martha had thirteen children:

1) Peter Fontaine Armistead II, (1810-1898) of Melrose, Franklin County;
2) William Bowles Armistead;
3) Patrick Henry Armistead;
4) Issac Coles Armistead;
5) Elizabeth Coles Armistead;
6) Elizabeth Virginia Armistead (1822-1849);
7) George Washington Armistead, twin;
8) Mary Ann Armistead, twin;
9) Martha Henry Armistead;
10) Sarah Armistead;
11) Nancy Armistead;
12) Lewis Armistead; and
13) Ellen O. Armistead.

The 1830 census of Lauderdale County lists 30 black slaves belonging to Peter Fountaine Armistead. In 1836, Peter Fontaine Armistead I was elected as the first senior warden of the vestry of Trinity Episcopal Church of Florence and was one of its original members.

Peter Fountaine Armistead I is not mentioned in the 1840 slave census. Sometime during or prior to the 1840s for whatever the reason, Peter Fountaine Armistead I left his wife Martha Armistead in the Tennessee Valley of Lauderdale County, Alabama and moved on to Panola County, Mississippi.

Peter Fountaine Armistead I was supposedly following a progressive westward migration pattern of cotton barons of that period. He was lured by the newer cotton country to the west; however, the circumstances of his departure are shrouded in mystery. According to folklore and oral traditions, Peter and Martha were having marital difficulties because of his illicit relations with slave women on the plantation that resulted in a number of mulatto offspring. One such son by the name of George Armistead was reputedly a natural black descendant of Peter Fontaine Armistead I.

Peter Fountaine Armistead died in 1866 in Panola, Mississippi. The location of his burial site is not known.

Martha and some of their children remained in Lauderdale County, Alabama. According to the 1850 slave census of Lauderdale County, Martha Armistead owned 22 black slaves. According to the 1860 slave census, Mrs. M. H. Armistead owned only 13 black slaves.

Martha Henry Winston Armistead continued to live at the Armistead Place and plantation home near Florence until her death on August 3, 1870, at the age of eighty eight. Martha Winston Armistead was laid to rest in the private cemetery beside the graves of other family members. In 1849, Peter and Martha's daughter, Ellen Armistead, married Reverend Jonathan B. T. Smith, who was a member of Trinity Church. A child of Ellen and Jonathan Smith, Martha, is buried in the family graveyard near the Armistead residence.

George Armistead

George Armistead, the son of Peter and Martha, married Ann Beckwith (1834-1889) and eventually moved to Arkansas. According to the 1840 slave census of Lauderdale County, George G. Armistead owned 103 black slaves.

In 1850, George Armistead owned 114 black slaves and Robert Armistead owned 14 slaves. In 1860, George Armistead owned 133 black slaves in various locations across Lauderdale County.

According to the court records of Lauderdale County, Alabama, "In 1861, George G. Armistead signed a $30,000 security bond in behalf of James B. and Young A. Gray, administrators of the estate of Elizabeth Childress, deceased. Now, Armistead asserts, the Grays are fighting between themselves, are insolvent, and Young Gray has left the state. Several estate slaves are imprisoned 'at expense.' He asks to be discharged from his responsibility; otherwise, he contends, he will sustain a substantial loss."

Armistead Plantation and Home

In 1877, Thomas S. Broadfoot purchased the plantation from the Armistead heirs. Afterwards, the Armistead house went through a long period of neglect before it was sold in the mid 1930's to Mr. and Mrs. Howard Wright. The Wrights were the parents of the present owner who undertook restoration work on the house in the 1970s.

According to the National Register, "The Armistead House is significant for its associations with the development of large slave based cotton plantations in Alabama's Tennessee Valley by descendants of wealthy Virginia planter families." The Peter Fountaine Armistead I home was added to the National Register of Historic Places.

The old Armistead home place is located approximately three miles west of Florence on the north side of the Waterloo Road in Lauderdale County, Alabama. From Wikipedia, "The Peter F. Armistead I home was placed on the Alabama Register of Landmarks and Heritage in1978 and the United States National Register of Historic Places in 1986."

According to National Register of Historic Places, "The Armistead home is a historic Tidewater Cottage built circa 1825. The outside of the house being a copy of the original owner's ancestral home in Culpepper County, Virginia, known as "Glen Ella." The house is one of the best examples in the group of the transfer of architectural tradition from the eastern seaboard into Alabama. It is the only double pile, wood frame example in this thematic group and the only one with a plan featuring a large center room at the back of the stair hall."

Peter Fontaine and Martha Henry Winston Armistead Home

Today, the historic grounds of the Armistead Place include 30 acres of land around the old plantation home. Also on the Armistead Place, there was a white cemetery for the slave owners and a separate black slave cemetery. During the early 1900s, the white Armistead Cemetery was destroyed by being plowed over except for two tombstones that are no longer located on their exact grave sites. The black slave Armistead cemetery has not been altered and is still being used as a burial site.

Bailey, Jonathan-Bailey Springs

Jonathan Bailey was born in Fauquier County, Virginia, in 1792; he was the son of Richard, a Revolutionary War soldier, and Margaret Bailey. Jonathan married Frances Herald about 1809; Frances was born around 1795 in North Carolina, and she died January 11, 1866.

Jonathan and Frances Bailey moved to the Pulaski, Tennessee, area around 1809 to Lauderdale County, Alabama. They came with their family from Tennessee in a covered wagon along Indian trails to the Indian crossing of Doublehead's Trace on Shoals Creek. A portion of Doublehead's Trace was upgraded as the first road created by the State of Alabama legislature on December 16, 1819. The widening of the Indian road was authorized two days after Alabama was admitted into the Union on December 14, 1819.

John Byler was given the contract to widen the Indian route into a wagon road; therefore, the new road was called the Byler Road. According to the Alabama legislation, the Byler Road started at Samuel Craig's place on the southwest side of Jackson's Military Bridge that crossed Shoals Creek on the ancient Indian trail. Byler Road ran south from Samuel Craig's place and passed by Bailey Springs which was named in honor of the Bailey Family.

From Bailey Springs, the road followed the old Doublehead Trace south by Tate Springs and on to Bainbridge Ferry where it crossed the Tennessee River. The old roads were laid out to go by everlasting springs where the people traveling during the dry seasons could replenish their fresh water supplies. According to the 1850 slave schedules for Lauderdale County, Milly Tate owned 21 black slaves, and in 1860, John S. Tate owned 17 black slaves.

On December 16, 1819, an act was approved by Alabama Legislature at Huntsville and signed by Governor William W. Bibb. The act identified the route of the Byler Road through Lauderdale County, Alabama, as follows: "Beginning on the great military road, leading from Columbia in Tennessee to Madisonville in Louisiana, at or near the place where Samuel Craig now lives, on the west side of Big Shoals Creek in Lauderdale County; thence, the nearest and best way to the Tennessee River, at the ferry opposite the town of Bainbridge, Franklin County."

The Baileys settled on Shoals Creek in Lauderdale County, Alabama, and they owned land on both sides of Shoals Creek just a mile or so downstream east of Jackson's Old Military Road Bridge. Jonathan Bailey was an owner of 16 black slaves who helped with his farming operations and at his resort.

David Curott and Butch Walker at red oak on Doublehead's Trace or Byler Road at Bainbridge Loop, Colbert County, AL

From March 6, 1818, through December 12, 1852, Jonathan Bailey entered 680 acres of land in Township 2 South and Range 10 West in Lauderdale County, Alabama. On September 26, 1850, Bailey entered 40 acres in Township 1 South and Range 9 West in Lauderdale County, Alabama (Cowart, 1996). In 1846, Jonathan purchased 40 acres containing the springs from Joseph Hough; Joseph entered a lot of land adjacent to Jonathan Bailey. According to the 1850 Lauderdale County, Alabama, census, Joseph Hough owned 28 black slaves.

After becoming owner of Bailey Springs, Jonathan began drinking its water and claimed it cured some of his ailments. He boasted of the healing qualities of the water, and before long, the medicinal properties spread far and wide. Bailey Springs became one of the most popular antebellum resorts and medicinal springs in the region; especially Lauderdale County, Alabama. Bailey built a huge hotel with a large ballroom to cater to and entertain his guests who came from all over the southeast to receive the healing powers of the spring water. The water from Bailey Springs was placed in jars and bottles to be sent to places all over the southeastern United States.

In 1854, the Bailey Springs Post Office was established with Jonathan Bailey as the first postmaster. The post office was closed permanently in 1901. Jonathan Bailey operated the Bailey Springs Hotel and Resort until his death in October 28, 1857.

According to Lauderdale County, Alabama, court records, accession number 20185717, "Richard A. and James J. Bailey, administrators of the estate of Jonathan Bailey, deceased, request to sell the sixteen slaves (one of them an unnamed three-year-old) and other personal property for a fair and equitable division thereof among numerous heirs." According to the 1860 Lauderdale County, Alabama, Slave Schedule, James J. Bailey owned ten black slaves, Richard A. Bailey owned 24 black slaves, and Mrs. Frances Bailey owned five black slaves.

After the Civil War, the resort lost its popularity and never regained the highly regarded status as a medicinal tourist destination. The resort was sold to A. G. Ellis whose daughter Virginia married Dr. Henry A. Moody; Moody had his medical practice at Bailey Springs until 1888. The 1860 slave census of Lauderdale County records that A. G. Ellis owned 24 black slaves.

According to the 1860 Lauderdale County, Alabama census, A. G. Ellis was a 54 year old male born in Virginia and owner of Bailey Springs properties. Also listed in his house number 120 was M. L. a 47 year old female born in Alabama, William P. a 19 year old male born in Mississippi who was clerk at the springs, Virginia A. a 17 year old female born in Mississippi, Martha J. a 15 year old female born in Mississippi, W. B. Holloway a 27 year old male wagon maker born in Georgia, Margaret J. a 22 year old female born in Tennessee, John W. a seven months old male born in Tennessee, and William Ellis a six year old male born in Arkansas.

Baker, Elijah Adam

The former Secretary of State James Baker's great-great grandparents, Elijah Adam Baker and Jane Casey Saxton Baker, were early settlers of the Gravelly Springs Community, about twelve miles west of Florence. From January 21, 1826, through December 16, 1839, Elijah enter 240 acres of land in Township 2 South and Ranges 12, 13, 14 West in Lauderdale County, Alabama (Cowart, 1996).

Elijah, a native of North Carolina, was born in 1792. Jane's maiden name was Casey, and she was also from North Carolina where she was born in 1798. A daughter, Mary Jane Baker, was married to Wilson Carroll whose family had purchased land in Gravelly Springs as early as 1821. Members of the Carroll family owned several black slaves. According to the 1860 slave census, Wilson Carroll owned 39 black slaves, Addison Carroll owned 15 black slaves, and John S. Carroll owned 106 black slaves.

Former United States Secretary of State, James A. Baker, has deep roots at the Muscle Shoals. Baker was much in the news during the Florida vote controversy when, as an attorney, he represented George W. Bush. Baker had previously served as Secretary of State in the administration of former President George H. Bush, father of President George W. Bush.

Following Elijah's death in 1845, his widow, Jane, was married first to Samuel Croft, and later, to Jabez Cobb. According to the 1860 Lauderdale County, Alabama, Slave Schedule, Jabez Cobb owned nine black slaves. Jane Baker Cobb moved to Huntsville, Texas, sometime prior to her death in 1884. Her final resting place is about fifty feet from the grave of the great Texas hero, Sam Houston.

The oldest son of Elijah and Jane Baker of Gravelly Springs was James Addison Baker who was the great grandfather of the former Secretary of State. He practiced law in Florence from 1843 until 1852. Born in 1816 in the Alabama Territory, Baker was admitted to the Alabama Bar in 1843, at which time he became a partner with a prominent Florence attorney, Samuel W. Probasco.

Samuel Probasco was married to Catherine Hightower; however he died in 1845. According to the 1850 Lauderdale County, Alabama, census Mrs. Catherine Hightower Probasco owned 30 black slaves. Florence attorney James Addison Baker was married to Caroline Hightower on May 30, 1849; she was a sister of Probasco's wife, Catherine.

Hardy and Harriett Hightower, from North Carolina, owned a 1,600 acre plantation which was located southeast of the Rhodesville Community near Gravelly Springs. Hardy and Harriett Hightower had the following known children that were born at Florence in Lauderdale County, Alabama:

1) Jane S. Hightower was born on February 27, 1812; she married Almon H. Mason.
2) Catherine S. Hightower was born on May 19, 1813; she married Samuel Probasco. Catherine died in 1877.
3) Mary Louisa Hightower was born on October 25, 1814; she passed away in 1833.
4) John Oldham Hightower was born on September 21, 1816; he married Apphia Lewis Allen. John died on May 10, 1848, in Texas.
5) Alfred Arnet Hightower was born on August 2, 1818; he married Emily Susan Jennings. Alfred died in 1867.
6) Harriet Margaret Hightower was born on January 28, 1820; she died in 1843.
7) Richard Donaldson Hightower was born on July 24, 1821; he married Virginia Norfleet Jones. Richard died in 1885 at Benton in Bossier County, Louisiana.
8) James B. Hightower was born on April 14, 1823; he married Sarah Ann Fowler and Eliza S. Dupree. John died in 1850 in Walker, Texas.
9) Martha Ann Hightower was born on December 31, 1824; she married Andrew Jackson McGown. Martha died in 1918 in Huntsville, Texas.
10) Caroline M. Hightower was born on August 14, 1826; she married James Addison Baker. Caroline died in 1852.
11) Darthula Tabitha Hightower was born on March 15, 1828; she married Edward Martin Branch. Darthula died in 1894.

**James Addison Baker III
U.S. Secretary of State**

According to the 1830 Lauderdale County, Alabama, census Hardy Hightower owned 43 black slaves. In the 1840 Lauderdale County, Alabama, census Hardy Hightower owned 56 black slaves and his son, John Oldham Hightower, owned 36 black slaves. John O. Hightower married Aphia Allen on January 3, 1838, in Lauderdale County, Alabama.

The Hightowers moved to Texas in 1841 after selling their plantation to the Reverend Mitchell Malone who had formerly lived south of the Tennessee River near Cherokee. According to the 1850 Lauderdale County, Alabama, census, Mitchell Malone owned 32 black slaves. In 1860, Mitchell Malone owned 43 black slaves.

Following Caroline Hightower Baker's untimely death in 1852, James A. Baker moved to Huntsville, Texas, where his deceased wife's family had settled. While in Texas, James married Rowena Crawford on September 27, 1853. His new wife Rowena was a principal of the Huntsville Female Academy, but she resigned when she started having children. At that time, it was not appropriate for a housewife to have a job.

James and Rowena Crawford Baker were the parents of five children. One of those children was James A. Baker, Jr. who was born on January 10, 1857; his son James Addison Baker (1892-1973) became the father of the former Secretary of State James A. Baker.

Names left in stone serve as faint records of the early Alabama roots of the internationally known James A. Baker, III. The lonely headstone of his great-grandfather's first wife, Caroline Hightower, is all but hidden among the weeds and bushes on the old Mitchell Malone Place southeast of Rhodesville, Alabama. The broken marker over the grave of his great great grandfather, Elijah Baker, is one of six gravestones in an abandoned cemetery on the Carroll Place north of the Waterloo Road in Gravelly Springs.

Barbee, Alfred Asbury

The Reverend Alfred Asbury Barbee was born in Lawrence County, Alabama, in 1841, and his young family lived on a small farm near Rogersville, Alabama. Alfred A. Barbee was a Methodist circuit rider preacher. His burial site is one of the unmarked graves in the Warmack Cemetery near Rogersville.

Alfred Asbury Barbee served with the Confederate States of America, Brady Company, Company E; even though he was a veteran of the Civil War, he was beaten and murdered. His brutal beating and assassination occurred some five years after Lee had surrendered to Grant in Virginia, at a time when old feuds were gradually fading amid the era called Reconstruction.

The Civil War ended in 1865. Yet, there were in families, and sometimes communities, with old conflicts that had not been settled. For some, the bitterness lasted a lifetime. This was especially the case in some areas of North Alabama where divisions between the North and South split communities and divided families and churches.

The Reverend Barbee was from a family of four sisters and five brothers. Four of the five boys became Methodist ministers. One, the Reverend James D. Barbee, was pastor of the Florence First United Methodist Church in 1855-59. The father of this large family was a veteran of the War of 1812. The religious persuasion of the four Barbee preachers was said to have come by way of their pious mother, Sarah Ready Barbee. She had united with the Methodists as a young girl in a log meeting house near Oakville in Lawrence County.

Alfred Asbury Barbee, the 1870 victim of terrorists, married Sarah Elizabeth Fuqua of Rogersville, Alabama, on October 13, 1865. The marriage was performed by Alfred's older brother James, a minister of the gospel in Lauderdale County, Alabama.

According to the 1860 Lauderdale County, Alabama, Slave Schedule, Susan Fuqua owned nine black slaves. Her parents were William Giles and Susan Taylor Fuqua, both natives of Prince Edward County, Virginia. The Fuquas were descended from French ancestors and were prominent farmers in Rogersville.

Alfred and Sarah Fuqua Barbee had three children:
1) Baldwin Barbee was born on November 17, 1867, and died on January 14, 1942. He married Belle Barbee(1870-1942).
2) Alice Barbee Lamb was born on October 2, 1868, and died on March 6, 1947. She married Arna Lamb (1841-1870); she is buried in the Cooper Cemetery at Rogersville (Find a Grave Memorial Number 55013297)
3) Hattie Barbee Graham was born on March 12, 1870, and died on February 5, 1948. She first married J. W. Haney and the A. Graham (Find a Grave Memorial Number 57709529).

Methodist archives show Alfred's appointment as pastor of the Shoals Circuit in 1866. This Circuit was organized in 1822 and covered a large area, extending from the Muscle Shoals eastward into Limestone County and across the state line into Tennessee. At one time, there were as many as twenty preaching places on the Shoals Circuit.

There was a strong bitterness in one of his churches over the issues that had divided the nation during the Civil War. According to a well-documented story in the book "The Heritage of Lauderdale County" (1999) by Shannon Teel of Framingham, Massachusetts, the pastor had probably been a member of the "southern sympathizer's faction." However, it was feared that Barbee had been a "government spy." Consequently, a trumped-up charge of "hog stealing" was made against him in Limestone County to destroy his ministry. Barbee's impeccable reputation as a Methodist preacher, Mason, and citizen of Rogersville was enough to win his acquittal by the Athens court.

However, as he was leaving the courthouse, eleven disguised riders appeared. At first, they were thought to be friends who had come to escort him back to Rogersville. These men, said later to have been members of an organization called the Loyal League, a precursor to the Ku Klux Klan, "pistol whipped" the preacher, then beat him with hickory sticks until he became unconscious. Afterwards, they renewed the charges against Barbee on the grounds that he had confessed.

Thus, the reverend Barbee was arrested again at his home in Rogersville. According to additional information submitted by Howard Stief, Las Vegas, Nevada, this is believed to have occurred in December 1870.

Alfred Asbury Barbee was a young circuit rider, husband, and father; Alfred was being returned to Athens to again face these trumped-up charges when he was assassinated. The assassination took place about ten or eleven miles west of Athens between Snake Road and what is now U. S. Highway 72. They were taking him to jail in Limestone County, when he was shot to death. A Negro boy who lived in the area found his body. This young man tied the dead circuit rider to the back of a mule and returned him to his wife and baby daughter. For the Barbee family, the Civil War had finally ended. Alfred Asbury Barbee was buried in the Warmack Cemetery in Lauderdale County, Alabama (Find a Grave Memorial Number 57701390).

After her husband was murdered, Sarah Elizabeth Fuqua Barbee married Samuel C. Hughes on May 13, 1888, in Florence. Sarah Barbee Hughes was going to Rogersville in her buggy, probably to visit her sister, Lucy Ann Fuqua Cooper, when she met with an accident. Some geese scared the horse pulling the buggy and Sarah went into a ditch. She probably broke her back because she was somewhat stooped after the accident. Lucy Haney, her granddaughter, was with her when Sarah died on July 14, 1930, in Limestone County, Alabama (Find a Grave Memorial Number 578402234).

Beckwith, Jonathan

Jonathan Beckwith was born on January 7, 1798. He was the oldest child of fourteen children born to Richard Marmaduke Beckwith (1775-1820) and Elizabeth Scott Buchanan Beckwith (1780-1834) of Fredericksburg, Virginia. Richard and Elizabeth had the following children:
1) Jonathan Beckwith was born on January 7, 1798, and died on May 5, 1856; he married Dolly Coles Winston.
2) Martha Beckwith was born on November 27, 1800;
3) Richard Marmaduke Beckwith was born on April 18, 1802; he married Pricella Turner.
4) Baby Beckwith died at birth on April 18, 1802.
5) Lawrence Butler Beckwith was born on March 13, 1804, and he died on November 29, 1874, at Brownstown, in Sevier

County, Arkansas; on February 28, 1857, he married Jennette Hill.
6) Andrew Buchanan Beckwith was born on October 20, 1805; on July 12, 1830, he married Adelaide B. Carter.
7) Mary Hewitt Beckwith was born on August 12, 1807; she died on September 19, 1808. She had another sister named after her.
8) Elizabeth Scott Buchanan Beckwith was born on March 7, 1809.
9) James Hewitt Beckwith was born on April 28, 1811, in Virginia; on February 27, 1845, he married Martha Daugherty.
10) Robert Wither Beckwith was born on March 15, 1813; he married Sarah B. Curtis.
11) Mary Hewitt Beckwith was born on May 27, 1815.
12) Hugh Mercer Beckwith was born February 8, 1817; on December 22, 1849, he married Maria del Refugia Estefana Micaela Rascon in Santa Fe, New Mexico.
13) Laura Brokenbrough Beckwith was born on March 30, 1818.
14) Rebecca Marmaduke Beckwith was born on October 17, 1819.

Richard and Robert Beckwith

Two of Jonathan's brothers, Richard M. Beckwith and Robert W. Beckwith, also came to Alabama. It is thought that his sister Rebecca Beckwith married Henry Smith of Alabama in 1842; Smith's will was proved in 1846.

Richard M. Beckwith married Pricella Turner; she was born about 1802 in Caroline County, Virginia. On October 5, 1846, Richard Beckwith was on a list of Grand Jurors for Lauderdale County; he was listed as a tanner on Bluff Creek.

Richard and Pricella had a daughter named Ann Beckwith who was born in 1834 and died in 1889. Ann married George G. Armistead; in 1860, he owned 133 black slaves. They also had a son William J. Beckwith who was born in 1825. William married his first cousin Virginia Beckwith, who was the daughter of Robert Wither Beckwith and Sarah B. Curtis. Virginia Beckwith was born in 1846 in North Carolina; she died 1879.

From December 28, 1844, through August 25, 1891, William J. Beckwith entered 520 acres of land in Township 1 South and Ranges 13, 14 West in Lauderdale County, Alabama. William J. Beckwith served in the Confederate Army.

Robert W. Beckwith was married to Sarah B. Curtis; she was born about1806 in North Carolina. In 1850, Robert is listed as a silversmith, and in 1860, he is a jeweler and watch maker; Robert died in 1873.

Jonathan Beckwith

In 1823 during the "Alabama Fever" epidemic for Tennessee Valley cotton lands, Dr. Jonathan Beckwith came to Lauderdale County, Alabama, with his some 30 black slaves. Jonathan Beckwith married Dolley Coles Winston (1749-1849); Dolley was born in Virginia to Isaac Winston (1745-1821) and his wife Lucy Coles (1741-1823). Prior to her marriage, Dolley lived for a while with her sister of Martha Henry Winston Armistead (1782-1870) and her husband Peter Fontaine Armistead (1778-1866) on their western Lauderdale County plantation until her marriage to Dr. Jonathon Beckwith.

Jonathan and Dolley had the following known children:
1) Isaac Winston Beckwith was born in 1824 and died in 1857.
2) Elizabeth Buchanan Beckwith, born in May 1829, and she died in 1912, married J. C. Conner but changed her name back to Beckwith on July 17, 1871.
3) Alexander Winston Beckwith was born October 4, 1830, died in 1905.
4) William Beckwith

According to an article by Ronald Pettus in the Journal of Muscle Shoals History, "Doctor Jonathan Beckwith (1798-1856) and his wife Dolly Madison Beckwith were prominent citizens of Lauderdale County in the antebellum period. In addition to large land holdings in the Waterloo and Gravelly Springs area, Doctor Beckwith had a good medical practice in the county. At his death in 1856, he owned over 1,600 acres of land, at least 83 slaves, and livestock valued at more than $3,500. Several people owed large medical bills to him. The estate of Henry

Smith of Sweetwater, for example, owed $2,837 for maintenance of slaves from 1847-1856" (Pettus, 1975).

According to the 1830 census, Jonathan Beckwith owned 29 black slaves; the 1840 census also gives Jonathan Beckwith with 29 black slaves. However, the 1850 Lauderdale County census recorded that Jonathan Beckwith owned 66 black slaves. According to Pettus (1975), by the time he died in 1856, Jonathan Beckwith owned 83 black slaves.

Jonathan Beckwith was an adventurous, well-educated, confident doctor, cotton planter, horse breeder, and owner of some 80 black slaves. He had plantations at Colbert's Reserve and near Gravelly Springs; the plantations were known as the "Beckwith Homeplace" and the "Johnson Place" and located in an area known as "the Bend of the River." On March 27, 1841, Jonathan Beckwith imported a stallion called Ragman that he advertised for breeding at his stable at his plantation at Colbert's Reserve.

According to the 1850 Lauderdale County, Alabama, Agricultural Census taken on December 5, 1850, Jonathan owned 670 acres of improve land and 950 acres of unimproved land with a real estate at $20,000.

Alexander and Elizabeth Beckwith

Dr. Jonathan Beckwith died on May 5, 1856, in Lauderdale County, Alabama. His son Alexander and his daughter Elizabeth took charge of the two plantations. On June 15, 1856, after Jonathan Beckwith's death, an inventory of his black slaves was taken on both of the plantations.

The tract of property called the "Beckwith Homeplace" was run by Alexander Winston Beckwith and listed some 55 black slaves as follows: 1) Henry, aged 35; 2) Little Sylvia, aged 32; 3) child, aged seven; 4) Charity, aged 60; 5) Sarah Jane, aged one; 6) Pleasant, aged 13; 7) Hannah, aged 17; 8) Calvin, aged five; 9) Alfred, aged three; 10) Abram, aged 35; 11) Matilda, aged 28; 12) Emily, aged four; 13) Almina, aged 20 and 14) child six months; 15) Zach, aged six; 16) Milly, aged four; 17) Caroline, aged 25; 18) Amos, aged 21; 19) Syfax, aged 65; 20) Mariah, aged 45; 21) Aggy, aged 17; 22) Luck, aged 21; 23) Mary, aged 35; 24) Lizzy, aged five; 25) Delilah, aged 16; 26) Yellow Susan, aged 16; 27) Fanny, aged 11, 28) Mitchell, aged seven; 29) Edmond, aged seven; 30) Wash, aged 45; 31) Jim, aged 56; 32) Black Susan, aged 14; 33) Ben, aged ten; 34) Donelson, aged 21; 35) Lucinda, aged 20 and 36) child six months; 37) Warren, aged six; 38) Jess, aged 40; 39) Peter, aged 35; 40) Martin, aged 50; 41) Patsy, aged seven; 42) Louis, aged 36; 43) Big Fanny, aged 25; 44) Dolly, aged 22 and 45) child six months; 46) George, aged 16; 47) Martha, aged 16; 48) Anderson, aged three; 49) Solomon, aged 45; 50) Eliza, aged 34; 51) Charlotte, aged 70; 52) Margaret, aged 33; 53) Big Sylvia, aged 40; and, 54) Phyllis, aged 13.

The Johnson Place was run by Elizabeth Buchanan Beckwith after her father's death. In 1856, the inventory of the Johnson Place recorded 20 black slaves as follows: 1) Elijah, aged 60; 2) Betsy, aged 35; 3) Alex, aged 20; 4) Sally Smith, aged 19; 5) Davy, aged two; 6) Amy, aged 26; 7) Ann, aged three; 8) Patience, aged seven; 9) Manda, aged five; 10) Mary, aged eight; 11) Isaac, aged 33; 12) Sally Lee, aged 24; 13) Judge, aged two; 14) Thomas Lee, aged six; 15) Delilah, aged 19 and 16) child nine months;17) Pass, aged 26; 18) Fred, aged ten; 19) Dick, aged four; 20) Judy, aged 22. The ten year old slave Fred was Alfred Beckwith (1846-1901) who grew up and married Sallie McDonald, by whom he had at least four children: Hannah; J. B.; Eliza or Emma; and Lizzie. Sallie McDonald Beckwith died sometime before Alfred's death in 1901. After the Civil War, Alfred worked as a carpenter and house painter; he died on Tuesday, February 19, 1901.

Jonathan Beckwith's son Alexander and his daughter Elizabeth greatly increased the value of his plantation estates and black slaves as given in the 1850 agricultural census. According to the 1860 Lauderdale County, Slave Schedule, Alexander owned 48 black slaves and his sister Elizabeth owned 45 black slaves; it appears that they equally divided the slaves of their father Jonathan Beckwith.

By 1860, four years after Jonathan's death, the census recorded Alexander and Elizabeth owned a total of 93 black slaves. The value of Alexander's real estate was $63,800 and his personal estate was $18,000. Elizabeth's real estate was valued at $55,000 and her personal estate was $26, 000. Therefore, the total value of the Jonathan Beckwith estate owned by his two children in 1860 was worth $162,800.00.

At the start of the Civil War, Alexander Winston Beckwith enlisted in Company C, 27th Alabama Infantry of the Confederate States of America where he served as a lieutenant before being promoted to captain. After the Civil War, Alexander sold his Lauderdale County plantation in 1866. He then moved to Helena, Arkansas, where he operated a plantation until 1874. Alexander and his wife Mary "Mollie" Mason (1846-1908) and their children moved to Spring Hill in Maury County, Tennessee. He died in Tennessee and is buried in the Spring Hill Cemetery.

Binford, Hugh

Hugh Binford was born in North Carolina on January 15, 1789. He was the son of John Mosby Binford and Eliza Frances Littleberry Lightfoot Hardyman. Hugh came from Madison County and settled in Lauderdale County, Alabama. Hugh married Susan Haraway; she was born in 1812. His second marriage was to Martha L. Stanton; she was born on May 31, 1788.

Hugh Binford fathered the following children with Susan Haraway and Martha Stanton:
1) John Henry Binford was born on April 9, 1838; he married Saleta Amanda Penelope Binford. John died on November 16, 1889.
2) Thomas Albert Binford was born on January 15, 1815; he died in 1831.
3) James A. Binford was born in Virginia on September 20, 1811; he married Margaret Binford.
4) John Frederick Binford was born in North Carolina, on March 12, 1813; he died in 1825.
5) Richard H. Binford was born on March 12, 1813.
6) Alfred Binford.
7) Peter Binford was born on January 13, 1817.
8) Francis Hardiman Binford.
9) John Binford was born in 1848 in Alabama.

10) Frances Binford was born on March 30, 1820; she married Theophilus Lacy.

11) William Cook Binford was born in 1827 in Alabama.

Hugh Binford is found in the 1830, 1840, and 1850 Lauderdale County, Alabama, United States Censuses. On August 6, 1831, Hugh Binford entered 80 acres of land in Section 4 of Township 3 South and Range 12 West in Lauderdale County, Alabama.

In the 1850 Lauderdale County, Alabama, United States Census, Hugh Binford is a 60 year old white male born in North Carolina. Also living in house number 494 of Hugh Binford is William Binford a 23 year old male born in Alabama, John Binford a 12 year old male born in Alabama, Thomas Binford a 10 year old male born in Alabama, Ann Binford an 18 female born in Virginia, and Martha Binford an infant female born in Alabama.

According to the November 8, 1850, Lauderdale County, Alabama, Agricultural Census, Hugh Binford owned 300 acres of improved land and 527 acres of unimproved land valued at $40,000. Hugh Binford had the fifth highest farm value on the 1850 Lauderdale County agricultural census. Also in the 1850 Lauderdale County, Alabama, Slave Census, Hugh Binford owned 20 black slaves located east of Jackson's Military Road; Hiram Kennedy was the enumerator of the census.

In 1860, Hugh Binford is not listed in the

Lauderdale County, Alabama, Agricultural Census. Hugh Binford died of typhoid fever on July 21, 1860, in Madison County, Alabama, at the age 71.

However, L. H. Binford was listed as owning 275 acres of improved land and 160 acres of unimproved land valued at $8,700. In 1860, L. H. Binford owned 28 black slaves according to the Lauderdale County, Alabama, Slave Schedule.

John Henry Binford

By 1860, the will with heirs, slaves, and court documents of Hugh Binford are found in the court records of Madison County, Alabama. John Henry Binford, the son of Hugh Binford, appears to be the executor of his father's estate. Hugh had died in July 1860 in Madison County, Alabama.

John Henry Binford was born on April 8, 1838, in Madison County, Alabama; he was the son of Hugh Binford and Susan Haraway. At the time of his birth, John had four half brothers and a half sister, all of whom were products of his father's first marriage, and all much older than he. In 1840 when John was only two, his mother died after giving birth to a second son Thomas Albert Binford.

Following their mother's death, John and Thomas lived for a brief time with their grandmother Haraway before rejoining their father. In 1850, the two boys were living in Lauderdale County, Alabama, with Hugh, half brother William Cook Binford, William's wife Ann, and the infant daughter of William and Ann. In 1853, John's brother Thomas died at the age of 14. When his father died in 1860, John became an heir to part of Hugh Binford's estate.

As the nation rushed toward the start of hostilities between the north and the south, John Binford was living on the land he had inherited in Madison County, Alabama. When war became certain in early 1861, John enlisted in a Huntsville, Alabama, militia company called the Madison Rifles which was to become part of the 7th Regiment, Alabama Infantry, Confederate States of America. He volunteered for one year, but he ultimately served until the war ended in 1865, spending a couple of months in a Chattanooga hospital with an unknown ailment. With an intense interest in medicine, he was also assigned to nursing duty in a Georgia hospital for several months.

John Henry Binford
4/8/1838-11/16/1889

At the conclusion of the war, John first returned to northern Alabama, but within a few years, he decided to follow his half brother William Cook Binford and William's brother-in-law, Dr. William Bell Burwell, both of whom had moved to Holmes County, Mississippi. Once there, John studied medicine under the guidance of Dr. Burwell, and then attended and subsequently graduated from Tulane University in 1871 with a degree at the age of 33.

On October 25, 1871, within a few months of receiving his medical degree, Dr. John Henry Binford married a 16year old girl from Yazoo County, Mississippi, whose full name was Saleta Amanda Penelope Brantley. She was the daughter of John Harrison Brantley and Mary Sophronia Cox.

John Henry and Saleta settled in the Community of Ebenezer in Holmes County, Mississippi. They had a large family of twelve children who were born to them between 1872 and 1888, including twin boys who died in infancy.

John Henry and Saleta had ten of their children who would live to adulthood:
1) Mary Susan Binford (1872-1904);
2) Hugh Binford (1874-1933);

3) John Henry Binford (1876-1899);
4) Thomas Albert Binford (1876-1931);
5) Fannie Lucy Binford Mann (1878-1940);
6) Ann Eliza Binford Truitt (1880-1949);
7) William Walker Binford (1882-1942);
8) Saleta Brantley Binford (1883-1904);
9) James Robert Binford, Sr.(1885-1938);
10) Foster Binford (1887-1887), twin;
11) Samuel Sample Binford (1887-1887), twin; and,
12) Louise Lacy Binford Oppenheimer (1888-1965)

Dr. John Henry Binford cared for his Holmes County patients until 1889 when his health failed at the early age of 51. Binford died in November 16, 1889, of Bright's disease, a kidney disorder now known as nephritis. He is buried in the Ebenezer Baptist Church Cemetery in Holmes County, Mississippi (Find a Grave Memorial Number 11202009).

Soon after John's death, his widow Saleta moved to Texas with nine of her children. Saleta was born on February 10, 1855, in Holmes County, Mississippi. She died on July 18, 1937, at San Antonio in Bexar County, Texas (Find a Grave Memorial Number 146895512).

Boddie, Nathan

Colbert's Reserve in west Lauderdale County was set aside in 1816 for the prominent Chickasaw Chief George Colbert. Two years later, the federal government acquired these some 31,000 fertile acres through a transaction between the Colberts and James Jackson at the Forks of Cypress Plantation near Florence. As the result of an act of the United States Congress, a portion of these new public lands was made available to the Deaf and Dumb Institute of Hartford, Connecticut, as a means of providing much-needed funding for this charitable organization.

Nathan Boddie was eager to leave the Carolinas. Nathan was born on October 17, 1795, in Nash County, North Carolina. Nathan Boddie married Mary Thomas Smith. Mary was born on February 14, 1803, in North Carolina. She

died on September 28, 1845, in Lauderdale County, Alabama, and is buried in the Florence Cemetery (Find a Grave Memorial Number 5549518). Nathan and Mary had the following children:
1) Mary Eliza Boddie (1823-1883)
2) George Bolivar Boddie (1825-1827)
3) Frances Drew Boddie (1827-1851)
4) James Smith Boddie (1830-1866)
5) Rebecca Boddie Jones was born on August 29, 1832; she died on April 28, 1887. Rebecca married Dr. Albert H. Jones.
6) Nathan V. Boddie
7) Mary E. Boddie (1836-1841)
8) Ann "Annie" Elizabeth Boddie (1842-)

Nathan Boddie's ancestors had been sympathetic to the British during the American Revolution. A generation or two had passed, but there remained considerable animosity and ill feeling between Tories and patriots, especially in the South. And so it came to pass, according to family stories, that Boddie loaded his family and possessions into wagons and headed to the new State of Alabama to carve out a new home in the wilderness.

Sizeable tracts on Colbert's Old Reserve were bought by wealthy planters who were seeking new agricultural lands. One was Nathan Boddie from North Carolina, who made a direct purchase from the Hartford Institution for his 1,600 acres. According to the 1850 Lauderdale County, Alabama, Agricultural Census, Nathan Boddie owned 900 acres of improved land and 800 acres of unimproved land worth $17,000. Nathan Boddie also entered additional land; from April 21, 1830, through August 29, 1839, he entered some 400 acres in Townships 2, 3 South and Range 10, 12 West in Lauderdale County, Alabama. According to the 1850 Lauderdale County, Alabama, Slave Schedule, Nathan Boddie owned 79 black slaves.

According to the 1860 Lauderdale County, Alabama, United States Census, Nathan Boddie was a 60 year old male planter born in North Carolina. Also listed in his house number 443 was Mary a 15 year old female born in Alabama, Nathan V. Boddie a 20 year old male born in Alabama, and Annie an

18 year old female born in Alabama. In the 1860 Lauderdale County, Alabama, Slave Schedule, Nathan Boddie owned 94 black slaves.

Nathan Boddie died at his plantation home on December 8, 1861. Nathan is buried in the Florence Cemetery at Florence in Lauderdale County, Alabama(Find a Grave Memorial Number 54632102).

Nathan Boddie Home

Nathan Boddie built a solid substantial house for his family in Colbert's Old Reserve. It was a two-story rectangular structure made from massive logs measuring 12 inches in thickness. Skilled servants, including family owned slaves along with those from nearby plantations, cut these primeval trees from the surrounding forests. It was said these logs were so well hewn that the interior rooms were easily plastered to provide warmth and elegance.

A kitchen, smokehouse, icehouse, and other buildings were added, including a brick office for the plantation owner. The nearby slave quarters were made up of 12 log cabins. The Nathan Boddie Plantation home was destroyed by fire in 1958 after standing as a formidable fortress in the old reserve for almost 140 years.

Maud Lindsey Free Kindergarten

Numerous stories have been handed down about the Boddie place. As with southern plantations, most of these tell about the hardships of the Civil War. The Boddies were especially vulnerable in that their lands almost joined a part of the reserve that was used as a training cantonment by Union Cavalry in the war's last few months.

One beautiful story that can be told about the Boddie plantation involved its connection with the "Maud Lindsay Free Kindergarten" in the cotton mill district of East Florence. Nathan and Mary Thomas Boddie were the grandparents of Lulie Jones and her sister, Susan Price, two of the founders of the kindergarten. Maud Lindsey (1847-1941), who was born in Tuscumbia, established the first free kindergarten in the State of Alabama at the East Florence. Maud taught at the kindergarten for 42 years and wrote several children's books.

Rebecca Boddie, the mother of Lulie and Susan, became the bride of a young physician, Albert H. Jones (1822-1884), who boarded and carried out his early medical practice at her family home. Jones later moved to Florence, where he became president of the Cypress Cotton Mill following the Civil War.

Rebecca Boddie Jones (Find a Grave Memorial Number 54047889) and Dr. Albert Jones had the following children:
1) Fred Jones (-1868)
2) Susan Hill Jones Price (1858-1935)
3) Mary Philippa Jones (1860-1941)
4) Percy Rivers Jones (1862-1927)
5) Emmitt Lee Jones (1865-1940)
6) Lulie Jones (1888-1923)

Thus, through family connections, the two Jones sisters, Lulie and Susan, became keenly aware of the needs of the mothers who worked in the cotton mills. This was the beginning of the free kindergarten. The family roots of these two gentle ladies reach all the way back to the Boddie Plantation in the old Colbert's Reserve.

James S. and Nathan V. Boddie

James S. Boddie and his brother Nathan V. Boddie were the administrators of their father's estate. According to the 1860 Lauderdale County, Alabama, United States Census, James S. Boddie is a 30 year old male planter born in Alabama. Also living in his house number was his wife Julia Turner Cassety a 21 year old female born in Alabama and R. H. Roberts a 22 year old male overseer born in Alabama. According to the 1860 Lauderdale County, Slave Schedule, James Boddie owned 21 black slaves.

According to the Lauderdale County, Alabama, court records, accession number 20186226, "James S. and Nathan V. Boddie, administrators of the estate of Nathan Boddie, deceased; ask to court to appoint commissioners to divide nearly one hundred slaves among several heirs. The estate, they explain, is solvent." Based on the court record, it appears that Nathan Boddie owned about 100 black slaves at his death.

According to the Lauderdale County, Alabama, court records, accession number 20186227, "James S. Boddie complains that neither the probate court minutes nor the docket pages include entries to show that he was appointed administrator of the estate of slave owner Nathan Boddie, deceased.

There are a number of court records concerning the case that have not been properly recorded, including: (1) the letters to petitioner and Nathan V. Boddie regarding their bond; (2) letters appointing appraisers; (3) returns of appraisers; (4) copy of inventory; (5) order for distribution of estate; (6) appointment of commissioners. Boddie asks that these and other missing entries be entered into the court minutes."

According to Lauderdale County, Alabama, court records, accession number 20186228, "Nathan V. Boddie, who resigned as one of the administrators of the estate of his father, Nathan Boddie, in February 1862, now discovers that his resignation was not recorded in the court minutes. He asks that the judge issue "an order discharging him from further obligations as administrator."

Casey, Elisabeth Duckett

Elisabeth Duckett Casey's grave is in an isolated grove of old trees about fifteen miles north of Florence. The inscription on her tombstone reads, "Sacred to the memory of Elizabeth Duckett wife of Gen. Levi Casey who departed this life on Dec. 1st 1839" (Find a Grave Memorial Number 46409564).

Elizabeth's grave is neglected, abandoned, and all but forgotten. In recent years, the sanctity of her burial has been desecrated by ruthless vandals. Elisabeth's husband, Brigadier General Levi Casey (1752-2/3/1807), a leader in the American Revolution, is buried in the Congressional Cemetery in Washington D. C. which is one of the most honored burial grounds in America.

At the time of his death on February 3, 1807, at the age of 58, General Casey was serving his third term in the U. S. Congress. He had previously represented Newbury County, South Carolina, in the state senate.

There was much strife in the Carolina back country before and during the Revolution. Many remained loyal to the British Crown, and were called "Tories." Guerilla groups were formed as outlaw gangs. They especially preyed upon the families of the soldiers who were fighting for independence. These pro-British Tories did not hesitate to maim, torture, kill, or burn the homes of the patriots. On January 15, 1778, they torched 232 homes in Charleston, South Carolina.

It was during this time of British terrorism that Levi Casey, a native of South Carolina at the age of 29, became an active partisan under Colonel Thomas Dugan. Casey was commissioned as a lieutenant and personally recruited many of his neighbors in Newbury and Laurens Counties, South Carolina.

Levi Casey experienced his baptism of fire on October 9, 1779, when French and American forces stormed Savannah which has previously fallen to the British. He not only served at the Siege of Savannah, but also fought at the battles of Rocky Mount (1780), Hanging Rock (1780), and Cowpens (1781). At the end of the war, he was given the rank of colonel in command of South Carolina's Little River Regiment, and eventually became Brigadier General of the state militia.

In 1802, Honorable Levi Casey served in the United States House of Representatives until he died. Brigadier General Levi Casey served to secure our freedom and Independence from an authoritarian and oppressive King. He fought in many of the pivotal battles in the Revolutionary War as did his father and five brothers. Elizabeth Duckett Casey served the cause as well by providing meat and other supplies to the military during the Revolutionary War. She and Brigadier General Levi Casey are patriots in the DAR records.

Brigadier General Levi Casey and wife Elizabeth Duckett Casey had seven known children:
1) John A. Casey (1775-1862) married three times to Sara Lowndes Berrien, Abigail Abby Marion, and Catherine or Amy Shell.
2) Nancy Ann Casey (1785-1860?) married Thomas Culver Davis.
3) Sarah Siner Casey (1789-1872) married Jacob Rhodes.
4) Levi Garrett "Old Flynn" Casey, Private (1791-1855) married Chloe Hill.
5) Elizabeth Betsy Casey (1795-1872) married Thomas Johnson. In the 1860 slave census of Lauderdale County, Mrs. Elizabeth Johnson owned eight black slaves.
6) Jacob Duckett Casey (1796-1853) married four times to Rachel F. Pennington, Charity Whitmire, Sarah Francis Lucas, and Rachel F Rice.
7) Samuel Otterson Casey (1801-1866) married Rachel Lawson.

After the death of her husband, Elizabeth Duckett Casey and her then minor children moved to Alabama with her nephew, John Duckett. From March 10, 1818, through April 10,1838, John Duckett entered some 750 acres in Townships 1, 2 South and Ranges 11, 12, 14 West in Lauderdale County, Alabama (Cowart, 1996). On April 1, 1844, Jacob Duckett Casey was listed as a farmer on Cypress Creek in Lauderdale County, Alabama.

Upon her death in 1839, Elizabeth Casey willed her property to her son Samuel Otterson Casey. She does not show up with him on the 1830 census; she may have been enumerated with son John A. Casey at that time in Lauderdale County. Samuel Otterson Casey is the only person in his household on the 1830 census.

Coffee, John R.-Hickory Hills Plantation

Hickory Hill Plantation in Lauderdale County, Alabama, became the home of General John R. Coffee, who was an American planter and great military leader. John was born in Prince Edward County, Virginia, on June 2, 1772. He was the son of Captain Joshua (January 26, 1745-September 8, 1797) and Elizabeth Graves Coffee (January 28, 1742-December 13, 1804). John Coffee was the grandson of Peter Coffee, Sr. (1716-November 1771) and Susannah Mathews (1701–1796).

The Coffee family moved from Virginia, to North Carolina where John spent his childhood. In 1798, John R. Coffee moved to Nashville, Tennessee. While living in Nashville, Tennessee, John became close friends to the Overton, Donelson, and Jackson families. John Coffee and Andrew Jackson formed a partnership in merchandising.

John Coffee challenged Nathaniel A. McNairy for publishing derogatory statements about Andrew Jackson. The duel took place on March 1, 1806, over the Tennessee line in Kentucky. During the course of the duel,

General John R. Coffee
6/2/1772-7/7/1833

McNairy unintentionally fired before the word, wounding Coffee in the thigh. In reparation, McNairy offered to lay down his pistol and give Coffee an extra shot. The weapons used in this duel were later used in the Jackson-Dickinson duel on May 30, 1806.

Before Coffee married Jackson's niece, Andrew Jackson sold his part of partnership to Coffee. John Coffee gave Jackson notes of debt for the purchase of the merchandise business. After the wedding, Jackson gave John and Mary Coffee the notes as his wedding present to the couple.

On October 3, 1809, in Davidson County, Tennessee, John Coffee married Mary Donelson, the niece of Andrew and Rachel Jackson. Mary Donelson was the daughter of Captain John Donelson III (1775-1830) and Mary Purnell (1763-1848). John Donelson III was one of the older brothers of Andrew Jackson's wife, Rachel. John and Mary Donelson Coffee had the following children:

1) Mary Coffee Hutchings
2) John Donelson Coffee (1815-1837)
3) Elizabeth Graves Coffee, (1817-1838)
4) Andrew Jackson Coffee (1819-1891)
5) Rachel Jackson Coffee Dyas (1823-1892)
6) Alexander Donelson Coffee (1821-1901)
7) Catherine Harriet Coffee (1826-1881)
8) Emily Coffee (1828-1829)
9) William Donelson Coffee (1830-1903)
10) Joshua Coffee (1832-1879)

John Coffee-War Hero

John Coffee was considered the most even-tempered and least selfish of Andrew Jackson's lifelong friends. He was described as a big awkward man, careless of dress, slow of speech, but kindly, tactful, and wise.

During the War of 1812, Coffee served as Andrew Jackson's cavalry commander in the campaigns against the Creek Indians at Horseshoe Bend and later against the British at New Orleans. In December 1812, Governor William Blount had called out the Tennessee Militia in response to a request from General John Wilkinson and the United States Secretary of War. Under Jackson's command, John Coffee raised the Second Regiment of Volunteer Mounted Riflemen, composed mostly of Tennessee militiamen and a few Alabamians.

In January 1813, Coffee led 600 men to Natchez in Mississippi Territory; Coffee's men traveled the Natchez Trace, in advance of the rest of the troops, who traveled by flatboats. After the two groups reunited in Natchez, General James Wilkinson ordered Jackson's troops back to Nashville; on the march back,

Jackson earned the nickname Old Hickory. On May 18, 1813, the troops arrived in Nashville.

In October 1813, John Coffee was promoted to brigadier general and placed in command of a large number of troops. The Second Infantry Regiment of Volunteer Mounted Riflemen and Colonel Cannon's Mounted Regiment was combined with the First Regiment of Volunteer Mounted Gunmen to form a military brigade of mounted infantry under the command of General Coffee.

General Coffee was Jackson's chosen advance commander in the Creek Indian War. Under Jackson's command, Coffee led his brigade at the Battle of Tallushatchee, the Battle of Talladega, the Battles of Emuckfaw and Enotachopo Creek where he was seriously wounded, and the Battle of Horseshoe Bend.

After the end of the Creek Indian War in March 1814, Coffee's brigade, including a large number of Indians and freed blacks, played a key role at the Battle of New Orleans. General John Coffee and his men were the first to engage the British, firing from behind the trees and other barriers; Coffee's men held the woods to the east of the British army.

John Coffee-Surveyor and Planter

For his war time service, General John Coffee was appointed surveyor general of the North Alabama district in 1817. One of his first jobs was to establish the land office and survey the Town of Huntsville. Coffee appointed James H. Weakley as Surveyor General of Alabama public lands.

After the war, John Coffee worked with the Chickasaws, Cherokees, and Creeks in surveying their tribal boundaries lines to eventually bring about Indian removal east of the Mississippi River. Coffee also began work as a surveyor in laying outs towns and lots including Melton's Bluff in Lawrence County, Town of Coldwater (Tuscumbia) in then Franklin County, and the Town of Florence, Alabama. In 1816, he surveyed the boundary line between Alabama and Mississippi. Several areas are named in his honor and include Coffee County, Alabama, Coffeeville, Alabama, Coffeeville, Mississippi, and Coffee County, Tennessee.

After helping form the Cypress Land Company in March 1818, John Coffee was engaged in acquiring large tracts of property. During this time, Coffee purchased 1,280 acres on Cox Creek north of Florence and established his Hickory Hill Plantation. In addition to being a surveyor, Coffee became a cotton planter and land speculator.

According to the 1830 Lauderdale County, Alabama, census, John Coffee owned 83 black slaves that farmed, planted, and picked cotton on his plantation. As a planter, businessman, and one of the most prominent citizens of Florence, John Coffee helped establish churches, schools, gins, mills and other commercial enterprises.

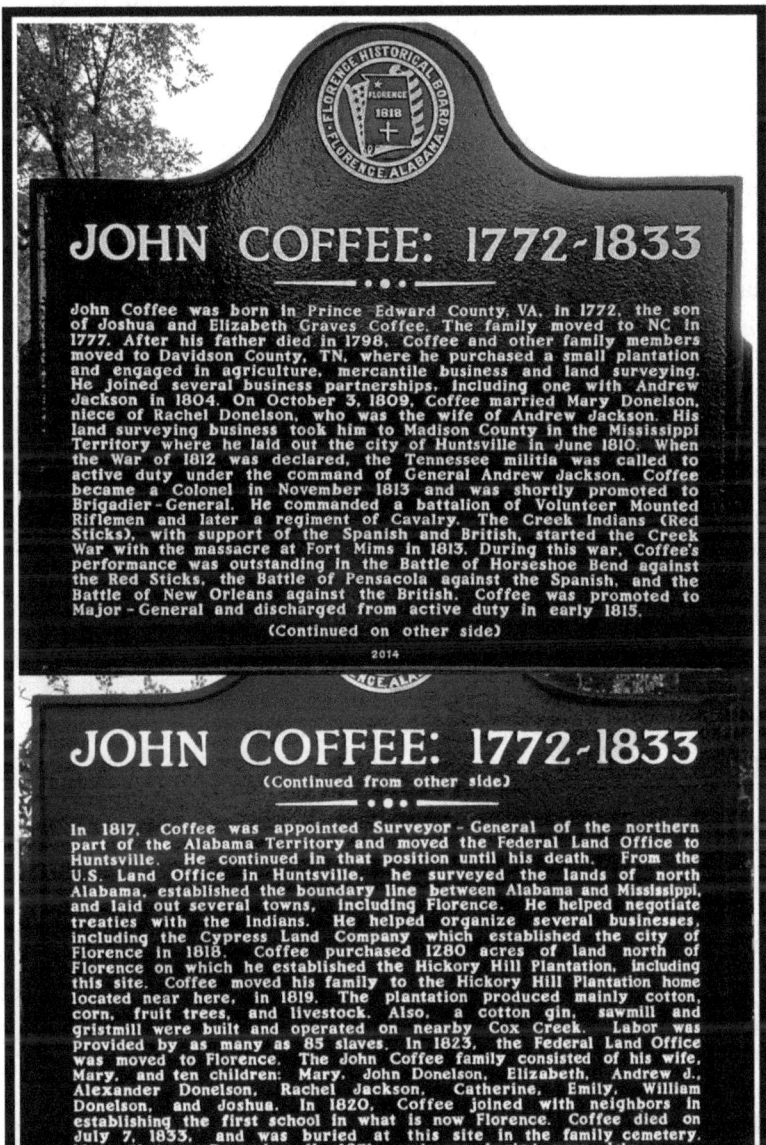

Death of John Coffee

After returning from a visit with President Andrew Jackson in Washington, General John R. Coffee became ill and died at the age of 61. On July 7, 1833, Coffee died at his Hickory Hills Plantation home on Coxe's Creek at Florence in Lauderdale County, Alabama. President Jackson wrote his epitaph, "As a husband, parent and friend, he was affectionate, tender and sincere. He was a brave, prompt, and skillful general, a disinterested and sagacious patriot and unpretending, just and honest man."

General John R. Coffee is buried in the Coffee Cemetery at Florence in Lauderdale County, Alabama. Today, the cemetery is adjacent to a Wal-Mart store in Florence. General John Coffee's tombstone reads, "Sacred to the memory of Gen. John Coffee, who departed this life on the 7th day of July A. D., 1833, aged 61 years. As a husband, parent, and friend he was affectionate, tender and sincere. He was brave, prompt and skillful General; a distinguished and sagacious patriot, an unpretending just and honest man. To complete his character, religion mingled with these virtues, her serene and holy influence gave him that solid distinction among his fellow men, which distraction cannot sully nor the grave conceal. Death could do no more than remove so excellent a being from the theatre he so much endorsed in this world to the bosom of the God, who created him and who alone has the power to reward the immortal spirit with bliss."

Other family members in the Coffee Cemetery include:
1) Coffee, Mrs. Mary, 13 Jun 1793, 11 Dec 1871, wife of Gen. John Coffee.
2) Coffee, Alexander Donel, 3 Jun 1821, 9 May 1901, "I am the resurrection and the life, he that believeth in me though he were dead, yet shall he live."
3) Coffee, Ann Eliza, 10 Sep 1824, 22 Mar 1871, dau of Rev Jas L & Lititia V. Sloss and wife of Alexander D. Coffee.
4) Coffee, John D. 15 Mar 1815, son of John and Mary Coffee.
5) Coffee, Elizabeth, 2 Feb 1817, 19 Jan 18, dau of Genl. John and Mary Coffee.
6) Coffee, Camilla, 1842-1928, Precious in the sight of the Lord is the death of his saints.
7) Coffee, Eliza Croom, 18 Aug 1879-5 Sep 1904, dau of Alexander D. and Camilla Coffee, Blessed are the pure in heart

for they shall see God. The dead live never more to die and often where we mourn them dead, they never were so high.

8) Precious Coffee, Emily, 23 Jul 1828-7 Aug 1829, dau of John and Mary Coffee.
9) Inf. Daughter, Dec 1857, In memory of our infant and beloved daughter.
10) Coffee, Infant Daughter, 1877, Infant daughter of A. D. & C. M. Coffee, As a flower she faded.
11) Coffee, Virginia Malone, 1840-1891, wife of William Coffee.
12) Coffee, William, 1830-1902, son of Gen. John Coffee and Mary Donelson Coffee.
13) Coffee, Catherine H., 24 Sep 1826-9 Nov 1881, dau of Gen. J. and M. Coffee; Blessed are the dead which die in the lord.
14) Coffee, Joshua, 19 Aug 1832-25 Jan 1879, son of Gen. J. and M. Coffee; Though he slay me yet will I trust in him.
15) Donelson, Capt. John, 23 Apr 1787-28 Apr 1840.

Mary Donelson Coffee

Mary Donelson Coffee was born on June 13, 1793, in Davidson County, Tennessee, and died on December 11, 1871, at Florence in Lauderdale County, Alabama. Mary Donelson Coffee's siblings include: Tabitha Donelson Smith (1781-1854), John Donelson (1787-1840), Lemuel Donelson (1789-1832), Rachel Jackson Donelson Eastin (1791-1822), William Donelson (1795-1864), Elizabeth Donelson McLemore (1796-1836), Catherine Donelson Martin (1799-1836), Stockly Donelson (1805-1888), and Emily Tennessee Donelson (1807-1836).

According to the 1840 Lauderdale County, Alabama, census, Mary Coffee owned 75 black slaves. In the 1850 Lauderdale County, Alabama, Slave Schedule, from October 22 through December 19, 1850, Mrs. Mary Coffee owned 76 black slaves, and her son Alexander D. Coffee owned 14 black slaves. The census was enumerated by M. T. Wilson.

According to the 1850 Lauderdale County, Alabama, Agricultural Census taken on November 26, 1850, Mary Coffee owned 500 acres of improved land and 1,420 acres of unimproved land worth $10,000. On October 30, 1850, ?hard Coffee owned 280 acres of improved land and 320 acres of unimproved land worth $4000. On November 26, 1850, Alexander D. Coffee owned 1200 acres of improved land and 1100 acres of unimproved land worth $45,000. On October 24, 1850, Caroline Coffee owned 90 of improved land and 30 acres of unimproved land worth $700. On October 30, 1850, Clayborn Coffee owned 30 acres of improved land and 30 of unimproved land worth $3000. On October 30, 1850, John C. Coffee owned 25 acres of land. On October 24, 1850, Joshua Coffee owned 80 acres of improved land and 40 acres of unimproved land worth $1000.

Mary Donelson Coffee
6/13/1793-12/11/1871

According to the 1860 Lauderdale County, Alabama, United States Census, District Number Two, Mary Coffee was a 67 year old white female plantress born in Tennessee. Also listed in household 599 was Catherine Coffee a 33 year old female born in Alabama, Joshua Coffee a 27 year old male born in Alabama, A. J. Dyas a 44 year old male born in Ireland, and Rachel J. Dyas a 36 year old female born in Alabama.

According to the 1860 slave census, Mrs. Mary Coffee owned 20 black slaves. Mary's son Joshua Coffee owned 12 black slaves, her daughter Catherine Coffee owned 18 black slaves, and her son Alexander D. Coffee owned 17 black slaves.

According to the 1870 Lauderdale County, Alabama, United States Census, Mary Coffee was a 77 year old female born in Tennessee. Also listed in household 1100 was C. H. Coffee a 44 year old female born in Alabama, Larien Coffee a 45 year old female born in Virginia, Edward Coffee an 18 year old male born in Alabama, William Coffee a 14 year old male born in Alabama, Alex Coffee a 12 year old male born in Alabama, Bettie Coffee a 10 year old female born in Alabama, Susan Coffee an eight year old female born in Alabama, Mollie Coffee a six year old female born in Alabama, and Layme Coffee a four year old female born in Alabama.

Alexander D. Coffee-Ardoyne Plantation

The son of General John and Mary Coffee, Alexander Donelson Coffee was born at the Hickory Hill Plantation on June 3, 1821. He first married Ann Elizabeth Sloss; after her death, he married Camilla Madding Jones.

Alexander married Ann Eliza Sloss on May 16, 1844, and she died March 22, 1871. Alexander and Ann had one child Mary Coffee; she married Edward Asbury O'Neal and William P. Campbell. In 1849, Alexander Coffee entered into a cotton mill business with Martin and Weakley.

According to the 1860 Lauderdale County, Alabama, United States Census, District Number two, Alexander D. Coffee was a 38 year old white male born in Alabama. Also listed was Anne Eliza Coffee a 35 year old female born in Alabama, and Mary Coffee a five year old female born in Alabama.

During the Civil War, Alexander D. Coffee served in Company C of the 16th Alabama until he was forced to retire due to ill health. Coffee High School in Florence was named in his honor.

According to the 1870 Lauderdale County, Alabama, United States Census, Alex Coffee was a 48 year old white male born in Alabama. Also listed was Sarah Jackson a nine year old female born in Alabama, Lena Jackson a 15 year old male born in Mississippi, Andrew Jackson a three year old male born in Alabama, John Jackson a three year old male born in Alabama, Aaron Jackson an infant male born in Alabama, Eliza Grisham a 38 year old female born in Tennessee, Eliza Coffee a 44 year old female born in Alabama, and Mary Coffee a 17 year old female born in Alabama.

On October 18, 1876, Alexander D. Coffee married Camilla Madding Jones. They had one child Eliza Croom Coffee (August 18, 1879-September 5, 1904; ECM hospital is named for her.

On May 9, 1901, Alexander Donaldson Coffee died and was buried in the Coffee Family Cemetery. He was a national hero and his father was one of the founding fathers of Florence, Alabama. Alexander lived to be almost 80 years old. He was well loved by the people of Florence area. At his funeral, a large crowd gathered on the grounds of Ardoyne his home place.

Collier, Wyatt-The Oaks Plantation

The Oaks Plantation

In 1836, Wyatt Collier purchased The Oaks Plantation from James Jackson of the Forks of Cypress. The Oaks was one of west Lauderdale County's large antebellum plantations with some 1,453 acres of land. This fertile cotton and corn land was part of the old George Colbert's Reserve near the Natchez Trace and Tennessee River.

The Oaks Plantation House was described as a handsome brick structure surrounded by a stand of majestic oaks. It had replaced an earlier dwelling that had been destroyed by fire. It is said that near the Oaks Plantation stood an oak of such great size and antiquity that it was used as a landmark.

In 1902, a local newspaper, the Florence Herald, offered lifetime subscriptions for six men who could prove that they had lived the longest in Lauderdale County, Alabama. Josephus Darby wrote that he "was born on June 15, 1828, in Colbert's Reserve…within 200 yards of the big oak tree." This was eight years before the tree became associated with Wyatt Collier of the Oaks Plantation.

Wyatt Collier

Wyatt Collier was a native of Lunenburg County, Virginia. He was born on August 19, 1791, to James Collier (1757-1832) and Elizabeth Bouldin Collier (1763-1828). Wyatt Collier (1791-1856) had brothers Charles Ephraim Collier (1805-1888), Henry W. Collier, and Thomas Bouldin Collier.

Wyatt Collier had moved to Florence from Madison County where his family was early settlers. Wyatt's father James served in the American Revolution as a sergeant. Seven of Wyatt's uncles were colonels under General George Washington during that time. Wyatt's brother, Henry W. Collier, of Tuscaloosa County, was elected the Fourteenth Governor of Alabama.

Not long after moving to Florence, Wyatt met his future bride, Janet Walker, who was born in 1805 at the gatehouse of Elect, Scotland. The event of their first meeting has been carefully preserved by their descendants.

During a visit to relatives in Florence, Janet is attending Sunday service at the First Presbyterian Church. While listening to the sermon, she rested her hand on the door that led to the high pew where she had seated. Although Wyatt could not see Janet, he became smitten by her small and delicate hand which seemed to be framed by the contour of the wooden door. According to this romantic story, Wyatt turned to his nearby friend and whispered, "I'm going to marry the lady attached to that hand."

Janet Walker never returned to her home in Scotland. She became the bride of Wyatt Collier and lived the remaining years of her life at "The Oaks Plantation" near the banks of the Tennessee River.

Wyatt married Janet Walker Collier; she was born on March 17, 1805, and died on August 8, 1869. She was the daughter of James Walker of Scotland. Janet Walker Collier was buried in the Florence Cemetery at Florence in Lauderdale County, Alabama, Plot 101 (Find a Grave Memorial Number 38552126).

Wyatt and Janet Walker Collier's only son, James died at the age of twelve years. Their daughter, Clara, was married to Captain William Simpson, who served on Confederate General Polk's staff. Another daughter, Mattie, was married to Will's brother, Captain Robert Tennent Simpson of the 63rd Alabama Regiment. A third daughter was engaged to be married to a third brother, John Simpson Jr., who was killed in action at the first battle of Bull Run.

Wyatt and Janet Walker Collier had the following children:
1) James William Collier was born on March 29, 1829, and died in 1833).

2) Clara Adeline Collier was born on November 13, 1834, and died in 1917. She married William Simpson, CSA of Florence.
3) Mary Elizabeth Collier was born on July 17, 1837. She married Nelson Maguire and Arthur Colyar.
4) Margaret "Mattie" Jane Collier was born on August 1, 1841, and died on May 22, 1908. She married Honorable Robert Tennent Simpson, CSA.
5) Janet Walker Collier was born on June 15, 1842, and died in 1936. She married Newton Estes, CSA.
6) Alice Walker Collier was born in 1845 and died in 1904.
7) Kate Collier was born in 1850 and died in 1853.

Wyatt Collier is listed in the 1840 Limestone County, Alabama United States Census. According to the 1850 Lauderdale County, Alabama Slave Schedule, Watt Collier owned 64 black slaves. According to the 1850 Lauderdale County, Alabama, Agricultural Census taken on December 5, 1850, Wyatt Collier owned 700 acres of improved land and 750 acres of unimproved land valued at $14,520.00.

According to the 1850 Lauderdale County, Alabama Census, District Number One, Wyatt Collier was a 58 year old white male farmer born in Virginia. Also living in the household was Janetta a 45 year old female born in Scotland, Clara a 16 year old female born in Alabama, Mary a 13 year old female born in Alabama, Martha a nine year old female born in Alabama, Jinnett seven year old female born in Alabama, Alice a five year old female born in Alabama,

Catharine a ½ year old female born in Alabama, and Julia Reynolds a 22 year old female born in New York.

Wyatt Collier died on October 6, 1856; he is buried in plot 101 in the Florence Cemetery at Florence in Lauderdale County, Alabama. The inscription on his tombstone is, "In Memory of Wyatt Collier born Lunenburg Co, Va, Aug 19, 1781, died in Lauderdale Co., Al, Oct 6 1856, The righteous hath hope in his death" (Find a Grave Memorial Number 38552165).

Janet Walker Collier

According to the 1860 Lauderdale County, Alabama, United States Census, Mrs. Janet Collier is a 56 year old female farmer born in Scotland. Also living in her house number 417 is Mattie an 18 year old female born in Alabama, Nettie a 16 year old female born in Alabama, Alice a 14 year old female born in Alabama, William Simpson a 29 year old male born in Alabama, Clara W. a 24 year old female born in Alabama, and Ann Stephens a 50 year old female born in Ireland.

Janet Walker Collier had reached the age of fifty six when her husband died. With great courage she took over management of the plantation, becoming one of the three ladies listed in the 1860 census as being in charge of large farming operations in Lauderdale County, Alabama. According to the 1860 Lauderdale County, Alabama, Slave Schedule, Mrs. Janet Collier owned 83 black slaves.

Janet Collier owned some 1,500 acres of land at The Oaks Plantation with half of that cultivated with six horses, thirty-two mules, and six working oxen. In 1860 with a work force of some eighty slaves, Janet Collier produced 106 bales of cotton, 7,500 bushels of corn, 150 pounds of wool, and 200 pounds of butter on her plantation.

Following Janet Collier's death in 1869, her oldest daughter, Clara, and husband, Captain Will Simpson, purchased the plantation from the other heirs. Thus, the Oaks Plantation remained in the family, but it became known as "one of the Simpson Places" in the Bend of the River.

Coulter, George-Mapleton

"Mapleton" is a relatively new name for an old house that has overlooked the Tennessee River from a strategic location for more than a century and a half. During most of its long history, it has been known by one or more names left by those who lived within its stately portals.

This grand mansion of the early 1820's was listed on the prestigious National Register of Historic Places in 1982 and the Alabama Register of Landmarks and Heritage in 1979. In recent years, it has been described as perhaps the finest frame house of the late Georgian style in the Tennessee Valley.

Mapleton

As one of Florence's oldest ante-bellum homes, its tall, slender columns at the front and back are a reminder of an earlier period when the town was noted for its white-pillared mansions.

Mapleton was built in the 1820's by Kentucky colonel, planter, and attorney, George Coulter. The house was also known as the George Coulter House. When Coulter located it on the heights west of Court Street, there was a large three-story brick mansion at about the same distance from the river on the east side of Court Street. That columned mansion, which was destroyed by fire before the turn of the century, was the home of John McKinley, one of the founders of Florence, who was later elected as a United States Senator and then appointed to the United States Supreme Court. It has been said that visitors arriving by steamboat at the Florence Landing could see the roofs of these two mansions above the thick forests, and consequently, they became identified with the entrance to the city.

Except for the large warehouse that later became the site for the Coca-Cola Bottling Works, and the public springs located in a hollow between Court Street and the mansion, the grounds of Mapleton fairly well covered the western part of the hill leading into Florence.

Old houses seem to acquire a ghost or two at some time or another. Mapleton's ghosts, it seems, made themselves a nuisance in the early 1850's when George Washington Foster purchased Mapleton. According to the 1850 Lauderdale County, Alabama, Slave Schedule, George W. Foster owned 67 black slaves. In the 1860 slave schedule, George is reported as owning 98 black slaves.

George W. Foster was the builder of Courtview or Rogers Hall at the north end of Court Street, as a wedding present for his daughter, Virginia, and her husband, James Bennington Irvine. According to the 1860 slave census for Lauderdale County, James B. Irvine owned 16 black slaves.

Virginia saw too many ghosts at her home; the house was isolated and too far from downtown Florence. The matter was resolved when her father purchased her a new home, which is now Colby Hall, on the University of North Alabama Campus.

Levi Todd-Todd's Hill

The next owner of Mapleton was a Lauderdale County physician, Dr. Levi Todd. For many years afterwards, the house and grounds were known as "Todd's Hill." Dr. Todd was a relative of Abraham Lincoln's wife, Mary Todd Lincoln. There had been such confusion through the years because Mary Todd Lincoln had a brother David Todd, who resided in Florence prior to the Civil War. According to the Louisville Kentucky Historical Society, Dr. Todd and Mary Todd Lincoln were cousins.

Todd's Hill was caught up in the Civil War and is mentioned by both Federal and Confederate reports of the capture of Florence on October 30, 1864. John Bell Hood's Army crossed the Tennessee both at Florence and at Old Bainbridge, which was located on the south bank of the river across from the mouth of Shoal Creek. Lieutenant Colonel R. H. Lindsey led the initial assault at the Florence crossing. Upon securing the beachhead, his men swarmed up Todd's Hill as the Federals retreated in the direction of Pulaski. One of Lindsey's lieutenants summed up the Confederate victory quite well in a letter he wrote a number of years later, "The town and all its pretty women, etc., was ours."

Mapleton or Todd's Hill was part of the scenario in one of the most remembered events of the Civil War period-the arrest of the pastor of the First Presbyterian Church. Dr. William H. Mitchell was serving also as President of Florence Synodical College; in the 1860 slave census for Lauderdale County, William H. Mitchell owned two black slaves.

William H. Mitchell prayed for the Confederacy and its leaders in a rather lengthy pastoral prayer at a Sunday morning service in July 1862. At the time, the Mapleton house was used as a command post by Union Army Colonel John Marshall Harlan and was occupied by the Tenth Kentucky Regiment. The location on the hillside overlooking the Tennessee River provided views of the town and river. Harlan's forces occupied the City of Florence, and his Provost Marshal's Headquarters was at Mapleton.

The Provost Marshal, Colonel John Marshall Harlan, and a number of other officers and men of the Tenth Kentucky, were in Dr. Mitchell's congregation. After the hymns were sung, Colonel Harlan and the other federals walked out of the church in protest. They returned, however, when the minister stepped into the pulpit to commence the sermon. With fixed bayonets, the soldiers placed him under arrest and took Dr. Mitchell away. He was charged with treason and confined in the Federal prison at Alton, Illinois.

During his absence, a loyal lawman, future governor Robert Miller Patton of the Sweetwater Plantation, filled Dr. Mitchell's pulpit on Sunday mornings. One sermon by Robert Patton was about all the Josephs of the Old and New Testaments. General U. S. Grant granted a full pardon for Dr. Mitchell after the end of the war. The arresting colonel, John Marshall Harlan, was appointed to the United States Supreme Court as an Associate Justice in his later years. He was also a grandfather of another Associate Justice of the same court known by the same name, John Marshall Harlan.

Robert McFarland

One of the heroes of Morgan's Raiders, Major Robert McFarland, became the next owner of Mapleton a number of years after the war. This family was associated with the mansion longer than any other owner, and even in the late years of the twentieth century, old timers more than likely will refer to Mapleton as "The McFarland Place." McFarland Bottoms and McFarland Park were a part of the farm, and, consequently, both honor the name of Major McFarland. The cotton fields of the farm extended west and included the area surrounding Eliza Coffee Memorial Hospital. Strawberries were also grown on the farm, and during the Great Depression, jobless families were encouraged to plant their vegetable gardens in McFarland Bottoms. Mapleton remained in this family until 1943.

Major Robert McFarland was a son of William and Jane McCulley McFarland of Londonderry, Ireland, where he was born August 6, 1836. He was educated in the best schools of Ireland, becoming especially prepared for a military career. However, he came to America in 1854, and entered what is now Washington and Lee University in Lexington, Virginia, where he graduated third in his 1860 class with a law degree. From Virginia, he came to Florence to enter into a partnership with James Bennington Irvine, Attorney at Law.

McFarland entered the Confederate Army in April 1861 as captain in the Fourth Alabama Infantry. He served under General Stonewall Jackson, whom he knew personally while living in Lexington. He was with Jackson at Harper's Ferry and was present when General Bernard Bee referred to Jackson at Manassas as a "stone wall."

Later, McFarland recruited a cavalry regiment and was placed under General John Hunt Morgan at Knoxville. He accompanied the renowned Morgan across the Ohio River and was the first man in the command to cross over into Indiana.

Following Morgan's capture, McFarland was assigned to General Cleburne's Division where he remained until the end of the war. He led Cleburne's famous charge at Dug Gap. McFarland was injured at Villa Rica, Georgia, when his horse was killed under him. He never fully recovered.

The Major opened his own law office following the war and became one of Florence's better-known attorneys. In March, 1868, he married Kate Armistead, daughter of Fontaine Armistead of Colbert County. Robert and Kate Armistead McFarland became the parents of seven children. The Major died in January 1892 and is buried in the Florence Cemetery (Find a Grave Memorial Number 38609887).

Foster, Thomas Jefferson-Malone House

The historic Malone House on Hawthorne Street in Florence, Alabama was built in 1832 by Thomas Jefferson Foster who was a local manufacturer, planter, and slave owner. On December 19, 1850, Thomas Jefferson Foster, Turner Saunders Foster, George Washington Foster, James Foster, and James Simpson, trading under the firm name of "Foster, Simpson, and Company," entered 79.69 acres in the west ½ of the northwest ¼ of Section 15 in Township 1 South and Range 10 West in Lauderdale County, Alabama. James Simpson first married Mary Ann Foster, and later he married Cornelia Foster. In the 1860 slave census, James Simpson owned 28 black slaves.

Thomas Jefferson Foster was born in Nashville, Tennessee, on July 11, 1809. Thomas was the son of a prominent politician Robert Coleman Foster (1769-1844) and Ann Slaughter Hubbard Foster (1770-1850).

On October 30, 1833, Thomas Jefferson Foster married Virginia Prudence Watkins. Shortly after their marriage, Thomas and Virginia Foster moved to Courtland, Alabama. Virginia was born on October 22, 1816, in Georgia. She was the daughter of the wealthy plantation owner Robert H. Watkins (10/1/1782-1855) of Rosemont Plantation in Lawrence County, Alabama. Robert H. Watkins is buried at Maplewood Cemetery at Pulaski in Giles County, Tennessee.

Thomas and Virginia were married less than four years before her death; she was only 21 years old when she died on May 12, 1837, in Lawrence County, Alabama. She was buried at the Foster Cemetery at Brickhouse Ford in Lawrence (Colbert) County.

Thomas Jefferson Foster made his fortune with the assistance of black slaves. According to the 1850, Lawrence County, Alabama, Slave Schedule, Thomas Jefferson Foster owned the Green Onion Plantation with 95 black slaves. According to the 1860 slave census of Lawrence County, Alabama, he owned 128 black slaves.

The Green Onion Plantation was near the mouth of Town Creek and was originally the home of Chickamauga Cherokee Chief Kattygisky. About 1818,

John Johnson, who had leased land from Doublehead, established the Green Onion Plantation and built his big brick home on a rise about 200 yards west of Kattygisky's Spring. The Chickamauga Chief Kattygisky lived near the spring which was about one mile southwest from the mouth of Town Creek where Foster had his plantation. Thomas Jefferson Foster's property was on the south side of the Tennessee River in present-day Colbert County at the mouth of Town Creek. The plantation was located at the Lower Cherokee Indian village called Shoal Town.

On Town Creek near the Tennessee River, Thomas Jefferson Foster owned and operated a grsit mill. The old bridge that crossed Town Creek near present-day Doublehead Resort was called Foster's Mill Bridge. Today, the road is known as Fosters Mill Road that connects the River Road to Highway 101.

When Alabama succeeded from the Union, Thomas Jefferson Foster raised the 27th Alabama Infantry Regiment for the Confederate Army and served as its first colonel. Colonel Foster was instrumental in the construction of Fort Henry to defend the Tennessee River. He served in the fort under General Lloyd Tilghman until his forces surrendered to General Ulysses S. Grant. Foster served two terms in the Confederate Congress and was later elected to the United States Congress, but was denied his seat because of his loyalty to the Confederacy.

Thomas Jefferson Foster died on February 24, 1887. He is buried in the Florence Cemetery at Florence in Lauderdale County, Alabama (Find a Grave Memorial Number 156611938).

Malone House-Spanish Flu History

During the summer of 1862 when Union General Don Carlos Buell occupied the town, the Malone House served as an improvised military hospital. About 1914, Dr. Lewis W. Desperez, a local physician who lived on North Wood Avenue, established a private city hospital that offered very limited health care for a small percentage of the desperately sick in the Malone House. However, most of the people were treated in their homes.

The Encyclopedia Britannica calls the 1918 influenza epidemic "the most destructive in history" and ranks it with the plague of Justinian and the Black Death as one of the severest holocausts of disease ever encountered. "More than 548,000 people in the United States succumbed to what became known as the "Spanish flu." It is estimated that more than twenty million persons perished around the world and that fifty times as many were sick.

The northwest corner of Alabama encountered its most severe impact from this fast moving infection in the autumn of 1918. No immunization and no effective medicine existed to combat the epidemic. During most of October and early November the newspapers of Colbert and Lauderdale Counties reported daily occurrences of deaths from this fast-moving virus.

Florence, Tuscumbia, and Sheffield, which prior to World War I were small rural towns, were especially vulnerable to the rapid spread of this disease. More than 19,000 defense workers were crowded into barracks, tents, and every available home and apartment in the surrounding Muscle Shoals area. One Florence lady on Seminary Street was said to have provided sleeping arrangements for eight workers in her parlor, "four sleep there in the day and four at night." An area of Maxwell Hill overlooking Florence Cemetery "was dotted by white tents which served as temporary homes for defense workers and their families."

The extent of the epidemic outbreak in the crowded worker's housing areas on Wilson Dam Reservation rapidly reached a crisis stage. An emergency hospital was quickly erected and additional physicians and nurses were brought in from other locations. Health squads were organized to report the location of the sick and remove the dead. As many as fifteen corpses was reportedly moved from the temporary housing areas in one day. The remains of the deceased workers whose home addresses were not known, or whose families could not afford to have them returned home, were buried on the Wilson Dam Reservation in unmarked graves.

It is estimated that in a little more than a month's duration one-half of the population of Florence was afflicted. Dr. David Wills Hollingsworth, who served as pastor of the Florence First Presbyterian Church from 1918 until 1953, and as pastor emeritus until his death in 1965, had many stories concerning the stark tragedy of this terrible epidemic.

On a number of occasions, following graveside services for his own parishioners, he would be approached by strangers requesting that he walk across the cemetery to say a few words over the remains of their loved ones. There were not enough preachers in Florence, Alabama, to officiate at all the funerals. To help cope with this tragedy, Dr. Hollingsworth and other Florence ministers organized and manned a station on Court Street where the families could seek help for their sick and dying.

From the darkest hour of this great tragedy was born the realization of an urgent need for health care facilities. This led to the building of the public hospitals that now serve the people at the Muscle Shoals.

Hannah, Alex John William

In the burying grounds at the Pisgah United Methodist Church near Cloverdale, Alabama, is a tombstone with simple carvings that show only a name, Alex Hannah, with dates of his birth and death, February 7, 1847, and January 11, 1930, and "His memory is blessed;" only these and nothing more. This cautious brevity of words seems to enhance the strange silence that surrounds his grave.

It would require volumes in paragraphs numbered by chapters to fill in between the dates of birth and death and to tell the story of his adventurous life. In the peaceful countryside of Lauderdale County is the grave of a veteran of the British Navy and a former soldier of Emperor Maximilian's Army in Mexico.

Alexander John William Hannah was born February 7, 1847, in Aberdeen, Mississippi. It is believed that he was descended from John of Hanna, master of one of the ships of King James of Scotland in 1424.

Alexander Murray Hannah

Alex's father, Alexander Murray Hannah, was born in 1814, at Wigtownshire Township in Whitehorn, Scotland. Soon after the birth of his son, Alex, on February 7, 1847, in Aberdeen, Mississippi, he and his young family were in Florence, Alabama. His wife, Elizabeth Sarah Downer Hanna, died in Florence on September 19, 1849, only two months after giving birth to her youngest son Malcolm.

According to the 1830 Lauderdale County, Alabama, United States Census, Sarah Hannah, a family member probably a sister to Alexander, is listed as owning 51 black slaves. From March 9, 1818, through July 5, 1830, Sarah Hannah of Tennessee entered some 1,210 acres of land just to the west of Florence, Alabama, in Township 3 South and Range 11 West. Sarah moved from Lauderdale County, Alabama, to Louisiana in 1836.

Alexander Murry Hannah, whose second marriage was to Mary E. Saffarans, became a prosperous merchant after forming a partnership with

Reverend Joseph L. K. Sloss. Sloss's daughter Ann Elizabeth Sloss Coffee was married to Alexander Donelson Coffee, son of General John Coffee. In 1860, Alexander D. Coffee owned 17 black slaves. Sloss's son Joseph H. Sloss was a member of the United States Congress.

According to family sources, the Hannah family at one time lived at Mapleton, one of the oldest mansions at the Muscle Shoals. On December 24, 1873, the Florence Times Journal referred to this residence as "the finest house in Florence."

The Hannas sent their three children-Gertrude, Alex, and Malcolm-to schools in Scotland between 1856 and 1860. Parish records at the Trinity Episcopal Church show the baptism of these young people prior to their leaving Florence.

According to the 1860 Lauderdale County census, Alexander M. Hannah was a 46 year old male merchant and tailor born in Scotland. In his house number 259 were Gertrude A. a 15 year old female born in Georgia and schooled in Scotland, Alex J. W. a 13 year old male born in Mississippi and schooled in Scotland, Malcomb M. a ten year old male born in Alabama and schooled in Scotland, and Mary S. a three year old female born in Alabama and schooled in Scotland.

Alex John William Hannah

Alex John William Hannah married Laura E. Cox. Laura was born on April 12, 1850, in Lauderdale County, Alabama; she died March 10, 1925 (Find a Grave Memorial Number 103449913). They had three children:
    1) Malcolm H. Hannah (1877-1945);
    2) William Cox Hannah (1879-1964); and,
    3) Gertrude Elizabeth Hannah Andrews (1895-1970).

The American Civil War commenced while Alexander Hanna was in Europe. It was at this time that he joined the British Navy and served for four years. Alex returned to Florence at the close of the war, and in 1866, he toured the far west. It was at this time that he enlisted in the army of Ferdinand Maximilian, archduke of Austria and emperor of Mexico. Maximilian's invitation to become involved in Mexico had been maneuvered by the French emperor Napoleon III who wanted to further his imperialistic ambitions.

With his young wife, Carlota, daughter of Belgian's Leopold I, Maximilian sailed for Mexico in May 1864. On June 10, the royal couple was crowned in the Cathedral of Mexico. A year later, with the aid of the French army, the Mexican troops were almost in Texas. However, Maximilian had not foreseen the ending of the Civil War and America's sudden demand that the Mexican army withdraw from the border of Texas.

> **AGED LAUDERDALE MAN IS VICTIM OF STROKE**
>
> Hannan, Was Native Of Scotland; Funeral Held Today
>
> A. H. M. Hannan, aged 82, of Florence, Route 3, died at the family residence Sunday from a stroke of paralysis.
> Funeral services were to be held from Cloverdale church this afternoon at 2 o'clock, followed by interment in Cloverdale cemetery with Brown's in charge.
> The deceased was born in Scotland, but had lived in this country a number of years.
>
> *The Florence Times - Alabama*
> *Monday - January 13, 1930*
> *Front Page*

It was at this time that Florence's Alex Hannah decided to become a soldier of fortune in Maximilian's army. However, the emperor's actions had become so rash and costly that the treasury was soon exhausted. The Empress Carlota rushed to Europe to plea for help and lost her sanity. Maximilian was executed in Mexico.

Alex, having served a brief two weeks in the emperor's army, made his way back to Alabama. It was said that conditions were so hard that he traded a diamond pin, a gift from his sister, for a pound of tobacco.

Alexander John William Hannah, the old sailor and soldier of fortune, returned to his farm in Cloverdale where it was reported that he became engaged in scientific farming. He died January 11, 1930, at the advanced age of eighty three years and was laid to rest in the cemetery at Pisgah United Methodist Church (Find a Grave Memorial Number 103449824).

Hough, Joseph

John Rueben Hough

John Rueben Hough was the son of Joseph Hough II and Jane McClendon. In 1800, John Rueben Hough (1775-1836) and Catherine Rebecca Allen (1780-) were married in South Carolina. By 1823, Rueben and Rebecca moved with their children to Lauderdale County, Alabama. John Rueben and Rebecca had at least eleven children:
1) John Hough was born in South Carolina in 1805; he married Sara Ray, probably the daughter of Green Ray. In 1830, he was living near Joseph and Stephen Hough; by 1840, he was living near Rebecca who had moved to Itawamba County, Mississippi, after the death of her husband John Ruben Hough
2) William Hough was born in South Carolina about 1806; in 1830, in Lauderdale County, Alabama, he was a single man living as a neighbor to John Ruben Hough. William married Mary Reese in February 1834, and they lived in Lauderdale County, Alabama.
3) Polly Hough was born about 1807; on June 2, 1838, she married Joshua S. Hale (Hail).
4) Frances Hough was born about 1808; on April 27, 1829, she married Washington Reese who was thought to be a brother to Mary Reese.
5) Elizabeth B. Hough was born about 1809; on December 31, 1829, she married Larkin Hendrix.
6) Josiah Hough was born between 1815 and 1820; he was given a slave in 1833.
7) Allen J. Hough was born about 1817, in South Carolina; he married Letty D. Justice. They lived for a while in Lauderdale County, Alabama, prior to moving to DeSoto County, Mississippi.

8) David Hough was born about 1819, in South Carolina; he came with his mother Rebecca on the Natchez Trace to Itwamba County, Mississippi, from Lauderdale County, Alabama. David married two times with his first marriage to Mary Ann Burch and second to Elizabeth Elliott Green.
9) Sarah "Sally" Hough was born about 1820, in South Carolina; on July 1, 1841, she married John Cockran.
10) Pleasant James Hough was born about 1821, in South Carolina; he married three times. His first marriage at age 23 was to Mary Elizabeth Harbour in Mississippi; second marriage at age 32 to Amanda Ray on March 10, 1853, in Lauderdale County, Alabama; and third marriage, at age 36 to Nancy Scott in Alabama; he fathered a total of twelve children.
11) Mary "Malsy" Hough was born in 1823, in Alabama; in 1850, she married James Page. In the 1850 census, Mary's mother Rebecca was living in the Page household and was listed as 70 years old. In the 1860 Itawamba County, Mississippi census, only James and his wife Mary Hough Page are listed with their seven children; her mother Rebecca Hough is probably deceased.

In December 1830, John Rueben Hough purchased a black slave from John Reeves Hough and sold the slave to Henry Garrard. In August 1831, John Rueben Hough administered the estate of Elijah Cockburn. In 1833, John Rueben and Rebecca Hough sold land on Shoals Creek to Francis Cockburn. On June 20, 1835, Rebecca Hough, a widow, sold land on Shoals Creek to John Wilson. John Rueben Hough died in 1834 or 1835 in Lauderdale County, Alabama; by 1840, his widow Rebecca was living in Itawamba County, Mississippi.

Joseph Hough

Joseph Hough was born in 1801, at Chesterfield in Chesterfield County, South Carolina. Some think that Joseph's parents were John Rueben Hough (1775-1836) and Catherine Rebecca Allen (1780-); however, he may have been a brother to John Reeves Hough whose father was an older Joseph Hough II. Based on the 1850 census Joseph Hough's children include:

1) Eliza A. Hough was born in 1829, and she married John S. Tate on December 7, 1854, in Lauderdale County, Alabama.
2) John Hough (1830-).
3) Tabitha Hough (1833-).
4) Joseph Hough Jr. (1834-).
5) Nancy "Nannie" Hough was the daughter of Colonel Joseph Hough; she was born on March 21, 1836, in Lauderdale County, Alabama, and she died on February 2, 1908, in Young County, Texas. Her father was a planter and slave owner. She married her husband James McLaren on June 2, 1858, in Lauderdale County, Alabama. Nancy is buried at Oak Grove Cemetery at Graham in Young County, Texas (Find a Grave Memorial Number 51541862).

6) Hetty Hough was born in 1837, and she married William M. Holleman on May 20, 1853, in Lauderdale County, Alabama.
7) William Hough (1838-). Some of the names of his children are the same names of Joseph Hough's siblings.

Colonel Joseph Hough was among the early settlers of Lauderdale County, Alabama; he was an 1812 war veteran in Welch's Company of the South Carolina Militia. Colonel Joseph Hough was awarded the 3,000 acres of land between Shoals Creek and present-day Highway 72 for his services in the war. According to family folklore, Joseph Hough was a direct descendant of Chickamauga Cherokee Chief Doublehead.

Colonel Hough also entered several hundred acres of land in Lauderdale County. From August 13, 1832, through September 13, 1854, Joseph Hough entered 2,440 acres of land in Lauderdale County, Alabama. The vast majority of the land he entered was in Township 2 South and Range 10 West along the Shoals

Creek area east of present-day Florence, Alabama (Cowart, 1996). Shoal Creek runs through Township 2 South and empties into the Tennessee River in the southeastern corner.

Joseph Hough sold a 40 acre tract to Jonathan Bailey, who had established a small settlement on Sycamore River known today as Shoals Creek. The land Jonathan Bailey bought from Joseph Hough contained freshwater springs around which Bailey developed a mineral springs resort. The resort became known as Bailey Springs and people from across the country claimed the springs contained curing agents in the mineral water. Many wealthy individuals and famous people visited the springs to enjoy their medicinal effects. During the early 1800's, Bailey Springs was one of the highest regarded resorts in the South.

According to the 1850 Lauderdale County, Alabama, United States Census, Joseph Hough was a 49 year old white male born in South Carolina. Also living in his house number 771 was Eliza Hough a 21 year old female born in Alabama, John Hough a 20 year old male born in Alabama, Tabitha Hough a 17 year old female born in Alabama, Joseph Hough Jr. a 16 year old male born in Alabama, Nancy Hough a 13 year old female born in Alabama, William Hough a 12 year old male born in Alabama, and Hetty Hough a 14 year old female born in Alabama. According to the 1850 Lauderdale County, Alabama, Slave Schedule, Colonel Joseph Hough owned 28 black slaves.

According to the 1860 Lauderdale County, Alabama, United States Census, Joseph Hough was a 58 year old male farmer born in South Carolina. Also living in his household was Saletha a 22 year old female born in Alabama, and William C. a 21 year old male farmer born in Alabama.

By 1860, Joseph Hough owned 47 black slaves. The 1860 federal census, slave schedules gives the gender and age of Joseph Hough's slaves: Female 65, Female 55, Male 40, Female 40, Male 35, Male 33, Female 30, Female 30, Male 30, Male 30, Male 30, Male 28, Male 28, Female 28, Female 28, Male 28, Female 28, Female 28, Female 28, Male 28, Male 22, Male 22, Male 18, Female 18, Female 18, Male 18, Male 16, Male 14, Male 13, Female 12, Female 12, Male 10, Female 9, Male 7, Male 6, Male 6, Male 6, Female 5, Male 5, Female 5, Female 4, Female 3, Female 2, Female 2, Female 1, Female 1, and Female 1.

John Reeves Hough

Joseph Hough (1801-) was probably a cousin or maybe a brother to John Reeves Hough who was born in Chesterfield District of South Carolina on May 7, 1799. John R. Hough died on May 3, 1849; he was probably the son of another Joseph Hough and a nephew of John Ruben Hough. On May 22, 1823, John Reeves Hough married Anna "Annie" Cockburn (1805-1892). They are buried at Jones Hill Cemetery in Lauderdale County, Alabama (Find a Grave Memorial Number 113930106).

According to the 1860 Lauderdale County, Alabama, United States Census, Annie Hough was a 54 year old white female born in North Carolina. Also living in her household was John a 20year old male born in Alabama, Nancy Bird a 23 year old female born in Alabama, Amos Hough a 17 year old male born in Alabama, Annie a 13 year old female born in Alabama, and Ann E. Bird a one year old female born in Tennessee.

John Reeves Hough was the son of Joseph Hough and probably a cousin or older brother of Colonel Joseph Hough. Annie Cockburn Hough was the wife of John Reeves Hough who died in 1849. According to the 1860 Lauderdale County, Alabama, Slave Schedule, Annie Hough owned eight black slaves.

According to the 1880 Lauderdale County, Alabama, United States Federal Census, Annie Hough was a 74 year old white female born in North Carolina. Her relation to head of the household was mother-in-law, her marital status was listed as widowed, her father's birthplace was North Carolina, and her mother's birthplace was North Carolina. Household members are Robert H. Smith age 40, Nancy Smith age 43, Johnie A. Bird age 21, Amos T. Smith age 14, William D. Smith age 11, Elizbeth E. Smith age nine, Nancy J. Smith age seven, Martha V. Smith age five, and Robert C. Smith age two.

Houston, David Ross-Wildwood Plantation

Wildwood Plantation

The Wildwood Plantation was about 13 miles west of Florence on the Waterloo Road in Lauderdale County, Alabama, near Gravelly Springs. David Ross Houston was the owner of Wildwood Plantation. The David Ross Houston family lived in Tennessee until they moved to Wildwood Plantation with their thirteen children. David Ross Houston first entered land for the plantation in Lauderdale County, Alabama, on October 21, 1820.

The plantation land extended from Gravelly Springs to the Tennessee River where they had a boat landing. The Wildwood Plantation home was located near Gravelly Springs; the springs were a stage stop on the original Natchez Trace and the road from Waterloo to Florence, Alabama.

Their Wildwood Plantation residence was a large, three-story brick structure, and a typical antebellum home. A huge water tank caught rain water and furnished the household with running water. The Wildwood Plantation home burned before 1900. The only remnants of the Wildwood home are portions of the old brick foundations of the mansion and remains of the once elegant garden house.

Civil War Era

Union General James Harrison Wilson made his headquarters at the Wildwood Plantation while his 22,000 cavalrymen were in training at Gravelly Springs during the winter of 1865. The General later described the Houstons as "having natural inclinations to the Union," but since they had large possessions in southern states, they had cast their lot with the Confederacy.

There is a historic marker erected by Florence Historic Board of Florence, Alabama, at the Union Camp Gravelly Springs which was Major General James Harrison Wilson's Headquarters. The marker is located at 34° 53.072' North, 87° 54.258' West at the intersection of County Route 14 and County Route 2.

The inscription on the marker reads, "At this site from mid January to mid March 1865, Maj. Gen. James Harrison Wilson, U.S. Army, assembled the largest cavalry force ever massed in the western hemisphere. Five divisions totaling 22,000 camped from Gravelly Springs westward to Waterloo. Wilson made headquarters a mile east of the springs at Wildwood Plantation, the boyhood home of Alabama senator and governor, George Houston. After intensive training Wilson's Cavalry crossed the Tennessee to invade South Alabama and Georgia, a campaign which included burning the University of Alabama at Tuscaloosa and the capture of Pres. Jefferson Davis at Irwinville, Georgia, in May 1865, after Lee's surrender."

David Ross Houston

David Ross Houston was born about 1774, in the Charleston District of South Carolina. David's father was John Houston, Sr., who was born in 1728, in County Tyrone, Ireland. John died in 1808, in the Newberry District of South Carolina. David's mother was Mary Ross, who was born about 1732 in Northern Ireland. Mary died in Feb 1811, in the Newberry District of South Carolina. In 1751, John Houston and Mary Ross were married in the County Tyrone in the north of Ireland.

David Ross Houston married Hannah Pugh Reagan around 1795, in the Newberry District of South Carolina. Hannah was born on November 3, 1776, in Tyrone County, Ireland. She died on December 1, 1847, in Lauderdale County, Alabama. After living in South Carolina for a while, David Ross Houston and Hannah Pugh Reagan resided in Greene County, Georgia, and Williamson County, Tennessee. The children of David and Hannah Reagan Houston are:

1) Jane Houston was born around 1797, and she died about 1873. She married General Phillip Jacob Irion on August 14, 1838, in Lauderdale County, Alabama. Phillip was born on November 25, 1796, in North Carolina, and died March 25, 1879, at Gravelly Springs in Lauderdale County, Alabama. General Phillip Jacob Irion first married Sally (Wall) Smith, then Jane Houston, and the third time to Victoria C. Wylie.

2) Sarah Houston was born in October 1798, in Williamson County, Tennessee. She died October 17, 1879, and is buried at Ocean Springs, Mississippi.

3) Dr. John Pugh Houston was born on January 25, 1803, in Greene County, Georgia. He married Lucinda Chisholm on December 23, 1830. He died on July 21, 1871, in Iuka, Mississippi.

4) William Ross Houston was born on June 6, 1805. Ross married Martha A. Bumpos on March 19, 1829. He died on December 22, 1863, in San Antonio, Texas. During this early period of the Civil

War, William R. Houston was captured and brutally murdered. There was also strong suspicion that local southern bushwhackers may have murdered him. Some thought that he was assassinated by either the Union Army or by a gang of Union sympathizers.

5) Rebecca Houston was born about 1810, in South Carolina. She died about 1864, in near the Wildwood Plantation. Rebecca married Henry Williams on December 21, 1841, in Lauderdale County, Alabama. Henry was born about 1810, and he died in 1850.

6) Judge Russell Houston was born January 10, 1810, in Williamson County, Tennessee. Russell Huston of Nashville was actively involved as a controversial political activist in support of the Union. Russell died on October 1, 1895, in Louisville, Kentucky.

7) Rebecca Floras Mary Houston was born about 1810, in South Carolina. Rebecca married James Lamb on December 17, 1840. Rebecca died about 1864, at the Wildwood Plantation in Lauderdale County, Alabama.

8) George Smith Houston was born January 17, 1811, in Williamson County, Tennessee. Wildwood Plantation was the boyhood home of George Smith Houston; he was a onetime member of Congress serving as chairman of the Ways and Means Committee, then the twenty-fifth Governor of Alabama, and later United States Senator. George Smith Houston stayed out of the Civil War at Athens, Alabama; however, his son David Houston raised a company of Confederate infantrymen. The young Captain Houston was arrested for being drunk on duty, but George, after a trip to Richmond, was able to get his son reinstated to his command. George Smith Houston died on December 31, 1879, at Athens in Limestone County, Alabama.

9) Dr. Gray Jones Houston was born in 1812, in Tennessee. He died around 1877, at San Antonio in Bexar County, Texas.

10) David Houston was born in 1815. He married Nancy Bromley on January 3, 1843.

11) Mary Alsis Charlotte Houston was born on April 4, 1815. She died on May 20, 1895, at the Wildwood Plantation. Charlotte married Allen Kirk on December 21, 1843. She married Ambrose Bourland Gilbert on March 21, 1847, in Lauderdale County, Alabama. Ambrose was born in North Carolina and died on August 19, 1849, in Cherokee, Alabama.

12) Lydia Louisa Houston was born about 1817, in Tennessee. She died in 1864, at Wildwood Plantation.

13) Anne Hannah Houston was born in 1819, in Tennessee and died in 1868. Anne married John Lamb on November 1, 1838. On July 27, 1846, Anne married John Bennington Boggs, a steamboat captain from Pennsylvania who was first cousin of Julia Dent Grant, wife of General Ulysses S. Grant. During the Civil War, the Boggs were living at the Wildwood Plantation.

The following is the will of David Ross Houston: "I, David Houston of the County of Lauderdale, State of Alabama, of a sound and disposing mind do on this 21st day of August 1836, made and publish this my last will and Testament.
Item 1: It is my will and desire that all of my just debts shall be paid out of my personal property.

Item 2: After the payment of my just debts, I will and bequeath until my daughter Jane a servant girl named Lize and her child and her sister named Jane.

Item 3: I will and bequeath unto my daughter Rebecca Floras Mary a servant girl and her two children Kitta and Perry.

Item 4: I will and bequeath unto my daughter Mary Alsis Charlotte a servant girl.

Item 5: I will and bequeath until my daughter Louisa Vinas eldest daughter Caroline a servant girl.

Item 6: I will and bequeath to my daughter Ann Floras Lise a servant girl that waits in the house.

Item 7: I will and bequeath to the three children Pugh, Nancy and Jane Ridley of Robert Ridley and Sarah Ridley his wife a servant girl named Frances now in the possession of said Robert and Sarah. Also the sum of Three hundred a piece.

Item 8: I will and bequeath to Robert Ridley one hundred and fifty dollars which is all I intend him to have of my estate.

Item 9: I will and bequeath to Sarah Ridley wife of said Robert One hundred and fifty dollars which is all I intend her to have of my estate.

Item 10: I will and bequeath to my son Ross Houston the servant girl named Easter now in his possession and three tracts of land lying in Lauderdale County the one on which he lives called the Gravelly Springs tract and two others now in his possession known as the Strong tracts to him and his heirs forever which is all I intend for him to have of my estate.

Item 11: The balance of my estate of every sort and description I want divided fairly and equally between my sons Pugh Houston, George S. Houston, Russell Houston and G.J. Houston and my daughters Jane Houston, Rebecca Houston, Mary Houston, Louisa Houston and Ann Houston share and share alike the mode of division to be such as my executors may adapt and agree upon.

Item 12: It is my will and desire that my property shall be kept together as it is now during the life of my beloved wife Hanna Houston under the control of my executors and that she is liberally supported out of the profits of the same during such her said life and that the profits of the labour of my servants on the farm and other places as my said executors may put them be put into and constitute a part of the general fund to be divided as aforesaid after taking out so much as may be required to support my beloved wife as aforesaid.

Item 13: I hereby appoint Pugh Houston and George S. Houston my sons my Exrs of this my last Will and Testament and it is my will and desire that they manage and control my Estate as I have above requested it to be done.

Item 14: I hereby authorize and empower my Executors if they think proper to do so to dispose of my surplus property real or personal at private sale or in any other manner they may agree upon and employ and use the proceeds of said sale or sales in the way they may think best for the benefit of the legatees."

Signed this 22nd day of August, 1936, by David Houston, Witnessed by Richard Baugh, Moses White and Jane Bromley Filed October 15th, 1836, Probate Court of Lauderdale County, Alabama, Recorded Will Book A, pages 26-27.

David Ross Houston died on September 24, 1836, in Lauderdale County, Alabama. In his will, David Ross Houston set aside five acres for the family cemetery and two acres for the slaves. Until recent years, an ornamental gazebo constructed in the shape of a Maltese cross stood as a sentinel near the center of the family burial grounds.

Jane Houston Irions

David Ross Houston died on September 24, 1836, leaving the bulk of his estate equally among most of his children. His sons sold their shares to their five sisters. Through an extraordinary arrangement with her sisters, Jane Houston Irions took over the management of the Wildwood Plantation and was highly successful as a planter.

On August 14, 1838, Jane Houston married Phillip Jacob Irions and settled on their small farm near the Wildwood Plantation. Phillip Irions and his brother, Thomas, arrived in Gravelly Springs around 1840. A third brother, Frederick

Augustus Irions, settled in this area nine years later. The Irion brothers ancestor, Frederick Witt Iron, came to America from Germany and settled in Rockingham County, North Carolina, where he died in 1794.

Along with the widows of James Jackson and Wyatt Collier, Jane Houston Irions was one of three ladies listed in the 1860 Lauderdale County, Alabama, United States Census, as being at the head of large plantations in Lauderdale County, Alabama. Jane's father had acquired his 2,760 acre farm in 1821. In 1860, with a workforce of 97 black slaves, Jane produced 172 bales of cotton, 5,500 bushels of corn, 260 bushels of wheat, 130 pounds of wool, and 365 pounds of butter.

Jane Houston Irions had reached her sixty-fourth birthday at the start of the Civil War with the firing on Fort Sumter. Her family endured considerable hardships curing the Civil War because of occupation of the Union army. During the Civil War, Gravelly Springs were the site of the formation of Wilson's large Union cavalry in late 1864, and early 1865, with the Cannon home serving as Wilson's headquarters.

Jane Houston Irions died in 1874, at the age of seventy-seven years. Her sister, Mary, was the last of the Houston family to reside at Wildwood. Jane Irions was successful during her years as planter on one of the very large cotton plantations that once played a major role in the economic base of the Tennessee Valley.

Ingram, Benjamin

Benjamin Ingram was born in Brunswick County, Virginia, on April 7, 1782. He was the son of Moses Ingram and Elizabeth Croft. Benjamin Ingram had one brother Henry Ingram. Benjamin Ingram's ancestors came to America from Northumberland, England.

Benjamin Ingram married Sarah "Sally" Mason; Sarah was born on February 10, 1789. Her parents were Joseph Mason (1757-1795) and Elizabeth Watson Mason.

Benjamin and Sally Ingram had the following children:

1) Mary Elizabeth Ingram (1809-1855) married Thomas F. Butler on December 21, 1824.
2) Emily L. Ingram (1810-1867) married Walter Haraway on September 6, 1831.
3) George M. Ingram (1814-1887) married Lucy Ann Crittenden on December 4, 1845. In 1860, George Ingram owned 32 black slaves.
4) Sarah Mason Ingram (1815-1843) married Thomas Binford on October 5, 1835.
5) Julia Ann Ingram (1817-1862) married John Fuqua on November 6, 1835. According to the 1860 slave census, Julia A. Fuqua owned 30 black slaves.

6) Octavia Ingram (1823-1861) married William H. Crittenden on June 24, 1843. In 1860, the William H. Crittenden estate owned 25 slaves.
7) Joseph Thomas Ingram (1825-1912) in the 1860 slave census owned 18 black slaves.
8) Moses Ingram (1829-1869) married Mary Crittenden on December 5, 1855. In the 1806 slave census, Moses Ingram owned 17 black slaves.

Benjamin first acquired land in Lauderdale County, Alabama, when he leased land in Doublehead's Reserve from Chickamauga Cherokee Chief Doublehead prior to his death in 1807. In 1818, Benjamin Ingram entered land in Township 2 South and Range 8 West in Lauderdale County, Alabama.

Benjamin Ingram is listed in the 1830 Lauderdale County, Alabama, United States Census. According to the 1840 Lauderdale County, Alabama, United States Census, Benjamin Ingram owned 25 black slaves.

In the 1850 Lauderdale County, Alabama, United States Census, Benjamin Ingram, Jr. is listed as a 30 year old white male. Also, living in house number 590 was Sarah Ingram a 61 year old female born in Virginia, Joseph Ingram a 25 year old male born in Alabama, and Benjamin J. Binford an eight year old male born in Alabama.

According to the 1850 Lauderdale County, Alabama, Slave Schedule, Sarah Ingram (widow of Benjamin Ingram) lived in the area east of the Military Road and owned 21 black slaves. Also, Henry Ingram, Benjamin's brother, owned 20 black slaves.

Even though Benjamin Ingram died in 1849, the 1850 Lauderdale County, Alabama, Agricultural Census that was taken on November 15, 1850, reports that his farm contains 600 acres of improved land and 900 acres of unimproved land worth $75,000. Benjamin Ingram's farm had the highest value of any cotton planter in 1850 in Lauderdale County, Alabama. The next highest farm value in the 1850 Lauderdale County, Alabama, Agricultural Census was $45,000.00.

The 1860 Lauderdale County, Alabama, United States Census of District One lists Benjamin Ingram, Jr. as a 39 year old white male born in Alabama and living in house number 267. Benjamin Ingram, Jr. is also found in the 1866 Lauderdale County, Alabama State Census. According to the 1860 slave schedule, Benjamin Ingram, Jr. owned 16 black slaves.

Benjamin Ingram settled at the crossing of Doublehead's Trace and the North River Road; these were two of the original aboriginal Indian trails through the area north of Shoal Town located near the middle of Big Muscle Shoals on the Tennessee River. After Benjamin, Moses, and George Ingram settled in the area, the early Indian trail crossing became known as Ingram's Crossroads.

Today, a historic marker stands near the crossroads; side one of the marker inscription is the following, "Settlement of this area began in the early 1800s. Gabriel Butler settled approximately two miles northwest of here on Bluewater Creek. His name is found on the 1810 petition for removal of white settlers leasing land on Chief Doublehead's Reserve. Gabriel Butler built a Baptist Church on his property which is believed to be the first church in the area. Other early landowners were John Bradford, Daniel White, Walter West, Robert Jackson, Aristides Jackson, Benjamin Ingram, George Ingram, and Moses Ingram. Huntsville Road (Highway 72) and Bellevue Road (Highway 101) was an important intersection. Huntsville Road was a major route from Chattanooga

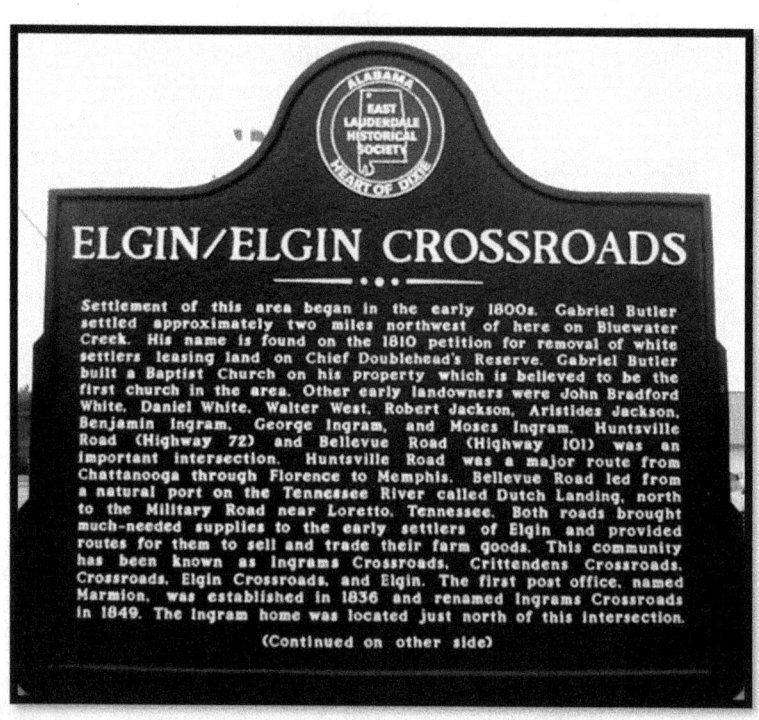

through Florence to Memphis. Bellevue Road led from a natural port on the Tennessee River called Dutch Landing, north to the Military Road near Loretto, Tennessee. Both roads brought much-needed supplies to the early settlers of Elgin and provided routes for them to sell and trade their farm goods. This community has been known as Ingrams Crossroads, Crittendens Crossroads, Crossroads, Elgin Crossroads, and Elgin. The first post office, named Marmion, was established in 1836 and renamed Ingrams Crossroads in 1949. The Ingram home was located just north of this intersection."

Side two of the historic marker reads, "Benjamin, George, and Moses Ingram are listed on the 1850 census as merchants. During the Civil War, Ingrams Crossroads served as a recruiting station for the Confederate States of America. Men enlisted into the 27th Alabama Infantry, 7th Alabama Cavalry, 9th Alabama Cavalry, and the 14th Alabama Infantry. Ingrams Crossroads Post Office was abandoned in 1868. The community was then referred to as Crittendens Crossroads until 1901 when a post office was re-established and given the name Elgin Post Office. Although this post office closed in 1905, the name Elgin has remained. The first Crossroads School was located here. It was a one-room structure built in the late 1800s. In 1917, a three-room school was built about 300 yards south of here on land given by F.E. Jackson to J.H. Belew. In 1939, four additional adjoining acres were donated by E.M. Jackson. In 1942, the Works Progress Administration completed a brick school here named Crossroads School, later renamed Elgin

Elementary School. The school closed in 1985. Today thanks to the Elgin Senior Citizens, the lunchroom and auditorium have been preserved."

The historic marker was erected by East Lauderdale Historical Society. The latitude and longitude of the marker is 34° 51.045' North, 87° 23.467' West. It is in Elgin, Alabama, in Lauderdale County, Alabama at the intersection of Alabama Highways 101 and 72.

Benjamin Ingram died on September 11, 1849 (Find a Grave Memorial Number 79394444); he is buried with Sarah and other relatives in the Ingram-Thornton Cemetery, Row 8. Sarah "Sally" Mason died on September 25, 1852; she is buried in the Ingram Cemetery at Thorntontown in Lauderdale County, Alabama (Find a Grave Memorial Number 79394537). The Ingram-Thornton Cemetery is found by following Highway 72 east of Elgin (Ingram) Crossroads and turning north on county road 569. The cemetery is on the right side of county road 569.

Elizabeth Perkins and James Jackson III

Jackson, James III- The Sinks Plantation

Colonel James Jackson, III was born on April 21, 1822, in Nashville, Tennessee. He was the son of James Jackson II (1782-1840) and Sarah Moore Jackson (1790-1879), the owners of the Forks of Cypress in Lauderdale County, Alabama.

On October 3, 1850, James Jackson III married Elizabeth "Lizzy" M. Perkins (1832 - 1872) on October 3, 1850, at Florence in Lauderdale County, Alabama. Elizabeth was the daughter of William O'Neal and Rebecca (Meredith) Perkins. James and Elizabeth lived in a large plantation residence, nine miles from Florence known as The Sinks Plantation.

James and Elizabeth had the following children:
1) William B. Jackson (born 1851) married Sarah Weakley;
2) Jane Jackson (1853-1853);
3) Mary Steele Jackson (1854-1861);
4) Sarah "Sallie" Moore Jackson (1856-1861);
5) Eleanora "Nora" Kirkman Jackson (1858-1937) married William H. Phillips;
6) James Kirkman Jackson (1862-   ) married Helen Gunter of Montgomery;
7) Charles Pollard (1863-   ) married Eliza S. Tatum;
8) Robert Andrew Jackson (1865-1936); and,
9) Elizabeth Perkins Jackson (1869-1871).

James Jackson III also had a daughter Queen Jackson Haley (1857-1941), by one of his father's black female slaves Easter Jackson (1816-1860). Queen was born at the Forks of Cypress Plantation. "After the Civil War, she made her way north. She settled in Savannah, working at the Cherry Plantation. She was the second wife of Alex Haley, a local ferry operator. Her grandson, author Alex Haley, would write the novel, 'Queen' about her life. It was later made into a miniseries." When writing 'Queen', Haley spent about three days in Florence, Ala. with co-author and Florence City Historian William L. McDonald. Queen was buried in the Savannah Cemetery at Savannah in Hardin

Queen Jackson Haley
1857-1941

County, Tennessee (Find a Grave Memorial Number 10780396).

James Jackson III's siblings included:
1) half sibling, Elizabeth McCulloch Kirkman (1809-1871);
2) Mary Steele Jackson Kirkman (1811-March 13, 1833);
3) Martha Jackson Mitchell (1812- August 15, 1879);
4) Ellen Kirkman Jackson Hunt (1814-1897);
5) Andrew Jackson (1816–1838);
6) Sarah Moore Jackson (1819-April 15, 1879);
7) William Moore Jackson (1824-December 21, 1899);
8) George Moore Jackson (1829-1883); and,
9) Jane Jackson (1831-August 1839).

James Jackson III was educated in private schools in Nashville, Tennessee, and Florence, Alabama. In April 1861 at the start of the Civil War, he enlisted in the Confederacy as an infantry private in the Fourth Alabama Infantry; he was shot through the lungs at the first Battle of Manassas. After recovery from a wound, James III helped organize the 27th Alabama Infantry, and he became Lieutenant Colonel after the death of Colonel Hughes. Colonel Jackson was captured with that regiment at Fort Donelson and was held prisoner for seven months. After a prisoner exchange, James III was with his regiment in the siege of Jackson, Mississippi.

Colonel James Jackson and his White Horse Cavalry participated in the Georgia campaign and lost an arm at Kennesaw Mountain; later, he was with General John Bell Hood at the Battle of Nashville. James was assigned to Confederate General Joseph Eggleston Johnson's Army of Tennessee, and he commanded a brigade under General Loving at the Battle of Bentonville in Johnson County, North Carolina. On April 26, 1865, Lieutenant Colonel James Jackson III was with Johnson when he surrendered, at the Bennett Place in North Carolina, to Union Major General William T. Sherman; Johnson's surrender effectively ended the Civil War.

Lieutenant Colonel James Jackson III was of ordinary stature, and reserved demeanor. His energy and decision of purpose were noteworthy traits; he preferred deeds to words. During his military service, James Jackson III was wounded 14 times, but he survived with the loss of his arm which did not slow him down.

Prior to James Jackson III serving in the Civil War with the Confederate States of American, his family was incredibly wealthy. He was initially an old line Whig, but became a democrat. However, after returning from the war to his Sinks home in Lauderdale County, Alabama, his family fell on hard times. He resumed his cotton planting operations, but had to go into public service to make ends meet. From 1865 through 1867, James III served as an Alabama State Senator. In 1870, James III got a job as probate clerk for Lauderdale County; later, he was elected Probate Judge of the county.

Colonel James Jackson, III died on August 14, 1879, at The Sinks Plantation in Lauderdale County, Alabama. He was originally buried at his Sinks home, but later, his grave was later moved to the Jackson Family Cemetery at the Forks of Cypress Plantation where he was born (Find a Grave Memorial Number 31712006).

James Kirkman Jackson

James Kirkman Jackson was born on April 7, 1862. He was the son of Colonel James Jackson III and Elizabeth Perkins Jackson of Florence, Alabama, and a business man who was born in Florence. On February 21, 1900, James married Helen Gunter in Montgomery. Helen was the daughter of William A. and Helen Poelnitz Gunter of Marengo County, Alabama. James and Helen had James Kirkman Jackson, Jr. and Helen Jackson.

He received his early schooling under a private tutor at Florence, and attended the state normal school at Florence. He was admitted to the bar, but never engaged in the practice of law. In 1883, he was appointed clerk of the

Alabama Railroad Commission, and held that position for four years. James served as private secretary for Governor Thomas Seay (1887-1890), Governor Thomas G. Jones (1890-1894), Governor Jelks (1902-1907), and serving the last three months under Governor Comer. He was elected secretary of state and served from 1894 to 1898.

Jackson, James-Forks of Cypress Plantation

In the early 1820's, James Jackson II was the builder and owner of the Forks of Cypress Plantation near the forks of Big Cypress Creek and Little Cypress Creek in Lauderdale County, Alabama. He supposedly purchased the property during the transition of the lands taken from the Cherokee and Chickasaw Indians from Chickamauga Cherokee Chief Doublehead's son, Doublehead Doublehead, who was allowed to continue to live on the plantation.

Forks of Cypress

James Jackson II was born on October 25, 1782, at Ballybay in County Monoghan, Ireland. The Irish Town of Ballybay was located in Northern Ireland at the junctions of roads going to Monaghan, Castleblayney, Carrickmacross, and

Clones. In the Irish uprising of 1798, James II enlisted in The United Irishmen at the age of 16 years old. The young man was captured by General Cornwallis and sentenced to be banned and transported as a felon to Botany Bay, Australia. With some intervention of the Kirkman family, James II was transported to Philadelphia in the United States. Later, Jackson moved to Nashville, Tennessee, where he became a successful merchant.

James II's father was James Jackson I and his mother was Mary Steele Jackson; his parents had been successful and were considered well to do. James Jackson I was born in 1743 at Ballybay, and he died on March 5, 1822, at the Town of Ballybay in County Monaghan, Ireland. James I's parents were Hugh Jackson (1709-1777) and Eleanor Gault Jackson (1711-1791).

James Jackson I and his wife, Mary Steele Jackson of Ireland, had the following children:
1) Hugh Jackson (1769-1806);
2) Walter Jackson (1770-   );
3) Henry Jackson (1771-   );
4) Sarah Jackson Hanna (1772-1843);
5) John Jackson (1773-1832);
6) Martha Jackson Hanna Cooper (1777-1806);
7) Henry Jackson (1780-   );
8) Mary Steel Jackson McDaniel (1781-   );
9) James Jackson (1782-1840); and,
10) Washington Jackson (1784-1865).

James Jackson I
1743-1822

James Jackson I's siblings were John Jackson (1744-1824), Alexander Jackson (1749-1796), Henry Jackson (1750-1817), and Hugh Jackson (1751 1810). James I is buried in Tullycorbert

Parish Church Cemetery in the Town of Ballybay in County Monaghan, Ireland (Find a Grave Memorial Number 133674929).

James Jackson II was a trustee in The Cypress Land Company along with LeRoy Pope, Thomas Bibb, John Coffee, John McKinley, and Dabney Morris. From February 6, 1818, through March 23, 1830, James Jackson II of the Forks of Cypress entered a total of approximately 16,800 acres of land in Lauderdale, Franklin (Colbert), Lawrence, and Limestone Counties. From March 3, 1818, through November 28, 1821, James Jackson II entered some 11,610 acres of land located in Township 2, 3 South and Range 11, 12 West in Lauderdale County, Alabama, with the majority entered in March 1818. He also entered some 950 acres in Lawrence County, over 2,260 acres in Franklin/Colbert County, and some 2,160 acres in Limestone County, Alabama. These are land record entries given in Old Land Records of Lauderdale, Lawrence, Limestone, Colbert, Franklin, and Counties (Cowart, 1984, 1985, 1986, 1991, and 1996).

James Jackson II
10/25/1782-8/17/1840

The Forks of Cypress Plantation Home of James Jackson and Sally Moore McCulloch Jackson was a Greek revival style house designed by William Nichols. The home featured brick columns spaced on each side completely around the entire house. The plantation mansion was constructed on a high flat rise between the forks of Big Cypress Creek and Little Cypress Creek north of Florence, Alabama.

Sarah "Sally" Moore was born on July 10, 1790; her father was George Moore (1746-1804). She was first married to Samuel McCullough who died around 1809. Sarah had one daughter Elizabeth McCulloch Kirkman (1809-1871) by Samuel McCulloch before he died in 1809. After the death of her first husband, she married James Jackson II, the owner and builder of the Forks of Cypress Plantation. The children of James and Sarah were Mary Steele Jackson Kirkman (1811-1833), Martha Jackson Mitchell (1812-1879), James Jackson (1822-1879), William Moore Jackson (1824 1899), George Moore Jackson (1829 1883), and Jane Jackson (1831-1839).

Rickey Butch Walker at columns of Forks of Cypress

For many years to come, the remnants of the Forks of Cypress Plantation Mansion of James Jackson II will be a reminder of the antebellum era cotton planters of Lauderdale County, Alabama. In March 1818, James II acquired tremendous tracts of property in the counties taken by the Turkey Town Treaty of September 1816. He made numerous friends who included General Andrew Jackson, to whom he was not directly related.

By early 1818, James II was acquiring land for his cotton plantation in Lauderdale County, Alabama. As a wealthy planter, he became influential in local politics, and entertained powerful politicians with princely hospitality at his Forks of Cypress Mansion. In 1822, he was a member of the general assembly; he also served as President of the Senate in 1830. James II served in both houses of the Alabama state legislature. Later, James Jackson II was twice beaten for the Senate by Honorable Hugh McVay.

In the years prior to his death, James Jackson II was described as a large portly man with very handsome features. Due to his wealth and status in the community, he experienced wide popularity and a great deal of political influence. James II possessed a great deal of energy, tact, and judgment which made him adept in dealing with people.

James Jackson II loved his horses and considered himself a horse breeder with a large number of excellent imported stock of the finest blood lines. James imported a dozen or more English thoroughbred horses for breeding his own horses in a effort to improve the overall bloodstock of his American thoroughbred. He was successful in his horse breeding with three particular

thoroughbred imports: Leviathan in 1830, Gallopade in 1835, and Glencoe in 1836. American turf historian John Hervey rates James Jackson II as the most successful importer in the history of the American thoroughbred.

James Jackson II enjoyed the best horse racing tracks and sought out those that were of highest quality. In 1836, James Jackson II imported a horse named Glencoe from England. The fine stallion Glencoe was one of the most famous horses to ever live at Forks of Cypress Plantation.

The Glencoe stallion's daughter, Peytona, won one of the most famous horse races of all time. During an 1845 race staged on Long Island in New York,

Peytona beat the best northern horse named Fashion which had a huge fan base. More than 65,000 people showed up to watch the horse race that was billed as a North versus South contest. The match was immortalized in a Currier and Ives print titled "Peytona and Fashion." A copy of the print is displayed at Pope's Tavern Museum in Florence, Alabama.

William Lindsey McDonald wrote about Glencoe, the famous English thoroughbred horse of James Jackson of the Forks of Cypress Plantation. Arriving in America in 1836, Glencoe stood at stud on James Jackson's Forks of Cypress Plantation in Florence, Alabama, until Jackson's death in 1840.

On September 15, 1840, the will of James Jackson II was recorded at the Lauderdale County Court House. His will directed that his nephew Thomas Kirkman to manage a trust which would control and gradually sell off all of James Jackson II's racehorses. Jackson's nephews, James and Thomas Kirkman then moved him to Thomas Flintoff's stud near Nashville, Tennessee.

In 1848, Thomas Kirkman completed his duties as described by the will with the sale of Glencoe. Glencoe was purchased by W. Frank Harper and sent to Woodford County, Kentucky. A few months before his death in 1857, he was sold to A. Keene Richards.

The 1830 Lauderdale County, Alabama Census for the James Jackson II household says there were seven white males with the oldest being between 40 to 50 years old and three white females with the oldest being between 40 to 50 years old. Also according to the census, James Jackson owned 75 black slaves which

Rickey Butch Walker at James Jackson's Tombstone

included 38 males and 37 females.

The 1840 Lauderdale County, Alabama, United States Census of the James Jackson II household gives one white male between five and ten years old, one white male between 50 and 60 years old, one white female between 50 and 60 years old. The 1840 census says that James Jackson owned a total of 86 slaves with 54 being black males and 32 being black females.

James Jackson II died on August 17, 1840, at the Forks of Cypress in Lauderdale County, Alabama. He is buried in the Jackson Family Cemetery on the Forks of Cypress Plantation in Lauderdale County, Alabama. He has an impressive marble tombstone in the Jackson Family Cemetery which is enclosed in a stone wall (Find a Grave Memorial Number 31602516).

James Jackson II has a historic marker erected in 2009 by the City of Florence. His marker is at Florence in Lauderdale County, Alabama, at Latitude 34° 48.406' North and Longitude 87° 37.88' West. The marker is located in River Heritage Park and can be reached from Hightower Place near Veterans Drive or Alabama Route 133, on the left when traveling west.

The inscription on James Jackson II's historic marker says, "Often referred to as the most successful breeder of thoroughbred horses in America, James Jackson imported Glencoe and Leviathan to

Sarah Moore McCollough Jackson
7/10/1790-12/24/1879

the U.S. in the early 1800's, leaving a permanent imprint on both the breed and American racing history."

Sarah Moore Jackson

After James Jackson's death in August 1840, his wife Sarah Moore Jackson took control of the Forks of Cypress Plantation. On October 9, 1840, Sarah Jackson, his widow, was the executor of his will and made bond in the amount of $400,000. According to the 1850 Lauderdale County, Alabama, Slave Schedule, Mrs. Sarah Jackson is the owner of 66 black slaves.

According to the 1860 Lauderdale County, Alabama, United States Census, Mrs. Sarah Jackson is a 68 year old female plantress born in North Carolina. Also living in her house number 610 is Sarah Polk a 40 year old female born in Tennessee, Sallie an 18 year old female born in Alabama, and Mattie Andrews a ten year old female born in Alabama.

On December 24, 1879, Sarah "Sally" Moore Jackson died at her Forks of Cypress Plantation home in Lauderdale County, Alabama. She is buried in the nearby Jackson Family Cemetery. On December 27, 1879, the Florence Gazette reported the following obituary of Sarah "Sally" Moore McCullough Jackson. "Died at her residence, The Forks of Cypress, at 8 o'clock on the morning of the 24th instant, Mrs. Sarah M. Jackson.

Mrs. Jackson was the daughter of Mr. George Moore of Orange County, North Carolina, and was born near Wilmington, on the 10th day of July, 1790. Her girlhood was spent with her guardian, Mr. Duncan Cameron, of Raleigh. She was married to Mr. Samuel McCulloch, and moved to Tennessee in 1808. Her second marriage was to Mr. James Jackson on the 28th of December 1810, and he settled The Forks of Cypress in this county in 1820. Which place was bought from the noted Indian, Chief Doublehead. From these facts it will be seen that Mrs. Jackson resided in the county nearly 60 years, and during that long period, held the most perfect respect and esteem of all her acquaintances and was never heard to speak disparagingly of anyone but ever espoused the causes of the weak and defenseless. A member of the Presbyterian Church, she was a devoted Christian and possessed a faith which enabled her to meet calmly, all the afflictions which were allotted her in her long and useful life. Almost all her life was spent in affluent circumstances, and it was ever her pleasure to relive suffering of those were under her notice. A modest, pure Christian woman, she was eminently endowed with that faith that suffereth long and is patient" (Find a Grave Memorial Number 31646381).

Forks of Cypress Burns

On June 6, 1966, the historic Forks of Cypress Plantation Mansion burned to the ground after being struck by lightning. Local rumor says that the brick columns survived the fire because the materials used in their construction contained ground horse hair which is said to be flame retardant.

Forks of Cypress on fire

      Hugh Scott owned the Forks of Cypress in 1935. By the 1940's, Scott sold the plantation to Rufus B. Dowdy (1897-1980). The Dowdy family restored the plantation mansion and surrounding grounds. After the fire, the historic mansion, which was built around 1820 by James Jackson II, was never rebuilt by the Dowdy family, but they preserved the brick pillars which are still standing in a high picturesque flat topped hillside setting.

Kernachan, Abraham and Robert

Kernachan Plantation

The Kernachan Plantation is located in Lauderdale County, Alabama. The plantation is displayed on the Sinking Creek United States Geographic Survey topographic map. The latitude and longitude coordinates of Kernachan Plantation are 34.7867554 North and 87.8347547 West with the approximate elevation being 495 feet above sea level.

The Kernachan Plantation was located in Chickasaw Territory that was ceded by the Turkey Town Treaty of 1816. In 1810, the Chickasaws complained that between 4,000 and 5,000 people had illegally invaded their territory. By 1816, Isaac Barker, a government agent, reported that 200 to 300 families were living around the Muscle Shoals of the Tennessee River including the area in Lauderdale County, Alabama.

Abraham Kernachan was a Scots Irish settler, who arrived prior or during the time of the American Revolution and immediately became patriots. Before 1820, Abraham moved south and is listed in the early land records of Lauderdale County, Alabama, as being from Giles County, Tennessee.

The "Inventory Book A" of Lauderdale County, Alabama, records 22 patents of land to Abraham Kernachan dated February 6, 1822, in Township 3 South and Range 12 West. This township borders Pickwick Lake on the Tennessee River to the south. It continues across the river into Colbert County, Alabama.

From October 18, 1820, through May 27, 1823, Abraham Kernachan entered some 1,360 acres of land in Township 3 South and Ranges 12, 13 West in Lauderdale County, Alabama. Most of the land he entered was within Chickasaw Chief George Colbert's Old Reservation along the Tennessee River. George Colbert and the Chickasaws were not removed from their land on the south side of the river until November 7, 1837.

Abraham is recorded as living in the Community of Smithsonia in Lauderdale County. On April 25, 1822, Abraham Kernachan recorded his livestock mark as a swallow fork in each ear.

Abraham Kernachan

Abraham Kernachan was born in 1783 at Corrigan in County Donegal, Ireland, and died March 12, 1833. The Irishman first arrived in Philadelphia, Pennsylvania, in 1799. Abraham married Martha Booth in Tennessee about 1820.

Martha Booth Kernachan was born in Mecklenburg County, Virginia, on November 3, 1791. She moved to Tennessee in 1818 and married Abraham Kernachan. Abraham Kernachan and Martha Booth had one son and five daughters with the first being twins:
1) Muriel G. Kernachan was born on April 6, 1822; she likely died as a child since there are no marriage records. Muriel is buried in the Kernachan Cemetery.
2) Mariah C. Kernachan was born on April 6, 1822. Mariah C. Kernachan married Isaac B. Williams; she died September 1, 1851, in the 30th year of her age. She is buried in the Kernachan Cemetery.
3) Eliza Ann Kernachan was born December 3, 1823. She married first cousin Francis Haywood Jones, son of Francis F Jones and Nancy Ann Booth Jones. She died a young bride at the age of 22 in 1845. The obituary of Francis Harwood Jones states that he and Eliza lived for a little while in Cincinnati. Francis Harwood Jones was also a cousin of Eliza Kernachan, being the son of Francis F. Jones and Nancy Ann Booth, sister of Martha Booth Kernachan. According to the 1850 slave census, Francis H. Jones owned 22 black slaves.
4) Matilda Bloomfield Kernachan was born May 16, 1826. She married James Carey Jones, also a first cousin and a brother to Francis H. Jones who married her sister Eliza.
5) Robert Thomas Kernachan II(Only son named for his uncle and probably his grandfather), was born on September 19, 1827. He was a Confederate soldier and veteran of the Civil War; he died in 1869. He married cousin Ann Elizabeth Ellen Simmons, daughter of John J. Simmons and Rebecca

Ann Charlotte Jones Simmons. Her mother would go on to marry John Nicholas Malone of Limestone County, Alabama.

6) Mary Lucy Kernachan was born on September 24, 1829. She was the first wife of John Nicholas Malone, who later married her cousin Rebecca Ann Charlotte Jones Simmons, mother of her sister-in-law, Ann Elizabeth Simmons. John and Lucy had three children together before she died in 1849: Algernon Kernachan Malone (1846), Robert Booth Malone(1847), and Sarah "Sally" A. Malone (1848).

In 1826, Abraham Kernachan filed a lawsuit in Lawrence County, Alabama, suing his brother-in-law, Harper Booth. Another party mentioned is a brother-in-law, Francis Jones, husband of Nancy Ann Booth Jones; Nancy was a sister to Martha. Abraham wins the suit and Harper Booth has to pay him the $1,279.25 that was borrowed in 1822.

In the 1830 census, Abraham was the head of household with a total of 55 persons living on his cotton plantation and listed in his household. According to the 1830 Lauderdale, Alabama, United States Census, Abraham Kernachan is listed with the following: Free white males Under 5: 1 (Robert Thomas Kernachan II age 3); 20 thru 29: 1; 30 thru 39: 1 (Abraham's brother Robert Thomas Kernachan age 34); and 50 thru 59: 1 (Abraham). Free white females under 5: 1 (Mary Lucy Kernachan); 5 thru 9: 3 (Mariah, Matilda, Eliza); and, 30 thru 39: 1 (Martha). The total free white persons are five under 20 and three free white persons 20 thru 49 for a total of nine free white persons.

According to the 1830 Lauderdale County, Alabama, United States Census, Abraham Kernachan owned 46 black slaves. His slaves are enumerated as follows: Male slaves under 10: 6; 10 thru 23: 9; 24 thru 35: 5; and 36 thru 54: 5. Female slaves under 10: 8; 10 thru 23: 6; 36 thru 54: 4; and, 55 thru 99: 3. Abraham owned a total of 46 black slaves in 1830. The total of all free white, slaves, and free colored persons equals 55.

Abraham Kernachan died in 1833 at his cotton plantation in Lauderdale County, Alabama. Abraham's tombstone inscription reads, "Abraham Kernachan, b. 1783, Corrigan, Co. Donegal, Ireland, d. 12 Mar 1833, in Lauderdale County Alabama."

A history of Lauderdale County states that the major Cotton mills were established between 1836 and 1840. The Cypress Creek area of Lauderdale saw the development of the Kernachan Mill and the Skipworth Mill, which would later be purchased by Mr. James Martin and Mr. Levi Cassity and renamed the Globe Factory or called the Cypress Mill.

John Kernachan, a brother to Abraham and Robert, remained in Ireland and is mentioned in Robert's will. Another brother, Andrew remained in Tennessee, and whose daughters the family still had interactions. Another possible relative mentioned as a Revolutionary War soldier was William Kernachan. William enlisted on April 13, 1791, as a private in the Pennsylvania line at Little York, Pennsylvania. He applied for a pension November 1, 1818, at age 68, in Bucks County, Pennsylvania. The 1820 record lists him with wife Grissel, 74, and possibly two grandchildren living in the home. William would have been born about 1750, and he may be the father, uncle, or some other relative of the Abraham and Robert Kernchan.

Robert Thomas Kernachan Sr.

Robert Thomas Kernachan, the younger brother of Abraham Kernachan, was born in 1796 in County Donegal, Ireland; he came to Philadelphia, Pennsylvania, at age six and then to Tennessee. In 1820, Robert Thomas Kernachan moved from Tennessee, to join Abraham and Martha at their cotton plantation in Lauderdale County, Alabama. Another younger brother, Andrew Kernachan, would remain in Shelby County, Tennessee.

Robert's brother Abraham died on March 12, 1833. In May of 1834, Robert Thomas Kernachan, Sr. married his brother Abraham's widow, Martha Booth Kernachan.

According to the 1840 Lauderdale County, Alabama, United States census, Robert Kernahan household had the following people: Free White Persons Males 10 thru 14: 1 (Robert Jr., age 13); Free White Persons Males 20 thru 29: 1; Free White Persons Males 40 thru 49: 1 (Robert Sr. age 47); Free White Persons Females 10 thru 14: 1 (Lucy age 11); Free White Persons Females 15 thru 19: 2

(Eliza 17, Matilda 15, Mariah married, Muriel 8: deceased); Free White Persons Females 40 thru 49: 1 (Martha age 48).

The 1840 census identifies the black slaves of Robert Kernachan: The male slaves are under 10: 19; 10 thru 23: 10; 24 thru 35: 9; 36 thru 54: 5; and 55 thru 99: 1. The female black slaves are under 10: 15; 10 thru 23: 10; 24 thru 35: 5; 36 thru 54: 4; and 55 thru 99: 3. In 1840, there were 40 persons employed in agriculture.

The totals for the 1840 census are free white persons under 20: 4, free white persons 20 thru 49: 3, with the total free white persons: 7. Robert Kernachan owned a total number of 81 black slaves in 1840. The total of all free white, free colored, and slave persons was 88.

Robert Kernachan was entrusted with the estate of Rebecca Elliott's will. His wife, Martha Kernachan, is named as an heir and near kin of Rebecca Booth Elliott, the aunt of both Mariah and her husband/first cousin, George W. Booth. Martha Booth Kernachan was married to Robert, and therefore an in-law of Mariah.

In the 19 page Divorce Settlement of Dr. George Washington Booth and his wife Mariah Booth Winfield Maffett Booth, Robert Kernachan is a major player. Robert is given the trusteeship of the property of Mariah Booth and her daughter Mary Ann Maffett, after it is taken from Dr. Booth and from Mariah's former brother-in-law Dr. William H. Maffett of Fayetteville.

The court records hold summons for Robert's service in several different years: April 4, 1844, Petitioned Jurors: Robert Kernachan, farmer, Sinking Creek, Sept 29, 1845, Summoned to Grand Jury: Robert Kernachan, farmer, Sinking Creek, 1850, Traves Jurors: Robert Kernachan, farmer, Sinking Creek, April 13, 1857, Robert Kernachan, farmer, Reserve. While the elder Robert was serving on the Jury, the younger Robert was appearing in court. He had multiple problems of his own.

In 1843, another mention of Robert Kernachan Sr., was in the court papers: In the matter of Robert Kernachan, Trustee, etc. of Mariah B Moffett, a decree was rendered by the chancellor removing the said trustee, and appointing James C. Malone in his stead. This decree led to the next phase in Mariah's life.

According to the 1850 Lauderdale County, Alabama, United States Census, District One, Robert Thomas Kernachan Sr. is a 56 year old white male born in Ireland. Also living in house 801 was John Crodock age 22, Robert Thomas Kernachan Jr. who was a 23 year old male born in Alabama. John Cradock was probably an employee who was living with Robert in 1850. Robert's wife Martha Booth Kernachan died on March 1, 1847.

According to the 1850 Lauderdale County, Alabama, Agricultural Census, Robert T. Kernachan Sr. owned 260 acres of improved land and 148 acres of unimproved land worth $6,000.00. Also Robert T. Kernachan Jr. owned 500 acres of improved land and 670 acres of unimproved land worth 10,593.00.

According to the 1850 Lauderdale County, Alabama, Slave Schedule, Robert T. Kernachan Sr. owned only 27 black slaves and Robert T. Kernachan Jr. owned 39 black slaves. In 1840, Robert Sr. owned 81 slaves, and within ten years, he and Robert Jr. owned only 66 slaves. By 1860, the number of black slaves had dropped to 49 for the two Robert T. Kernachans.

According to the "Nashville Christian Advocate," Volume 29, Number 6, February 6, 1869, "Robert Kernachan died on January 14, 1869, aged 73rd year, native of Ireland. Where he died; joined the Methodist Episcopal Church in 1821 or 1822. Sister (Martha) Kernachan was born in Mecklenburg County, Virginia, on November 3, 1791; died March 1, 1847. She moved to Tennessee in 1818 and married Abram Kernachan who died March 12, 1833. In 1820, she settled in Lauderdale County, Alabama. She had four daughters and one son. She married as a widow to Robert Kernachan in May 1834."

Robert T. Kernachan Jr.

The "Nashville Christian Advocate" reported that, "Robert Thomas Kernachan died near Florence, Alabama, November 20, 1885, in his 31st year of age of accidental gunshot wound; married Blanche Moore, Jan. 18 1881, two children. The two children were John Simmons Kernachan and William J. Kernachan, both who grew up to be distinguished men."

From Newspaer Abstracts from "The Huntsville Daily Mercury," contributed by K. L. Stacy, "Florence Notes," November 22, 1885, "A Young Man Kills himself accidentally: "Mr. Robert T. Kernachan, one of our most popular and worthy young men, was wounded Thursday evening by the accidental discharge of his gun, and from the effects of which he died yesterday. He leaves behind a wife and two little children, and a host of friends to mourn his sad and untimely end. He will be buried today at the family burying ground in Colberts Reserve in this county."

Kernachan Cemetery

The Kernachan Cemetery contains the remains of Abraham and his brother Robert lies in Colbert County. The Kernachan Cemetery is in George Colbert's Old Reservation in Lauderdale County, Alabama, and is located off of Gunwaleford Road. The legal description of the cemetery is southeast ¼ of the northeast ¼ of Section 18 of Township 3 South and Range 13 West. Inscriptions on the grave tombstones for the interments are as follows:
1) Kernachan, Robert 14 Jan 1869 aged 76 years;
2) Williams, Isaac B. 5 Apr AD 1812-5 Mar AD 1853 aged 39 yrs 11 mos 10 das;
3) Williams, Maria C. 6 Apr 1822-1 Sep 1851 aged 29 yrs 4 mos 25 das Consort of Isaac B. Williams & daughter of Abram & Martha Kernachan;
4) Kernachan, R. T. 28 Mar 1868 aged 40 yrs 6 mos. 9 days;
5) Jones, Martha Tazewell 7 Apr 1845-15 Jun 1846 aged 1 yr 2 mos. 8 days;
6) Jones, Infant 22 Sep 1843-1 Oct 1843, inf. son of James C. & Martha B. Jones;
7) Jones, William Edward 2 Aug 1860-15 Oct 1882, son of James Carey & Matilda Bloomfield Jones;
8) Jones, Sallie Bloomfield 11 Aug 1868-29 Mar 1883, dau of James C. & Matilda B. Jones;

9) Jones, James Carey 30 Jul 1819-12 May 1885 father; Matilda Bloomfield 16 May 1826-11 Oct 1885 mother; nee;
10) Kernachan, Abraham 12 Mar 1833 aged 50 yrs, born in County Donegal, Ireland.

Key, William Henry-Buck Key Plantation

Buck Key Plantation

The Buck Key Plantation consisted of some 2,800 acres of fertile farmland near the Tennessee River about eight miles west of Florence. The area of the old plantation along the Tennessee River and at the nearby Coffee Slough is rich in both historic and prehistoric Indian lore.

One summer, I, Rickey Butch Walker, participated in archeological digs at the Smith Bottom Cave, Dusk Cave, and Basket Cave sites conducted by Dr. Boyce Driskell of the University of Alabama. Beginning in 1989 and continuing for several summers, Dr, Driskell surveyed the surrounding caves and area that revealed early Indian people were here seeking shelter in nearby caves along the river before the ancient pyramids were built in Egypt. Some of the caves were occupied by aboriginal Paleo-Indian people as much as 12,600 years ago.

On the Buck Key Plantation, William H. Key built a rather unusual house for this area of North Alabama. Its exterior walls were built with slave made bricks. These were stacked behind board and batten siding. A wide central hallway had large double doors at both ends. Every room in the house, except the hallway, had its own brick fireplace.

William Henry "Buck" Key

William Henry Key was born in Sussex County, Virginia, in December 1819. William married Susan Hill Boddie; she was born on December 4, 1821, in North Carolina.

William H. "Buck" Key, was a native of Virginia. He came with his parents to Lauderdale County, Alabama, in his early youth. There are two marked graves in a small family cemetery on the grounds of the old Key Plantation. One is the tomb of John Key, father of William H. Key. John was born in 1790, and died in 1844. The other lonely grave is that of Ann Key, who was perhaps the mother of John Key and grandmother of Buck Key. She was born January 5, 1766, and died August 27, 1845.

William Henry Key and Susan Hill Boddie Key had the following children while living in Lauderdale County, Alabama:
1) Mary Hill Key Conner was born on December 25, 1845, in Lauderdale County, Alabama. She married Joseph Cable Conner (1838-1913). Mary died on September 11, 1913, at Florence in Lauderdale County, Alabama (Find a Grave Memorial Number 52539116).
2) Elizabeth "Bettie" Blow Key Stewart was born on March 2, 1848, at Florence in Lauderdale County, Alabama. Bettie married Malcolm Graeme Stewart (1837-1883); she died on February 3, 1900, at Nashville in Davidson County, Tennessee. Elizabeth Stewart is buried in Florence, Alabama (Find a Grave Memorial Number 51007345).
3) Susie Key (1849-   ).
4) Fannie Key Murdock was born in July 1853, and died in 1902. Fannie married James Murdock; she died on July 27, 1902, at Florence in Lauderdale County, Alabama (Find a Grave Memorial Number 153231429).
5) William H. Key, Jr. was on February 5, 1857, and died on June 10, 1919. He is buried in the Florence Cemetery at Florence in Lauderdale County, Alabama (Find a Grave Memorial Number 93132932).

6) Charlotte "Lottie" C. Key Watson was born on December 16, 1859. In October 1884, Lottie married Dr. Charles McAlpin Watson (1859-1917); she died on April 28, 1904, at Birmingham in Jefferson County, Alabama. She is buried in the Florence Cemetery at Florence in Lauderdale County, Alabama (Find a Grave Memorial Number 97164600).

In 1850 Lauderdale County, Alabama, United States Census, William H. Key is a 30 year old white male born in Virginia. His household includes Susan Key a 28 year old female, Mary Key a five year old female, Elizabeth Key a three year old female, Martha Lane a 25 year old female, and James Key a 40 year old male.

According to the 1850 Lauderdale County, Slave Census, William H. Key owned 74 black slaves. By the 1860 Lauderdale County, Alabama, Slave Census of District 2 and enumerated by Peter R. Garner on June 1 through July 3, 1860, William H. Key owned 131 black slaves.

In the 1860 Lauderdale County, Alabama, United States Census, District 2, William H. Key is a 40 year old male born in Virginia. Living with him is S. H. Key a 38 year old female, Mary H. Key a 14 year old female, Bettie B. Key a 12 year old female, Susie Key a 10 year old female, Fannie Key a seven year old female, William H. Key a three year old female, Charlotte C. Key a 6 months old female, and Martha Lane a 54 year old female.

At the beginning of the Civil War, there were 149 black slaves on the Buck Key Plantation according to the 1860 slave schedule. The slaves were residing in a small village consisting of thirty houses. According to the 1860 census, these black servants produced 240 bales of cotton, 12,000 bushels of corn, 300 bushels of wheat, 100 pounds of wool, and 500 pounds of butter. That year, the Key Plantation had 15 horses, 114 mules, eight working oxen, 200 swine, and 35 sheep. The total value of Key's personal property was estimated to be almost $164,000.

In the early Spring of 1864, Union Colonel William D. Hamilton apologized to William Key as he sat at the dining table at the Buck Key

Plantation, "This is the most embarrassing situation I've ever been in." As a guest, he was being entertained in appreciation of his kindness by returning their silver that had been taken away by the Colonel's Cavalrymen. However, during the course of the meal, one of Key's servants rushed in to warn the family that the Yankees had returned and were demanding keys to the smokehouse. Colonel Hamilton explained that the raiders were his men and that were carrying out his orders to "exhaust or destroy all foods and supplies in the area so as to prevent such from falling into the hands of the Confederates." In that he had issued these orders, there was nothing he could do to stop them from what they were doing.

When the Federal troops occupied Lauderdale County, Alabama, Buck Key had an excellent hiding place to store its goods, far from the enemy's reach. The secret place was a large underground chamber known as Key Cave. It worked well until one of his servants informed the Yankees where Key's farm products and other valuables were hidden.

After the Civil War, the 1870 agricultural census indicates that William H. Key owned 1,300 acres of improved land and 900 acres of woodlands valued at $32,000. The farm was located in Township 3 South and Range 3 West in Lauderdale County, Alabama.

After the war, William H. Key's daughter Elizabeth "Bettie" Blow Key Stewart moved with her husband and children to Texas. According to the 1880 census of Gertrude in Jack County, Texas, M. G. Stewart is a 42 year old male. Also, living in his household was Elizabeth B. Key Stewart a 32 year old female, Willis T. Stewart a 20 year old male, Walter P. Stewart a 17 year old male, Bessie K. Stewart a nine year old female, and Joel P. Gibson a 28 year old male. During the 1870's, M. G. Stewart founded the Town of Gertrude in Lost Valley in the far western portion of Jack County, Texas.

Death of Mrs. W. H. Key.

Our community was surprised and shocked on Tuesday morning last to hear that Mrs. W. H. Key after a brief illness of but little more than two days, had fallen a victim to the grim monster Death. Mrs. Key had contracted a cold, which gave no special concern to her family; but on Monday her symptoms became worse, pneumonia developing, and at 6 o'clock in the evening she peacefully passed away. Thus has gone to her reward one of the most estimable ladies of our community. For many years a faithful member of the Presbyterian church, zealous in good works in connection with it, and in all life's relations maintaining the highest standard of Christian and womanly excellence, she leaves a record without spot or blemish, hallowed by the memory of a pure and elevated life.

Mrs. Key (whose maiden name was Miss Susan Body) was married nearly fifty years ago, and she and her husband were anticipating a joyous reunion at an early day with their friends in the celebration of the golden anniversary of their marriage. She is survived by her husband and five children, Mrs. Dr. J. C. Conner, Mrs. Dr. C. M. Watson, and Mrs. Bettie Stewart of this city, and Mrs. James Murdock of South Florence, and Mr. W. H. Key, Jr., of St. Louis.

The funeral, conducted by Rev. John A. Preston, D. D., took place in the Presbyterian church at 3 o'clock on Wednesday afternoon and the mortal remains were interred in the city cemetery.

The Buck Key Plantation was acquired during the 1870's by Frank M. Perry, who came to North Alabama from Tennessee during the Reconstruction Era following the Civil War. The Perry's made their home here until sometime after 1902, hence it became known as the Perry Place. Perry became a prosperous planter and Florence merchant. Frank Perry, Sr. was born in 1843 and died in 1929. His wife, Kate Glenn, was born in 1853 in Rogersville, and died in 1924 in Florence. The Key-Perry Plantation House, one of the rare historical treasures to survive the Civil War, was dismantled in recent years.

On January 23, 1893, William Henry Key's wife Susan died at Florence in Lauderdale County, Alabama. Susan Boddie Key is buried in the Florence Cemetery at Florence in Lauderdale County, Alabama (Find a Grave Memorial Number 97167175).

On December 7, 1895, William Henry Key died at the residence of his son-in-law, Mr. James Murdock, of South Florence (Find a Grave Memorial Number 97166591). He was one of the oldest citizens of Lauderdale County.

The obituary of William Henry Key was published in The Florence Times on Friday, December 14, 1895, as follows, "Death of Mr. W. H. Key. On last Saturday evening, Mr. William H. Key, one of the oldest citizens of our county, died, at the residence of his son-in-law, Mr. James Murdock of South Florence.

Mr. Key was born in Sussex County, Virginia, in December 1819, but removed when very young, perhaps 70 years ago, with his parents to Alabama. For many years before the war, he was one of our largest and most successful planters. Since the close of the struggle between the States, which brought to him, in common with all our people, terrible financial loss, he has worked manfully, diversifying his crops and using improved implements, and leaves a place in capital condition. Though always taking an active interest in politics and public affairs, he never sought nor accepted any public position.

Mr. Key was a man of fine mind, excellent business qualifications, great energy and force of character, warm hearted, generous and social in disposition, courtly in manners, a typical gentleman of the old Southern school.

At a comparatively young age, he married Miss Susan Boddie, one of Lauderdale's noblest daughters, who was, until her lamented death a few years ago, to him indeed a help meet and counselor. He leaves four daughters, Mrs. Dr. Conner, Mrs. Dr. Watson and Mrs. Bettie Stewart, of this city, and Mrs. Murdock of Colbert; and one son, W. H. Key, Jr., of St. Louis. Several winters ago he had a severe attack of la gripe, from which he never fully rallied, and lately has sunk rapidly.

On Sunday evening his remains were interred in our cemetery, after appropriate services at the Presbyterian Church, by Rev. J. H Lacy. One by one, our old landmarks are passing away."

McDonald, James T.-Glenco Plantation

There is an old Scottish ballad that urges all McDonalds to remember the bloody massacre of the McDonalds at Glenco on the morning of February 13, 1692. King William, wanting to make an example of the "Popish" Glenco McDonalds, ordered that, "All under seventy are to be killed, and the Chief must not escape." The eighty-year old Chief was killed while he attempted to dress.

His lady was driven naked into the street and died later from her wounds. The massacre at Glenco was made worse in that the McDonalds had offered food and shelter to the tired and hungry soldiers. Even more grievous to the McDonalds was that the leader of the King's men was Robert, a member of the Campbell Clan, the ancient enemy of all McDonald Clans of Scotland.

In 1817, Lieutenant Colonel James T. McDonald, known as "Bully McDonald," was sent to Tuscumbia by Andrew Jackson to survey that section of the Jackson Military Road in North Alabama. While here, he resigned from the army because of health problems. According to historian Nina Leftwich in her book, "Early Beginnings of Colbert County," Colonel McDonald was appointed Tuscumbia's first postmaster in 1817. Colonel McDonald was born to Scottish parents at Chillouch, Ohio, in 1781. McDonald's brother-in-law, Joshua Prout, later became governor of that state.

When James McDonald reached his fifteenth birthday, he enlisted in the United States Army and quickly gained recognition as a leader of men. On September 17, 1814, during the Battle of Lake Erie, he was decorated for "gallantry in action" and promoted to the rank of Lieutenant Colonel. According to another source, he received recognition for distinguished service in the battles of Lindy Lane and Chippewa. Chippewa is often used to refer to the Ojibwa, one of the important Algonquian Indian tribes of Canada and the United States.

McDonald's first presence at Muscle Shoals was noted in the August 24, 1810, edition of the Democratic Clarion and Tennessee Gazette, Nashville, Tennessee, "…We have learned that Captain James McDonald's and Captain John Regan's companies have arrived at the Rifle Company a few miles from the mouth of the Elk River from containment near Natchez…The object for the assembling of soldiers is conjectured two-fold, first to remove intruders from Indian lands, and secondly to open a road to Tombigbee."

Colonel James T. McDonald's wife was Eliza Adylette Keller, a sister of David Keller, who was Helen Keller's grandfather. Eliza McDonald was also a granddaughter of Governor Alexander Spotswood of Virginia.

The McDonald's had a daughter who was married to Oakley Bynum Oakley Bynum was a cotton baron from Lawrence County, Alabama, and owned 151 black slaves in 1850. Nina Leftwich, in her "Early Beginnings of Colbert County," wrote that following his appointment as Postmaster of Tuscumbia, "He bought a farm west of town and built a house which he called Glenco." Other papers show that Glenco Plantation was purchased jointly by McDonald and his brother-in-law, David Keller, who became the grandfather of Helen Keller, who is loved and respected around the world.

David Keller, native of Maryland, had moved to Tuscumbia from Knoxville, Tennessee, where he had been a merchant. David's wife was Mary Fairfax Moore whose great-great grandmother was a first cousin of Martha Washington. Mary Fairfax Moore's uncle was married to a daughter of Patrick Henry.

Colonel James McDonald died on December 23, 1828, and is buried with family members, including David and Ann Keller, on the grounds of the modern Vulcan Materials Company, west of Tuscumbia. At one time, the area was part of the Glenco Plantation. One of the crypt tombs in the Glenco Cemetery belongs to Colonel James T. McDonald and has a War of 1812 service medal attached to the stone.

The grounds of Glenco now serve the Shoals as an important industrial site. The management of Vulcan Materials is complemented for the beautiful restoration and continuous upkeep of the Glenco Cemetery.

McVay, Hugh-Mars Hill Plantation

Hugh McVay

Governor Hugh McVay's ancestors came from Scotland. His father, Hugh McVay, was a veteran of the American Revolution. In 1807, the future Alabama Governor settled in what is now Madison County, Alabama.

In 1818, following the federal land sales, Hugh McVay moved with his family to Lauderdale County. From March 2, 1818, through May 27, 1831, Hugh McVay entered 2,800 acres in

Townships 1, 2 South and Ranges 7, 9, 10, 11, 14 West of land in Lauderdale County, Alabama (Cowart, 1996).

Hugh was a major political figure in Lauderdale County of North Alabama. In addition to his short tenure as governor, Hugh served almost a quarter of a century as a representative in the territorial, and later, the state legislature.

According to the 1830 Lauderdale County, Alabama Census, Hugh McVay owned 24 black slaves. In the 1840 Lauderdale County, Alabama Census, Hugh owned 35 black slaves, and by 1850, McVay owned 42 black slaves. Governor McVay died in 1851, and was buried in the McVay-Moore Cemetery at the old Mars Hill Plantation located now in the Industrial Park.

Lewis Capit Moore Sr.

Lewis Capit Moore, Sr.'s wife, Atlantic Pacific McVay Moore, preferred to be called "Attie." Atlantic Pacific McVay married Lewis C. Moore on November 3, 1831; she died a year prior to the beginning of the Civil War. Attie was a daughter of Alabama's ninth governor Hugh McVay, and, as with her sisters, had married well.

Lewis and Attie had the following children:
1) Hugh McVay Moore (1835-1912)
2) Lewis Capit Moore Jr. (1837-1917)
3) James K. Polk Moore (1845-1887)

Lewis Capit Moore Sr., a Kentucky native, owned 29 black slaves according to the 1860 slave census for Lauderdale County. His wife probably had inherited some of her father's slaves after his death in 1851.

Two of the sons of Lewis C. Moore Sr. were killed in that terrible conflict between the North and the South. Samuel H. Moore died in the Second Battle of Manassas. John H. Moore was killed while riding with Forrest in Pulaski, Tennessee.

Lewis Capit "Chris" Moore Jr.

According to family stories, Lewis Capit Moore Jr. was with his brother John at the time of his death at Pulaski, Tennessee, during the Civil War. Lewis returned to Pulaski at the end of the war in an effort to recover John's body but was unable to locate his grave.

Lewis Capit Moore Jr., grandson of Governor Hugh McVay, was born on Christmas day December 25, 1847. He was known as Chris; the name was used by several generations in the Moore family. His parents were Lewis Capit Moore, Sr. (1810-1864) and Attie McVay Moore (1815-1860).

Lewis Capit "Chris" Moore Jr. married Martha Price. Chris Moore Jr. built his home near Governor McVay's log house. Lewis, Jr. and Martha (1844-1907) had the following children:
1) Jane Moore Lucas (1870-1969)
2) Bird Moore Finley (1871-1963)
3) Albert Howe Moore (1874-1956)
4) Mattie Moore Cunningham (1877-1936)
5) Claude Lillard Moore (1880-1965)
6) James Thomas Moore (1882-1961)
7) Velma Moore Cleere (1884-1922)
8) Loulie Moore Prosser (1886-1957)

A descendant of the McVay Moore family recently restored the beautiful Mars Hill landmark. It is one of the few homesteads in Alabama that has remained in the same family for almost 200 years.

Harry John Wesson

Lewis Capit Moore Sr. was fifty-four years old when he fell victim to Harry John Wesson during the Civil War. Not much is known about "Harry" John Wesson other than he was a loyal unionist and, hence, branded as a "Tory." During the early war years, Wesson sold beef to both Union and Confederate armies as they came and went through the Muscle Shoals. Dr. Wade Pruitt, in his book "Bugger Saga," says that Lewis Capit Moore Sr. had at one time accused Harry John Wesson of stealing one of his calves. It was later learned that it was John Martin who stole Moore's calf and sold it to Wesson. Martin and his sons were notorious outlaws.

Wesson joined the Union cavalry after being "roughed up" by an overly zealous Confederate recruiting officer. It seems that Wesson remained with the Federal Cavalry until the end of hostilities. Most of his military assignments were in and around Clifton, Tennessee. Their main mission was to prevent General Forrest from crossing the river at Clifton. Wesson's commanding officer was Captain Risden Deford who was very familiar with the area. His father was a Methodist preacher whose circuit at one time included Moore's Chapel located near the present Mars Hill Church of Christ.

As Captain Risden Deford's Sixth United States Cavalry was entering Florence in February 1864, Private Harry John Wesson slipped away from his post and made his way to what is now the Mars Hill Community. There, he ambushed and murdered Lewis Capit Moore Sr. Moore, a successful and highly respected farmer, was also Lauderdale County's appointed agent to work with families of confederate soldiers who were away at war. Many of these dependants were in need of food, clothing, and other basic necessities of life.

When the war was over, Harry John Wesson did not remain long in Lauderdale County. His former neighbors could not forget or forgive his crimes. In cold blood, he had killed Lewis Capit Moore Sr. a highly respected citizen. One of Wesson's descendants was a popular educator in Florence long after he had moved away.

Nichols, John Martin-Nichols Hill

Although a world apart, Reeder Nichols Mountain in Western Australia and Nichols Hill in East Florence have one thing in common. Both have names that were derived from the same family.

Until a few years ago, Nichols Hill was a steep, wooded spur connected geographically with the west side of Cherry Hill. Beginning at Thurman Avenue, this high ridge ran westward to Railroad Hollow which separated Nichols Hill and Billy Goat Hill. Bulldozers and earth movers, while constructing the north approach to the Singing River Bridge, have all but eliminated Nichols Hill.

The Nichols family, including sons and daughters, were factor workers associated with the Cherry Cotton Mill and earlier cotton factories in the area. A number of this same Nichols family is shown in a rare 1885 photograph of the employees of Florence's historic Cypress Cotton Mill.

Reeder Nichols was born in 1904 within the sight of Nichols Hill in East Florence. It is believed that Reeder's father, John Martin Nichols, was named for James Martin who established one of North Alabama's earliest cotton factories. According to the 1860 Lauderdale County slave census, James Martin owned 11 black slaves.

John Martin Nichols was a charter member of St. James United Methodist Church which had its beginnings at the foot of Nichols Hill. John's brother, William Thomas Nichols, was a Baptist minister and often preached at the Central Baptist Church which was located across the creek from Nichols Hill. Reeder Nichols' great grandfather Nichols was a Methodist circuit rider who preached in Lawrence, Limestone, and Colbert Counties in Alabama and Wayne County in Tennessee.

In 1923, Reeder Nichols left East Florence to enlist in the U. S. Marine Corps at the age of 19. This was during the period following World War I when the army, navy, and Marine Corps were adjusting to the introduction of the airplane as a major component in modern warfare. With what is to believe to have been a limited formal education, Reeder gained great professional knowledge of aeronautics and communications. After leaving the Marines, Reeder made a name for himself as the navigator for Roscoe Turner in the famed air race from England to Australia.

Reeder re-entered the armed forces during World War II as a captain. Assigned to the South Pacific he rose rapidly in rank and was placed in charge of coordinating the highly successful island-hopping campaign against the Japanese. By the war's end Reeder Nichols was wearing the star of a brigadier general. Accompanying General Douglas McArthur on this history-making return to the Philippines was one of Reeder's most memorable assignments.

In 1950, Reeder Nichols became a permanent resident of Australia. Employed by several iron-mining companies, he worked out a communications system for Western Australia.

Brigadier General Reeder Nichols died May 24, 1975, in Sidney, Australia, at the age of seventy-one years. Seventeen months later, the government of Western Australia named one of their iron ore mountains Mount Reeder Nichols in his memory.

In a letter to Nichol's widow, dated October 1, 1976, the following statement was made by the premier of Western Australia, "This imposing feature will, I am sure, become quickly associated in the minds of the local people with the man whose name it bears. It will be a lasting memorial to his outstanding endeavors, for which we in Western Australia will always be grateful."

Thus ends the story of a remarkable journey from Nichols Hill in East Florence to Mount Reeder Nichols in Western Australia. The author is grateful to Dr. Darrell A. Russell for his extensive research in the life of Brigadier General Reeder Nichols.

Noel, James Alexander

James Alexander Noel was born about 1780 in Virginia. In 1816, James married Mary Webb Downey (b.1794) in Granville County, North Carolina. While living in Granville County, North Carolina, James and Mary had three children: William Alexander Noel, Mary Jane Noel, and Sarah Ann Noel. They had more children after they moved to Alabama including another son, Samuel Noel, plus several daughters. James Alexander Noel died in Alabama in1859.

By 1830, James and Mary moved to Lauderdale County, Alabama. According to the 1830 Lauderdale County, Alabama, United States Federal Census, James Noel and his family are reported as living in the county. On June 1, 1835, James Noel entered 240 acres of land in Sections 28 and 34 of Township 3 South and Range 12 West in Lauderdale County, Alabama.

According to the 1840 Lauderdale County, Alabama, United States Census, James A. Noel owned 43 black slaves. By the 1850 census of Lauderdale County, Alabama, James A. Noel owned 53 black slaves and Edmond Noel owned 25 black slaves.

According to the 1850 Lauderdale County, Alabama Agricultural Census, James Noel owned 400 acres of improved land and 30 acres of unimproved land worth $6,450.00. In addition, Edmond Noel owned 300 acres of improved land and 300 acres of unimproved land worth $6,000.00.

According to the 1850 Lauderdale County, Alabama, United States Census, James Noel is a 70 year old white male born in Virginia. Also living in James household was Mary Noel a 56 year old female born in North Carolina, Samuel Noel a 20 year old male born in Alabama, Cornelia Noel a 16 year old female born in Alabama, John Noel a 14 year old male born in Alabama, Elizabeth Claiborn a 23 year old female born in Alabama, and William Claiborn a five year old male born in Alabama. Cornelia married Samuel Tillman on November 7, 1850.

Patton, Robert Miller-Sweetwater Plantation

Sweetwater

At one time, the Sweetwater Plantation covered some 3,800 acres of land. The plantation and manor house was named Sweetwater because of its location on a hill above Sweetwater Spring east of Florence in Lauderdale County, Alabama. The spring forms the head of Sweetwater Creek. The mouth of this creek enters the Tennessee River across from Patton Island.

According to stories handed down by the Patton Family, the ancient shell mounds on the island were carted away by the black slaves of the Sweetwater Plantation. The Patton servants crushed the shells and spread over the driveways and walks of the Sweetwater Plantation.

The Sweetwater Mansion was an eight room plantation house built of slave made brick in 1835. The bricks used in construction of the main house were made on site by the plantation's black slaves at Sweetwater Creek which ran just below the house. The mansion residence had marble mantels from Italy and boxwood hedges from London.

The Sweetwater plantation home is located at the corner of Florence Boulevard and Hough Road in Florence, Alabama. The Sweetwater Plantation consisted of the Sweetwater Mansion, an overseer's house, and sixteen slave cabins.

The Civil War years were rough at Sweetwater. The big spring at the rear of the home made an ideal campsite, and both armies used it as Lauderdale County changed hands time and again when the tide of war washed to and fro.

Sweetwater Mansion in 1934
E. W. Burkhardt and W. N. Manning

Robert Miller Patton

The Sweetwater Plantation Mansion was the home of Major General John Brahan of the Alabama Militia; Brahan owned some 4,000 acres in eastern Lauderdale County. General Brahan was a veteran of the War of 1812. On January 31, 1832, Brahan's daughter Jane Locke Braham married Robert Miller Patton; Sweetwater would become the home of the general's daughter Jane and his son-in-law Robert.

Robert Miller Patton and Jane Locke Braham would have nine children with seven of his children living to adulthood:

1) John Brahan Patton served with the Florence Guards.
2) William Anderson Patton (1837-1862) died at the Battle of Shiloh.
3) Mary Jane Patton (1840-1908) married J. J. McDavid, attorney at Huntsville.
4) Mattie Hays Patton (1842-1933) married Colonel John Weeden, a lawyer in Huntsville.
5) Robert Weakley Patton (1844-1865) died at the Battle of Selma.
6) John Simpson Patton (1847-1849) died at an early age.
7) Charles Hays Patton (1850-1891) was a banker in Florence.
8) Andrew Bierne Patton (1855-1883) was an invalid seven years before his death.

Robert Miller Patton was born on July 10, 1809, in Russell County, Virginia. His father William was a native of the north of Ireland and his mother of Virginia. In 1812, the William Patton family including three small children came to Huntsville, Alabama in Mississippi Territory. William Patton operated a mercantile business in Huntsville, Alabama.

In addition, William Patton had founded the Bell Factory Cotton Mill on the Flint River some ten miles from Huntsville. The cotton mill continued in successful operation during the lifetime of William Patton. At the death of William, the ownership of the cotton mill was given to Dr. Charles Patton, brother of Robert Miller Patton.

Charles operated the mill with success during his lifetime, and after his death, the cotton mill was operated and owned by his children. Robert M. Patton, in one of his letters, writes, "This mill has enriched three generations of the Pattons, and I am inclined to think that my worthy and enterprising brother-in-law, Colonel Edward Richardson, was encouraged from his knowledge of the success of this factory to take hold of the Wesson Mills, which have proved in all respects so valuable to him, and, for that matter, to the whole South."

Robert Miller Patton apprenticed in his father's cotton mill and attended Green Academy in Huntsville, Alabama. In 1829, at the age of 20 years old, Robert Miller Patton moved to Florence, where he became a merchant. At an early age he joined the Presbyterian Church and always took an active interest in the affairs of the church and Sabbath school. For one year prior to his death, he was the senior elder of the church and Superintendent of the Sabbath school at Florence. After their marriage in 1832, Robert Miller Patton and Jane Locke Braham Patton lived in the Sweetwater Mansion.

After his marriage, Robert Miller Patton began his political career; he ran and was successfully elected as a Whig candidate for a seat in the Alabama State Legislature. He was elected to the special legislature that convened in 1837 in response to the financial panic and depression of that year. Robert Miller Patton would serve in both legislative houses and was twice elected President of the Senate. Patton continued to serve in one branch or the other of the state legislature until the outbreak of the Civil War.

Shortly after arriving in Lauderdale County, Robert Miller Patton became a large land holder, a cotton planter, and owner of black slaves. In the 1850 Lauderdale County, Alabama, Agricultural Census, Robert M. Patton owned 1,200 acres of improved land and 400 acres of unimproved land worth $30,000.00. According to the 1840 Lauderdale County, Alabama, United States Census, Robert Miller Patton owned 24 black slaves. By the 1850 Lauderdale County, Alabama, Slave Schedule, he owned 73 black slaves.

According to the 1850 Lauderdale County, Alabama, United States Census, Second Division east of the Military Road, Robert Miller Patton is a 40 year old white male merchant born in Virginia. Also living in his household is Jane a 35 year old female born in Alabama, John a 16 year old male student born in Alabama, William a 13 year old male born in Alabama, Mary a 10 year old female born in Alabama, Martha an eight year old female born in Alabama, Robert a six year old male born in Alabama, Charles a six month old male born in Alabama, and Martha Pettepool a 17 year old female born in Alabama.

In 1859, his mercantile business was turned over to his sons; John Brahan Patton and William Anderson Patton who were merchants in Florence, Alabama, until the Civil War. In 1860, Robert Miller Patton represented the State of Alabama at the national convention in Charleston, South Carolina and was present at the secession convention in Montgomery. Patton opposed secession but supported the state's efforts through time and money and as a commissioner for the Confederacy.

Robert Miller Patton

According to the 1860 Lauderdale County, Alabama, Largest Slave Holders List, Robert Miller Patton owned 113 Slaves. In the 1860 Lauderdale County, Alabama, Agricultural Census, Robert Miller Patton owned 2,000 acres of improved land and 1,800 acres of unimproved land worth $80,000.00.

According to the 1860 Lauderdale County, Alabama, United States Census, Robert Miller Patton is a 50 year old male planter and merchant born in Virginia. Also in his household is Jane L. Patton a 45 year old female born in Tennessee, Elizabeth McClusky a 40 year old female born in South Carolina, William A. Patton a 22 year old male merchant born in Alabama, Mary a 19 year old female born in Alabama, Mattie H. a 17 year old female born in Alabama, Robert W. a 15 year old male born in Alabama, Charles H. a ten year old male born in Alabama, and Andrew B. a six year old male born in Alabama.

During 1861, Robert Miller Patton had three sons to join the Confederacy, but two were killed during the Civil War. On April 6, 1862, First Lieutenant William Anderson Patton, educated at the LaGrange Military College, was killed at Shiloh. Robert Weakley Patton, educated in the Cadet Corps at the University of Alabama, was wounded at Selma, April 3, 1865, and died in the hospital on April 6, 1865. By the war's end, he suffered not only the loss of his sons but the destruction of his estate in Lauderdale County. During the Civil War, his Sweetwater home was used by both the Union and Confederate Armies.

After the war, Governor Robert Miller Patton served as the twentieth Governor of Alabama from 1865 through 1867. He represented Lauderdale County at the constitutional convention in September 1865. He was elected Governor of Alabama in November and was inaugurated on December 13.

During his time as Governor, Patton worked closely with the assistant commissioner of the Freedmen's Bureau, General Wager Swayne. He helped Swayne procure rations for the thousands of indigent families in the state. His greatest contribution was his success in reducing the state debt. He issued "Patton certificates" in 1867 to offset state expenses in anticipation of the collection in taxes.

Despite Patton's efforts, he was largely stripped of his authority in March 1867, when presidential reconstruction ended with the passage of the Reconstruction Acts by Congress. Major General John Pope was placed in charge of the Third Military District which included Alabama, Georgia, and Florida. Swayne continued as the commanding officer of Alabama. Patton was allowed to remain in office and draw his salary but he was mainly a figurehead who could do no more than make recommendations to Swayne. Patton was officially the head of the state until William H. Smith became Governor in July, 1868.

According to the 1870 Lauderdale County, Alabama, Agricultural Census, Robert Miller Patton owned only 200 acres of improved land and 618 acres of unimproved land worth only $1,000.00.

After his political career ended, Patton became involved in several commercial ventures to establish and build railroads in the state. Robert was one of the leading directors of the State Bank at Decatur. He also served as a trustee of several schools and colleges, including the University of Alabama. He was instrumental in rebuilding the university after it was burned by Federal troops during the war. He was President of the Board of Trustees of the Florence Synodical Female College and also of the Board of Directors of the State Normal College at Florence.

In 1876 he received an appointment as a member of the honorable Board of Finance for the Centennial Exposition at Philadelphia. He was also appointed Vice President of the National Cotton Planters' Association, and a member of the Board of Management of the World's Industrial and Cotton Exposition at New Orleans. He organized an association of Eastern capitalists to connect Chattanooga, Mobile and New Orleans by rail. He was made President of the road from Chattanooga to Meridian, a distance of three hundred miles, and subsequently succeeded John Whitney as President of the South and North Alabama Railroad Company extending from Decatur to Montgomery. He was active in building the Memphis & Charleston Railroad.

Robert Miller Patton died on February 28, 1885, at Sweet Water near Florence. He was buried in the Maple Hill Cemetery at Huntsville in Madison County, Alabama.

Patton Island

The new Tennessee River Bridge, which connects Lauderdale and Colbert Counties, crosses over historic Patton Island. This island was once a part of the vast land holdings of an early Alabama Governor: Robert Miller Patton. Patton Island is one of the few surviving islands at the Muscle Shoals. Most of its neighboring islands were inundated when the local dams were built in the early part of the 20th century.

The earliest settlers knew Patton Island as Cane Island because of its abundant growth of cane. It was said that local American Indians used the cane to weave baskets. This cane was important material, along with poles, used in the construction of their homes. Numerous shell mounds once existed on Patton Island indicating that primitive inhabitants called the "Shell Mound People" were on this island as early as the last stages of the Ice Age.

The first owner of this historic island was Colonel Benjamin Sherrod who in 1821, purchased most of its approximately 600 acres. Sherrod, an early planter of Courtland, owned a number of plantations that were worked by about 700 black slaves and servants. Confederate General Joseph Wheeler was married to the widow of Colonel Benjamin Sherrod's grandson also known as Benjamin Sherrod.

Patton Island was identified on an 1844 map as Tinnin's Island. Its owner was said to have taught in an early Florence school in the early 1830s. Prior to the Civil War, Andrew Blair, whose home was located at the intersection of Mobile and Seminary Streets, farmed Patton Island. In 1861, while returning from the island, Blair was thrown from his horse. His body was discovered the next day at the foot of the Florence Indian Mound.

Following the burning of the old Florence Bridge in 1862, Patton Island played an important role in the river crossings of various Union and Confederate troops. In her diary, Eliza, wife of Alabama Militia General Samuel Weakley, told of going onto the island to watch the crossing of General John Bell Hood's Army in November 1864.

Over the next fifty years, until the coming of TVA in 1933, Patton Island was farmed by a number of local tenants. A large community barn was erected on the island. The farmers made use of a ferry located near the mouth of Sweetwater Creek to cross the old Florence Canal onto the island.

Robert Linsey told of how, on a spring day in 1927, the river began to rise so fast that he barely escaped with his two mules from the island. William L. Teas lived on the island with his daughter in the early 1920's. He had many scary tales about the floods on the Tennessee River, how they often had to flee the island during the night and in heavy storms.

Patton Island, perhaps, is as old as the river that surrounds it. Its presence at the foot of the Muscle Shoals has been a landmark for as long as the earliest people have called this part of the great Tennessee Valley their home. Some archaeologists have described it as untouched archives whose pages are yet to be read, and its hidden history properly deciphered.

Uncle Champ

His body lies alongside the new four-laned Florence Boulevard in an unmarked grave on the grounds of his beloved Sweetwater. "Uncle Champ" they called him, and what a pity a monument does not tower as high as his memory did in the hearts of those who knew him. Nearby rests the original builders of the plantation, Major John Brahan and his wife Mary Weakley.

Uncle Champ was the body servant of Governor Robert MillerPatton. Patton, through his wife Jane Locke Brahan, inherited Uncle Champ along with the then unfinished mansion. Patton and his wife became owners of the vast 2,500 acre estate from Major Brahan, a comrade of Andrew Jackson and a veteran of the war of 1812.

It was often said in the family that although the records showed that the Pattons owned Uncle Champ, the fact was that Uncle Champ really owned the Pattons. Originally and formally his name was Edmond. He earned the name 'Champ" in his vigorous youth through hard work and determination. He won every contest from dancing to horseshoes and was always the champion among the contestant in the fields. He could pick the most cotton on any autumn day.

When the Civil War broke out, Uncle Champ had graduated from the fields and had assumed command of all the servants. He looked the part, too, in his formal attire as he opened the door and bowed to the distinguished visitors at Sweetwater.

The Governor's beautiful daughters were always proud to show off such a distinguished servant, and they were quick to call him by his formal name Edmond. But the three Patton boys, Brahan, William, and Robert, were Uncle Champ's special charges. It was his solemn duty to see them off to the war. He drove them to Florence in the family carriage one by one as they left to join their units. Uncle Champ always said that although the boys did the fighting, his was the hardest task; for it fell his lot to break the news to "De Massa" and "Ole Missa" when words were received that William died at Shiloh and Robert fell in the heat of battle in Selma.

When Sweetwater smokehouses were raided during the Civil War, Uncle Champ had to use his special skills to find food. He had to prepare food for the table at the main house, as well as tables in the overseer's house and the sixteen little slave cabins about the place. Most times it was meager and sometimes there just wasn't enough.

It was a frightening experience when smallpox broke out among the Union troops. As a safeguard, those soldiers who died from the dreaded disease were placed in two cabins and cremated. Furrows were added to Uncle Champ's brow as he worried about the spreading of small pox among his loved ones. It was weight of many burdens that slowly stooped his broad shoulders.

Uncle Champ must have chuckled on the night of a party when a General stumbled into the fountain on the front walk. No one recorded who he was, but confederate General Gideon Pillow showed up for the Battle of Franklin with a broken arm. Rumors have it that the General was drunk when he broke it; and Willie Smith recorded in his diary that General Pillow fell into a fountain while at Florence.

Uncle Champ's proudest hour occurred on a night of terror at Sweetwater in 1865. This is the story as told so many times through the year by descendants of the Patton family: The "Buggers," dressed in Yankee uniforms, stormed into the house, plundered it of all valuables not previously buried, and even insulted the mistress of the plantation by attempting to search her personally. When they started up the steps where the Governor's daughters were hiding, Uncle Champ immediately blocked the stairs with outstretched arms. He stated that they would have to walk over his dead body to get up those stairs. For some unknown reason, they did not kill the faithful old servant, and forever after, the family never forgot the bravery of the slave who really owned the Pattons.

Emancipation day was "Jubilee Day" for the newly freed slaves. Uncle Champ, however, refused to leave Sweetwater, and he made arrangement to stay on as the gardener for what few pennies the family could afford. Times were hard then. The Pattons had lost their fortune in the war. And although Sweetwater was put up for public auction on December 20, 1869, they did manage to save it and hold on. Uncle Champ lived out the remainder of his days taking care of the vegetable and herb gardens, and with his tender care made the formal flower and shrubbery arrangement around the old mansion, a scene of beauty to behold.

It was during these years that the renowned poet and artist, Howard Weeden of Huntsville, painted Uncle Champ. Stooped and bent he stands immortal with his hoe in that life-like water color. When shown this painting Uncle Champ said, "Laws Miss, if I'd known you was takin my picture, I could a stood heap straighter'en dat."

The artist, related by marriage to the Pattons, told about this proud Negro. He was the usual combination of dependence and loyalty. He venerates the family name and possessions with a lordly air that bespeak half-ownership. Often when working in the garden, he will shoulder his hoe, and coming around the house, under my nephew's window, will call up "You Mister Robert! I want fifty cents!" He always get it, and Robert has never yet thrown it to him, but always bring it down and puts it in his out stretched hand.

Miss Howard Weeden

Artist, poet and author, Miss Howard Weeden of Huntsville was a frequent guest of Sweetwater, an ante-bellum plantation east of Florence. Howard was a small, delicate, frail maiden whose dress and demure befitted one who was reared to prefer her masculine name, Howard; it was bequeathed to her by her father whose death occurred six months prior to her birth. She was Christened Marie Howard Weeden.

Howard was the author of four books; "Shadows on the Wall," "Songs of the Old South," "Bandanna Ballads," and "Old Voices." These are collections of beautiful poetry illustrated by paintings that seem almost alive through her creative genius as an artist.

Joel Chandler Harris, author of "Uncle Remus," was an admirer of Howard Weeden's delicate and realistic portraits of the servants who worked in the big house, and especially those who cared for the children on the plantation. Harris noted in his introduction to "Bandanna Ballads," "…never before has an artist caught with such vital and startling characteristics, such moving fidelity, the characters which gave to the old plantation, if not its chiefest charm, at least one of its most enchanting features." Some contended that Miss Weeden patronized and characterized Negro servants. Others, such as Joel Chandler Harris, pointed to Miss Weeden's interpretation of the plantation servants as individuals with stories she presents through her delicate brush and pen.

Howard Weeden's brother, Confederate Colonel John D. Weeden, was married to Governor Robert Patton's oldest daughter, Martha. Their son, John D. Weeden Jr., a Florence Real Estate Agent who died in the 1950s, was the last of the Patton heirs to live at Sweetwater.

Miss Howard Weeden was born in 1847 and died April 12, 1905. Her father, Dr. David Weeden, was a native of Baltimore. After the end of the War of 1812, in which he had served as a Colonel, he established his first plantation, "Weeden Mountain Plantation," now part of the Redstone Arsenal. Miss Howard's mother, Eliza, was a daughter of Dr. David Urqhart, whose ancestors came from the wild mountain country of Cromarty on the boarder of Loch Ness in Scotland. The Weeden townhouse in downtown Huntsville is now the Howard Weeden Museum. During the Civil War, when Huntsville was occupied by federal troops, Miss Howard and her mother and sister were forced to live in the slave quarters at the rear of the mansion.

The enchanting stories about Florence's ante-bellum Sweetwater Plantation will continue to live through the brush and pen of Miss Weeden long after the brick walls of the old mansion have crumbled and fallen into ruins. Miss Howard Weeden was especially fascinated with Edmund, whom she called Uncle Champ. No less than four paintings exist to tell how Edmund risked his life to save the Patton girls, when Sweetwater was invaded and terrorized by General Sherman's soldiers in 1863. In her poem, "The Worst of War," the horrors of Shiloh are recalled when the corpse of young Billy Patton was recovered and carried home by his body servant who was also his boyhood friend. The writer quotes Sam as saying, "I led his horse back home where they sat expecting him- and I saw Mistis and Master's hearts when they broke-that was the worst of war."

In her poem, "The Old Boatman," Miss Howard describes the bond that existed between Governor Patton and his servant who rowed the boat to and from Patton Island where the tall corn grew. After freedom, the old boatman changed his name as so many of the slaves did. Following Governor Patton's death, Old Rome took his former name back. He reasoned that the old Governor has "passed Heaven's River now, and soon he'll call across the foam: Rome, loose your boat and come on home."

Peters, John

John Peters

John Peters was born on August 11, 1801. He married Temperance who was born on October 14, 1784. John was the largest slaveholder in Lauderdale County, Alabama. He lived on Gunwaleford Road, about five miles west of Florence.

According to the Lauderdale County, Alabama, Agricultural Census taken on December 5, 1850, John Peters owned 2,200 acres of improved land and 440 acres of unimproved land valued at $34,000.00. In 1859, Peters was the largest producer of cotton with 681 bales. In addition, he produced 25,000 bushels of corn, 1006 bushels of wheat, 500 bushels of rye, and 11,000 bushels of oats.

According to the 1860, Lauderdale County, Alabama, United States Census, John Peters was living in house number 420. He was listed as a 57 year old male born in Virginia and owned three cotton plantations in Lauderdale County. In 1860, he owned 6,620 acres of land, some 340 black slaves, and a large number of cattle and hogs. In that year, Peters fattened, killed, and salted down 960 hogs which amounted to almost three hogs per person on the plantation.

John Peters of Lauderdale County was one of the wealthiest cotton planters and slave owners in Alabama, but he lived in relatively a simple modest home which was a two story frame house. His plantation home some five miles west of Florence on Gunwaleford Road was the site of a Civil War skirmish.

During the Civil War, the son of James Jackson of the Forks of Cypress Plantation, Confederate Colonel James Jackson Jr. of the Sinks Plantation made a raid from Franklin into Lauderdale County, Alabama. He attempted to end the raiding and plundering of the infamous Union Ninth Infantry of the Ohio Cavalry.

Colonel Jackson's troops rode 150 strong white steeds of that group giving them the name "White Horse Cavalry." Finding the enemy camped on the John Peters Plantation, Jackson's volunteers from the 27th Alabama Infantry routed them, killing two, taking 42 prisoners, and capturing livestock and food stolen from local residents. Jackson's men returned into Franklin but ironically, two Ohio Cavalry members escaped to Florence and the Federals evacuated the city, fearing a large invasion force.

John Peters died on March 14, 1869, and John Peters' wife Temperance Peters died on January18, 1850. According to the family, John and Temperance were buried next to the porch of the Peters plantation home which is no longer standing. It is thought that John Peters' mother is buried in the Peters Cemetery in Lauderdale County, Alabama. The cemetery is predominately a black slave cemetery with only two white burials. The cemetery is located in the southeast ¼ of the northwest ¼ of Section 14 in Township 3 South and Range 12 West.

John L. Webb

John L. Webb was one of a number of hog drivers during pre-Civil War times. He was busy most of the year on his farm in Perry County, Tennessee, fattening large numbers of pigs. Just prior to hog killing weather, which commenced at the first cold spell in November, Webb could be seen with his hired hands driving herds of these animals into Alabama. He counted on the large plantations, such as those that belonged to John Peters and other planters along the Tennessee River, needing extra swine to supplement their own herds. It was sometimes impossible for them to raise enough meat for their families and slave communities.

John L. Webb could count on one planter to purchase hogs that he and his men drove out of Tennessee. That was Mary Coffee, the aged widow of General John Coffee, hero of the War of 1812. The slave population on her plantation dwindled to only twenty by 1860.

In 1925, Barney DePriest of Linden, Tennessee, recalled working as a hog driver for John Webb during those antebellum years. "Just after Christmas we drove to General Coffee's place about three miles north of Florence, killed and salted about 40 or 50, then drove down into what they called Colbert's Reserve and sold out. This was my first trip out of the State of Tennessee."

About 1860, on John L. Webb's last trip to Alabama, he was almost out figured in his financial arrangements by a widow Rogers who lived at what is now known as Colbert's Reserve in West Lauderdale County. This was perhaps the Martha Rogers who, according to the slave census that year, was operating a plantation "by Campbell employers."

DePriest wrote an interesting account of Webb's dealings with the widow Rogers, "…We left home with 150 hogs an went direct to the Reserve, stayed at the widow Rogers there, we killed and sold two days, then moved over about three miles from Gravelly Springs; however, I stayed with Mrs. Rogers with our camp outfit. That old lady was sure boss of her cotton farm, had her own gin and I guess 50 or 60 Negroes working on the farm. The old lady bought about 2,000 pounds of pork and had me in the kitchen helping and showing them how we cooked lard, made sausage in Tennessee, and she talked all the time asking a thousand questions. She sure had a fine dinner and I enjoyed it too. Mr. Webb and the whole crew came in about dark. I had their supper ready. We bundled our outfit and started for home the next morning. Mrs. Rogers came in for settlement, and had her account made out and here is the way it ran: Rent on room 3 days and nights, $5.00; use of water out of pond, 50 cents: use of butcher knife, 20 cents; use of balance for weighing hogs, 24 cents; and the young man's dinner, 50 cents; total, $6.45. I did not say anything then but told Mr. Webb when we got away that he should have charged her $1.00 for my days work."

Barney DePriest, who wrote these accounts when he was seventy-six years old, forgot to mention how much John Webb charged Mrs. Rogers for her 2,000 pounds of pork. He emphasized, however, that "(this) was our last hog driving in Alabama."

Rapier, Richard-Merchant Prince of Cotton

Richard Rapier was known as the Merchant Prince of Cotton. He moved his already expanding trading empire to the new town of Florence at the head of navigation on the Tennessee River about the year 1820. And, Captain Richard Rapier created quite a boom when he did it.

As early as 1807, he was operating out of Nashville. His vans of prairie schooners roved the wilderness to establish trading centers with settlers and Indians. His barges piled the river down to New Orleans to bring back sugar and staples. He made history with one large boat called Rapier's Barge by making the round trip in a record breaking ninety days. This created so much excitement that Nashville gave a public dinner in his honor. Normally, it took four long months to make such a trip.

So, one can readily see what it meant to the developing Town of Florence when the Merchant Prince of Cotton moved his base of operations. Judge William Basil Wood, one of Florence's outstanding citizens, remembered before his death that Rapier established the second house of merchandise on the corner of Court and Tennessee Streets, where a restaurant is now located. He recalled, too, that the first commercial barge to navigate the lower shoals into Florence landing belonged to Richard Rapier.

The Prince erected commodious brick warehouses at the Florence dock. He added to his fleet of keelboats and one of them had the astronomical capacity of hauling ninety tons of cotton! Rapier's boats could transport very large loads containing many bales of cotton grown by the cotton barons of the Tennessee Valley to New Orleans.

For that day and the Town of Florence, there was nothing quite like it. He monopolized the shipping of cotton and other produce to the markets. His prairie schooners operated on both sides of the river to carry his goods into nearby towns and communities and returning farm products to be sent to distant markets. His empire was originally the Richard Rapier Company, and later with a partner, it became the House of Rapier and Simpson.

Richard Rapier was corpulent; he weighed over 200 pounds. He was a bachelor and had an African American housekeeper named Suson; she was born a slave on December 25, 1811, in Baltimore, Maryland. The Rapier home stood at the corner of seminary and Mobile Streets. She had several children probably all by Richard Rapier; among them were Jackson, Alexander, and John.

John Rapier became a free Negro when his father Richard Rapier died. John was a prominent citizen of Florence and was the town's barber for over forty years. He became the founder of a proud Negro lineage of Alabama. One of his sons, Jim Rapier, was elected to the United States House of Representatives from Montgomery on the Republican ticket during Reconstruction.

The old prince of the merchant fleet and prairie schooners died early in January 1826. In his will, he specified that $1,000 be paid to his executors, his bay horse to John Simpson, and "freedom to my mulatto boy John Rapier, who waits on me." As requested, he was buried in his backyard. Today, somewhere under the modern Shoals Theatre is the dust of this wealthy leader of early Florence.

His housekeeper and consort, Suson, lived modestly in wealth until 1841, and to the dismay of her white neighbors, became the first and only Negro buried in the white section of the old Florence Cemetery. Her grave is not difficult to locate. It lies at a peculiar angle among some of Florence's proud first families.

No doubt about it, the Merchant Prince of Cotton who lived in Florence was intelligent, wise, shrewd, clever, crafty, peculiar, impendent, and rich. Regardless of what others may have thought, he always had the last word, even in death.

Rowell, Neal-Alba Wood Plantation

One of the most interesting antebellum cotton farms was Alba Wood Plantation in Colbert's Reserve in west Lauderdale County, Alabama. It was called "Alba Wood," because the name comes from the ancient Celtic, meaning "Wood of Scotland." The old manor house at Alba Wood was on a knoll overlooking its surrounding cotton and corn lands. Its solid brick walls were laid in English bond design, with a cross foundation of yellow poplar logs. The house's most unique architectural features were its crow-step gables with double chimneys at both ends that were an intrinsic part of the wall design. Similar to Wakefield on North Court Street and The Hickory Place on North Pine Street in Florence, Alabama.

Alba Wood was built in the early 1840's by physician, Dr. Neal Rowell. His wife, Martha Ann, had inherited the original 1,000 acres of Alba Wood from her father, Christopher Cheatham, following his death in 1839. In the 1830 slave census of Lauderdale County, Cheatham owned 49 black slaves.

Christopher Cheatham had earlier operated the Twickenham Hotel in Huntsville, Alabama, and was part owner of that city's historic Bell Tavern. In 1824, he moved to Lauderdale County, Alabama, and established a ferry across the Tennessee River at Smithsonia. Cheatham lived in a simple log house which he constructed on his Alba Wood Plantation. He lies buried in an abandoned cemetery on the former grounds of Alba Wood.

According to the 1840 Lauderdale County, Alabama, United States Census, Neal Rowell owned 27 black slaves. In the 1850, Lauderdale County, Alabama, Slave Schedule, Neal Rowell owned 72 black slaves. According to the 1850 Lauderdale County, Alabama, Agricultural Census, Neal Rowell owned 750 acres of improved land and 1890 acres of unimproved land worth $35,000.00.

In the 1860 Lauderdale County, Alabama, Slave Schedule, Neal Rowell owned 89 black slaves. The 1860 census shows the cash value of Alba Wood in excess of $100,000 make its owner one of the four wealthiest planters in the county. There were 90 black slaves living in a community of 21 small cabins on the plantation. In 1860, Alba Wood produced 269 bales of cotton, 6,000 bushels of corn, 500 bushels of wheat, 150 pounds of wool, and 400 pounds of butter.

Dr. Rowell was born in 1796 in what is now Wood County, West Virginia. He was widely known for his cultural interests and had an exceptionally large library at Alba Wood. He was also a delightful conversationalist. One of the things he enjoyed talking about was an old gun which he kept on display in the large entrance hall at Alba Wood. Part of this relic had rusted away. Yet, on the gun's cover was clearly engraved the inscription "Liberty or Death." This antique gun had once belonged to Dr. Rowell's father, Dr. Daniel Rowell, whose wife Nancy was a daughter of Captain James Neal, a Revolutionary War Officer. Captain Neal, whose Irish ancestors spelled their name as O'Neal, had led a party of settlers to the mouth of Little Kanawha River, in Moore County, West Virginia in 1785.

While hunting along this river, Dr. Rowell's father was attacked by hostile Indians. His two companions, including a brother-in-law, Henry Neal, were killed. Dr. Rowell's father escaped by diving into the Little Kanawha River, leaving behind his gun which he had hidden in a hollow log. This gun was discovered 67 years later; its muzzle had been caught in a young Dogwood tree that had taken root where the log had since rotted away.

Dr. Neal Rowell died in 1886 at the age of 90 years. Martha Ann lived until 1890. After they went away, their beloved family home degenerated to a condition that was almost beyond repair. It is gone now, and all that remains of the "Wood of Scotland" is a lonely structure that once stood near the rear of the old manor house.

Simpson, John

Margaret Patton Simpson
9/30/1794-8/22/1851

John Simpson was born on August 17, 1790, in Belfast, Tyrone Ireland. John came to America in 1818, and settled in Florence, Alabama. He became involved in the mercantile business.

After living in Florence for seven years, John Simpson went back to Ireland and married Margaret Patton on October 21, 1824, in Belfast, Tyrone Ireland. They returned to Florence, Alabama. Margaret was born on September 30, 1794, in Belfast, Ireland. John and Margaret Patton Simpson had the following children:

1) Isaac P. Simpson was born on July 26, 1825, and died on June 22, 1841.

2) James Patton Simpson was born on January 21, 1827, and died on August 6, 1924. He married Mary Ann Foster on September 27, 1846; she was the daughter of George Washington and Sarah Independence (Watkins) Foster. Mary Ann was born October 15, 1830, and died March 30, 1853. James and Mary had one daughter, Sarah Foster Simpson (December 16, 1851-May 26, 1852. After the death of Mary Ann, James married Cornelia Foster on July 26, 1855; she was the daughter of Ephraim and Jane Lytle Dickinson Foster. James and Cornelia had a daughter Mary W. Simpson (1864-1956). James and both wives, Mary and Cornelia, are buried at Florence Cemetery.
3) Mary Ann Simpson Walker was born on June 9, 1828, and died in 1911. Mary Ann married Richard Wile Walker (1828-1914).
4) John Cotton Simpson Jr. was born on November 12, 1829, in Lauderdale County, Alabama. He died on July 21, 1861, in the Civil War at the first Battle of Manassas in Virginia. John was a First Lieutenant of the Lauderdale Volunteers, Company H, Fourth Alabama Infantry.
5) William Simpson was born on April 14, 1831, and died on June 3, 1897; he married Clara Adeline Collier, the daughter of Wyatt and Janet (Walker) Collier.
6) Hugh Simpson was born on November 3, 1832, and died on February 19, 1834.
7) Thomas Simpson was born on February 3, 1834, and died on February 3, 1834.
8) Margaret Simpson was born on June 30, 1835;

John Cotton Simpson
8/17/1790-12/13/1865

she married J. Peter Dux.
9) Robert Tennent Simpson was born on June 5, 1837, and he died August 6, 1912. Judge Robert married Margaret Jane Collier; she was born on August 14, 1841, and died on March 20, 1908. Margaret was the daughter of Wyatt and Janet (Walker) Collier.

In the 1840 Lauderdale County, Alabama, United States Census, John Simpson owned 83 black slaves. According to the 1850 Lauderdale County, Alabama Slave Schedule, John Simpson owned 111 black slaves. By the 1860 Lauderdale County, Alabama Slave Census of District Two, John Simpson owned 107 black slaves.

According to the 1850 Lauderdale County, Alabama, Agricultural Census taken on December 13, 1850, John Simpson owned 1,200 acres of improved land and 976 acres of unimproved land worth $28,640.00.

According to the 1850 Lauderdale County, Alabama, United States Census, John Simpson was a 59 year old white male merchant born in Ireland. Also listed in his household was Margaret Simpson a 55 year old female born in Ireland, John Simpson a 20 year old male born in Alabama, William Simpson a 19 year old male born in Alabama, Margaret Simpson a 15 year old female born in Alabama, Robert Simpson a 13 year old male born in Alabama, and Hugh Simpson a 54 year old male born in Ireland (Hugh is most likely a brother to John). John Simpson was listed as a merchant worth $48,640. The 1850 census also gives the household of G.W. and Sarah Foster which includes James Simpson age 23 and Mary Ann (Foster) Simpson age 19.

In the 1860 Lauderdale County, Alabama census, John Simpson is a 69 year old male planter born in Ireland. Also listed in his house number 153 is R. W. Walker a 37 year old male court judge and farmer born in Alabama, John Simpson Jr. a 30 year old male merchant born in Alabama, Mary A. Walker a 30 year old female born in Alabama, Margaret Simpson a 24 year old female born in Alabama, John S. Walker a ten year old male born in Alabama, Margaret P. an eight year old female born in Alabama, and Rich W. Jr. a three year old male born in Alabama.

John Simpson House or Colby Hall, Lauderdale County, Alabama

The historic marker for the "Simpson House-Irvine Place-Colby Hall" has an inscription that reads, "Built by John Simpson in 1843, on the site of his earlier home, this residence was occupied at various times by both armies during the Civil War. The house was purchased in 1867 by George W. Foster, builder of Courtview, for his daughter, Virginia, and her husband, James B. Irvine. Their daughter, Virginia, left the home to her great-niece Harriett Rogers King in 1939. Mrs. King and her husband, Madding, restored Irvine Place in 1948. Acquired in 1990, by David Brubaker, and donated to the University of North Alabama in memory of his wife, Colby Stockard Brubaker. Listed: National Register of Historical Places."

The historic marker is located at Latitude 34° 48.247' North and Longitude 87° 40.838' West. The marker was erected on Pine Street on the Campus of the University of North Alabama by the Florence Historical Board, Florence Alabama.

John Simpson died on December 13, 1865. John is buried in the Florence Cemetery at Florence in Lauderdale County, Alabama (Find a Grave Memorial Number 18747906).

Margaret Patton Simpson died August 22, 1851. Margaret is buried in the Florence Cemetery at Florence in Lauderdale County, Alabama (Find a Grave Memorial Number 18747960).

Simpson House/Colby Hall-1834

Smith, Henry D.

On May 9, 1826, Henry D. Smith married Martha Peters in Greensville, Virginia. In the 1830 Lauderdale County, Alabama, United States Census, Henry Smith owned 105 black slaves. In 1840, there were two Henry Smiths; Henry Smith owned 120 black slaves and Henry D. Smith owned 105 black slaves. In the 1850 Lauderdale County, Alabama, Slave Census, Henry D. Smith owned 137 black slaves. From October 22 through December 19, 1850, M. T. Wilson was the enumerator for the west end of the county.

According to the 1850 Lauderdale County, Alabama, United States Census, Henry D Smith is a 47 year old white male born in Virginia. Also living in house number 769 is Martha Smith a 42 year old female born in Virginia,

Etheldred Smith a 22 year old male born in North Carolina, John Smith a 20 year old male born in North Carolina, Elizabeth Smith an 18 year old female born in Alabama, Martha Smith a 13 year old female born in Alabama, Hanna Smith an 11 year old female born in Alabama, Henry Smith a nine year old male born in Alabama, Caroline Smith a seven year old female born in Alabama, Mary Smith a five year old female born in Alabama, Jerry Smith a two year old male born in Alabama, and Margaret Jalls a 10 year old female born in North Carolina.

By 1850, Henry D. Smith owned 27,875 acres of land in Lauderdale County, Alabama. According to the 1850 Lauderdale County, Alabama, Agricultural Census taken on December 5, 1850, Henry D. Smith owned 1,850 acres of improved land and 26,025 acres of unimproved land worth $43,040.00. Henry D. Smith has the fourth highest farm value in the 1850 Agricultural Census for Lauderdale County, Alabama.

According to the 1860 Western Division of Lauderdale County, Alabama, United States Census, Henry Smith is a 56 year old white male born in Virginia. Also living in the household number 256 is Martha Smith a 51 year old female born in Virginia, Martha Smith a 20 year old female born in Alabama, Henry Smith a 17 year old male born in Alabama, Caroline Smith a 15 year old female born in Alabama, Mary Smith an 11 year old female born in Alabama, Jerry Smith a nine year old male born in Alabama, Margaret Sauls a 17 year old female born in Alabama, and Joseph Phillips a 23 year old male born in North Carolina.

According to the 1860 Largest Slaveholders of Lauderdale County, Alabama, Henry D. Smith owned 54 slaves. His overseer was a man by the name of Burns. Henry D. Smith is also listed in the 1866 Lauderdale County, Alabama, State Census.

The Henry D. Smith Cemetery is located in the southeast ¼ of the southeast ¼ in Section 23 of Township 3 South and Range 12 West in Lauderdale County, Alabama. Internments in the cemetery include:
1) Hamilton F. Smith, 5 Oct 1833, 7 Apr 1835.
2) Hannah D. Smith, 15 Dec 1839, 5 Jun 1865.
3) John H. Smith, 7 Jun 1830, 8 Jun 1851.
4) Absalom C. Smith, 5 Dec 1835, Jul 1836.

5) Henry D. Smith, Sr., 5 May 1803, 25 Dec 1869.
6) Martha P. Smith, 29 Oct 1809, 23 Nov 1868.

Thompson, Joseph

Joseph Thompson was born on May 25, 1788. Joseph married Mary Elizabeth Maverick; Mary Elizabeth Maverick Thompson was born on December 26, 1807, at Charleston in Charleston County, South Carolina. Mary's parents were Samuel Maverick (1772-1852) and Elizabeth Anderson Maverick (1783-1818). Mary had a brother Samuel Augustus Maverick (1803 1870). Mary was married first to Joseph Turpin Weyman (1795-1834), and then she married Joseph Thompson.

Mary had the following children:
1) Elizabeth Anderson Maverick Weyman Houston was born on December 17, 1826, in Anderson County, South Carolina. She was a daughter of Joseph Turpin Weyman and Mary Elizabeth Anderson Maverick Weyman Thompson. She married Dr. Gray Jones Houston (1812-1878); she died on August 15, 1895, in the City Cemetery at San Antonio in Bexar County, Texas (Find a Grave Memorial Number 16319628).

2) Josephine "Joey" Thompson Bryan Hardin was born in 1837; she married William Ferdinand Hardin (1814-1885) on September 18, 1872, in Manhattan, New York, New York. Josephine died on May 2, 1923, and is buried at Rose Hill Cemetery at Columbia in Maury County, Tennessee (Find a Grave Memorial Number 42836200).

The Joseph Thompson estate in the 1850 Lauderdale County, Alabama, Slave Census owned 87 black slaves. On December 13, 1850, the 1850 Lauderdale County, Alabama, Agricultural Census says that the estate of Joseph Thompson had 900 acres of improved land and 1,300 acres of unimproved land worth $44,000.00. This estate had the third highest value during 1850 in Lauderdale County, Alabama.

According to the 1860 Largest Slaveholders in District 2 of Lauderdale County, Alabama, Joseph Thompson owned 106 black slaves. His overseer was J. J. Howell.

Josephine "Joey" Thompson
1837-1923

Joseph Thompson died on January 25, 1849. He is buried in the Florence Cemetery at Florence in Lauderdale County, Alabama (Find a Grave Memorial Number 65525079).

Mary Elizabeth Maverick Thompson died on May 30, 1842; she is buried in the Florence Cemetery at Florence in Lauderdale County, Alabama (Find a Grave Memorial Number 65525234).

Waits, James-Grandfather of T. S. Stribling

Thomas Sigismund Stribling (T. S. Stribling), the 1933 Pulitzer Prize Winner, was born on March 4, 1881, in Clifton, Tennessee. The noted author had special ties to Lauderdale County in northwest Alabama. In 1902 and 1903, he attended Florence Normal College, now the University of North Alabama, where he was an esteemed graduate. Later, he practiced law in Florence for a brief time on Short Court Street, known then as "Intelligence Row," because of the number of attorneys there.

T. S. Stribling's mother was Amelia Ann Waits (9/9/1849-6/7/1927); his maternal ancestors, James and Lydia Waits, were early settlers of Gravelly Springs, located between Florence and Waterloo. James Waits was born November 9, 1801, in South Carolina. James was the son of William and Mary Bright Waits of Newberry District, South Carolina. James married Lydia Wilson; Lydia's parents were William and Elizabeth Darby Wilson.

James Waits met his wife, Lydia Wilson, who was a native of Indiana, in Charleston, South Carolina. Soon after their marriage, they made their way to Alabama. According to the 1860 census, there were four daughters and two sons in the household. According to the 1860 Lauderdale County Slave Schedule, James Waits owned 15 black slaves.

James Waits, a farmer and blacksmith, built his house, not facing the road as did his neighbors, but with its gable end facing the road. He claimed that this was the way the early settlers of South Carolina built their homes. The Waits home was a two-room log house that had been chinked with red clay mud and whitewashed with a solution made of lime and water. James, the builder of the old family home place, was Tom Stribling's grandfather,

Two of James Waits' boys, Shelton Waits and Leonidas Basdale Waits, served as soldiers in the Confederate Army during the Civil War. Leonidas served in the 4th Alabama Cavalry Regiment and later became the captain of the scouts. According to historian Richard Sheridan, when word was received that their regiment had been almost annihilated near Atlanta, Georgia, their older sister, Martha Waits, joined with two other ladies from Gravelly Springs to make the hazardous trip to Georgia to find their loved ones.

Grandma Lydia Waits had not the education to read or write. Yet, this gracious lady was said to have possessed a rare gift of being able to recite poetry and hymns for the younger members of the family.

During his early school days, Tom Stribling made his home with his parents in Clifton. During the summer months he lived with his mother's older sister, Martha Waits, whom he called "Aunt Mom." She made her home in the old Waits place located about two or three miles east of Gravelly Springs near Rhodesville Crossroads.

Tom Stribling was too young to remember his grandmother Lydia Waits who died July 30, 1883, at the age of 79 years. His faint remembrance of his grandfather James Waits was seeing the old gentleman on his bed of affliction during the last years of his life which came to an end on April 4, 1889. Both were buried in the small Cannon Cemetery near their old home place.

Florence, Alabama, was the home of Stribling's favorite uncle and aunt, Lee and Etta Waits, who rented the old Burtwell Place on North Pine Street. Stribling's prize-winning novel, "The Store," and the other two companion books in his popular trilogy, "The Forge" and "Unfinished Cathedral," had their historical and fictional settings in Florence and Lauderdale County, Alabama.

The small Cannon Cemetery near Gravelly Spring, although recently vandalized, speaks softly of T. S. Stribling's ties to Lauderdale County, Alabama, through the legacy of his grandparents, James and Lydia Waits.

Some of the novels written by T. S. Stribling were "Some Bright Metal" (1928), "Strange Moon" (1929), "Clues of the Caribees" (1929), Backwater (1930), "The Forge" (1931), "The Store" (1932), "Unfinished Cathedral" (1934), "The Soundwagon" (1935), and "These Bars of Flesh" (1938). In January 1964 after "The Store" came out in paperback, T. S. Stribling accepted a speaking invitation at the University of North Alabama from English Professor Nickolas Winn. Within a year, T. S. Stribling and his wife moved to Florence, Alabama.

Thomas Sigismund Stribling only lived for a short time in Florence before he died on July 8, 1965. He was carried back to his home town where he was buried. Carved on his gravestone that overlooks Clifton, Tennessee, are these meaningful words, "Through This Dust These Hills Once Spoke" (Find a Grave Memorial Number 57477692).

Weakley, James H.

James Harvey Weakley was born in 1798 in Halifax County, Virginia. His parents, Samuel and Sarah Vaughn Weakley, were of Irish and Welsh lineage. As an infant in 1799, James was brought to Davidson County, Tennessee. Eventually, in 1831, Samuel D. Weakley moved to Lauderdale County, Alabama, where his older brother James resided. According to the 1860 slave census of Lauderdale County, Samuel D. Weakley owned 15 black slaves.

In 1817, James H. Weakley was appointed by General John Coffee as Surveyor General of Alabama Public Lands. He was first assigned to the position in Huntsville, Alabama. James was Surveyor General of Alabama until the office was abolished in 1851.

In 1830, James H. Weakley married Ellen M. Donegan from the City of Cork, Ireland, in Huntsville. After James died, Ellen moved to Nashville, Tennessee, where she spent the remainder of her life.

Prior to moving to Nashville, Ellen had to become a citizen of the United States in order to dispose of the property of her late husband. The following is the

Lauderdale County court record for her obtaining citizenship. "On October 5, 1844, this day, Ellen M. Weakley in open court makes oath that she bona fide intends to become a citizen of the United States and renounces forever all allegiance and fidelity to any foreign prince potentate state or sovereignty whatever and particularly to Victoria Queen of the United Kingdom of Great Britain and Ireland, and her successors in whose dominion she was born and whose subject she now is. She further declares on her oath that she was born in the City of Cork, Ireland, and that she sailed from that city in August 1818 a minor and landed in Philadelphia, State of Pennsylvania, in October following, a minor aged 14 years and has resided in the United States since that period and in the Town of Florence, State of Alabama, for the last fourteen years. Sworn to and subscribed in open court Oct 5th 1844. Ellen M Weakley. Tester R. B. Baugh, Clerk

This day came in open court Ellen M. Weakley who upon oath states that she emigrated to the United States of America from Ireland three years preceding her arrival at Twenty one years of age and that she resided therein three years next preceding her twenty first year and that she hath resided therein up to the present period of time being more than five years and that she has resided in the State of Alabama more than one year prior hereto and that it has been her bona fide intention for three years next preceding the present period of time to become a citizen of the United States and that she doth here now renounce and abjure all allegiance to any foreign Prince power or potentate and particularly to Victoria Queen of the United Kingdom of England, Ireland, and Scotland of whose Kingdom she is a native born subject and that she will hereafter support the constitution of the United States of America.

And it appearing to the satisfaction of the court from the testimony adduced upon this application that the said Ellen M Weakley is a native of Ireland and that she emigrated to the United States of America three years preceding her arrival at twenty one years of age and has resided therein five years previous to this time and has resided in the state of Alabama one year previous to this time and that it has been for three years past bonafide her intention to become a citizen of the United States of America and that during her residence in the United States she has behaved as a person of good moral character attached to the principles of the constitution of the United States. It is therefore ordered by the court that the said Ellen M Weakley be admitted and she is hereby declared to be a citizen of the United States of America with all the rights privileges and immunities thereunto belonging."

After receiving citizenship, Ellen begins the process of selling her deceased husband's estate. According to the Lauderdale County, Alabama, court, accession number 20185810, "Ellen M. Weakley and other executors of the estate of James H. Weakley, deceased, request permission to sell thirty slaves to pay off debts. Most of the other property in the estate consists of stocks, which could not be sold for a profit. The slaves, primarily young children and teenagers, on the other hand, will bring returns "fully up to their market value."

The advertising notice for the sale of James H. Weakley's Estate is given in the Florence Gazette, Friday, November 19, 1858, page 2. "The State of Alabama-Lauderdale County Probate Court, November 3rd, 1858, "Ellen M. Weakley, James J. and James H. Donegan, Executrix and Executors of Ja's H. Weakley, have this day filed in said Court, their petition, representing that the said James H. Weakley departed this life leaving his last will and testament, that the said James H. Weakley left a large personal and real estate; his personal property consisting principally of slaves: That it is necessary to resort to a sale of said personal or real estate, and believing that a sale of a portion of said slaves, would be less injurious to said estate than a sale of the real property, and having no power by the will of their testator to sell said slaves, they therefore file this petition praying an order of the Court, authorizing said sale for the purpose of paying debts. It is therefore ordered that said petition be set for hearing at a term of said Court to be held for said County, at the Court House in the town of Florence, on the 22d day of November, instant: that publication be made in the Florence Gazette, for three consecutive weeks, notifying all persons interested in said Estate, that they may attend on said day and contest said application if they see proper. Attest, W. T. Hawkins. Probate Judge, Nov. 5, 1858."

The sale of James H. Weakley's black slaves is from the Florence Gazette, Friday, November 26, 1858, page 3, "Executors' Sale of Negroes. BY virtue of an order of the Probate Court for the County of Lauderdale and State of Alabama, we will proceed to sell, at public auction, to the highest bidder, at the Court House door, in the town of Florence, on Monday, the 3d day of January, 1859, the following valuable slaves: Harvey, 32 years old; Aleck, 25; Sandy, 36; Martha, 19; Jim, 19; Paralee, 16; Narcissa, 13; Lotty, 52; Robert, 16; Bill, 21; Isaac, 14; Charles, 34; Margaret, 23; Sallie, 3; Becky, 7 months; Mary, 3; Richard, 2; Susan, 22; Walker, 2; Chaney Ann, 18; Charlotte, 3; Anne, 3; Aleck, 4 months; Martha, 36 years; Fanny, 14; Rachel, 11; Kesia, 9 months; Johnny, 9 years; and, Clara ,6 years. Terms-14 months credit with approved security. Ellen M. Weakley, Executrix, James J. Donegan, and James H. Donegan, Executors of James H. Weakley, Nov. 26, 1858."

Wood, Alexander Hamilton

Brigadier General S.A.M. Wood-CSA
3/17/1823-1/26/1891

Alexander Hamilton Wood was the first Worshipful Master of the Florence Masonic Lodge number 14. He is buried in the historic Florence Cemetery. Wood served in this high office in 1821, 1822, and 1823, and again in 1842.

Alexander was born on July 22, 1796, in Richmond County, Virginia. He married Mary Evans Wood (1796-1871). Alexander and Mary had the following children:
1)   Margaret C. Wood Smith was born May 3, 1818; she married John A. Smith. Margaret died on October 4, 1863.
2)   William Basil Wood was born on October 31, 1820, at Nashville in Davidson County, Tennessee. He married Sarah Briscoe Leftwich (1823-1898). William was a Colonel in the 16th Alabama Infantry with the Confederate States of America; he died on April 3, 1891.

3) Sterling Alexander Martin "S.A.M." Wood was born on March 17, 1823, in Florence, Alabama. He married Lelia Elizabeth Leftwich (1825-1891). S.A.M. was a Civil War Confederate Brigadier General; he died on January 26, 1891, at Tuscaloosa in Tuscaloosa County, Alabama.
4) Alexander Hamilton Wood was born on August 25, 1828; he married Mary A. Evans (1826-1867). Alexander died on October 30, 1880.
5) Henry Clay Wood was born on February 5, 1831. He married Sallie Sheppard (1838-1917). Henry Clay Wood was a Major in the 16th Alabama Infantry with the Confederate States of America; he died on December 2, 1906.

According to the 1860 Lauderdale County, Alabama, Slave Schedule, three of the Wood brothers owned 27 black slaves. Alexander Hamiliton Wood owned 11 black slaves, Sterling Alexander Martin Wood owned ten black slaves, and William Wood owned six black slaves.

Alex Wood was also Florence's first mayor, following incorporation of the city in 1826. A native of Richmond, Virginia, and veteran of the War of 1812, Wood arrived in Florence with his family from Nashville in 1821. Wood Avenue, one of the town's major thoroughfares, was named for his oldest son, Judge William Basil Wood. Judge Wood was often referred to as "Mr. Florence," and "Father of East Florence." Alex Wood's father, Leighton Wood, served as secretary to Alexander Hamilton, America's first Secretary of the Treasury.

Alexander Hamilton Wood died on November 15, 1860, in Florence. Mayor Wood's tall memorial obelisk was knocked over and broken a number of years ago by vandals. Under the current

Alabama Statues, grave markers seventy-five years and older are classified as historic and can be restored or repaired with private or public funding if members of the family of the deceased cannot be located.

Old Florence Cemetery

The old Florence City Cemetery remains as one of the most historic treasures in the Muscle Shoals area. General John Coffee's 1818 plans for Florence included provisions for a cemetery "outside the city proper" but inside the legal limits of the town. The original two-acre plot has gradually grown to its present size of about 30 acres.

In the oldest section of the burying ground are a number of unmarked graves of the area's earliest settlers. One of these is thought to be the final resting place of William Garrard Sr., who served in the American Revolution as a private in the Virginia State Troops.

The tombs of a son and a brother of Ferdinand Sannoner, one of the surveyors of Florence, are located in this original two acre plot. Sannoner's work was so appreciated that the directors of the Cypress Land Company gave him the honor of naming the town.

Resources:

1830 Lauderdale County, Alabama, United States Census

1840 Lauderdale County, Alabama, United States Census

1850 Lauderdale County, Alabama Agricultural Census

1850 Lauderdale County, Alabama, Slave Schedule

1860 Lauderdale County, Alabama, United States Census

1860 Lauderdale County, Alabama Slave Schedule

1870 Lauderdale County, Alabama, United States Census

1880 Lauderdale County, Alabama, United States Census

Ahern, L. R. Jr., and Hunt, R. F. Jr., "The Boatyard Store, 1814-1825," Tennessee Historical Quarterly, Volume XIV, March-December 1955.

Bracey, John H., Jr., and Sharon Harley, Editors, "Race, Slavery, and Free Blacks," Series II, Petitions to Southern County Courts, 1775–1867 Part A: Georgia (1796–1867), Florida (1821–1867), Alabama (1821–1867), Mississippi (1822–1867).

Brewer, Willis, "Alabama Trails, History of Lauderdale County, Alabama, Her Resources and History," 1872.

Brown, John P., "Old Frontiers: The Story of the Cherokee Indians from Earliest Times to the Date of Their Removal to the West, 1838," Southern Publishers, Kingsport, Tennessee, 1938.

Carter, Clarence Edwin, "The Territorial Papers of the United States," Volumes IV, V, VI, and XVIII, United States Printing Office, 1936.

Coffee, Eliza, "Eliza Coffee Papers," Coffee High School Library, Florence, Alabama.

Coffee, John, "General John Coffee Papers," Collier Library, University of North Alabama, Florence, Alabama

Cotterill, R.S., "The Southern Indians," University of Oklahoma Press, Norman, Oklahoma, 1954.

Cowart, Margaret Matthews, "Old Land Records of Lauderdale County, Alabama, Huntsville, Alabama, 1996.

Davidson, Donald, "The Tennessee," Volume I, Rinehart and Company Inc., New York, 1946.

Edwards, Cris, and Axford, Faye, "The Lure and Lore of Limestone County," Portals Press, Tuscaloosa, Alabama, 1978.

Find a Grave Memorial, www.findagrave.com

Gaines, George Strother, "Gaines Reminiscences," Alabama Historical Quarterly, Volume XXV, Fall, 1963, pages 206-212.

Gibbs, Lewis C., "The Oats or Newport Plantation," Colbert County, Alabama History, May 2004.

Gibson, Arrell M., "The Chickasaws," University of Oklahoma Press, Norman Oklahoma, 1963

Hathorn, Stacye and Robin Sabino, "Views and Vistas: Traveling Through the Choctaw, Chickasaw, and Cherokee Nations in 1803," The Alabama Review, Volume 54, Number 3, The University of Alabama, July 2001.

"Historic Muscle Shoals: Buildings and Sites," Journal of Muscle Shoals History, Volume X, 1983.

Malone, Henry Thompson, "Cherokees of the Old South: A People in Transition" (1956)

McDonald, William Lindsey, "A Walk Through the Past: People and Places of Florence and Lauderdale County," Bluewater Publishing

McDonald, William Lindsey, "Beginnings of The University of North Alabama, Early Map of North Alabama," Birmingham Publishing Company, 1991

McLoughlin, Wm. G., "Cherokee Renascence in the New Republic." Princeton: Princeton University Press, 1986

Pettus, Ronald, "Journal of Muscle Shoals History," Volume III, 1975.

Pickett, Albert James, "History of Alabama" 1851.

Saunders, James Edmonds, "Early Settlers of North Alabama," Willco Publishing Company, Tuscaloosa, Alabama 1961

Wallace, Harry E., "Lauderdale County, Alabama, History of the Shoals," Times Daily, Thursday, February 25, 1999.

White, Kate, "John Chisholm, A Soldier of Fortune Chronicles of Oklahoma," Volume 8, No. 2, June, 1930.

Woodard, Grace Steele, "The Cherokees," University of Oklahoma Press, 1963.

Index

Adair, James, 28
Adams, John Quincy, 34
Alabama Fever, 40, 74, 92
Alba Wood, 204, 205
Alba Wood Plantation, 204
Alexander, Edward M., 64
Andrews, Gertrude Elizabeth Hannah, 131
Appalachia, 6
Appalachians, 74
Ardoyne, 115, 116
Armistead Cemetery, 80
Armistead Place, 78, 80
Armistead, Elizabeth Coles, 77
Armistead, Elizabeth Virginia, 77
Armistead, Ellen O., 77
Armistead, George, 41, 77, 78
Armistead, Issac Coles, 77
Armistead, John, 75
Armistead, Lewis, 77
Armistead, Martha Henry, 77
Armistead, Mary Ann, 77
Armistead, Nancy, 77
Armistead, Patrick Henry, 77
Armistead, Peter Fontaine, 75, 76, 77, 92
Armistead, Sarah, 77
Armistead, William Bowles, 77
Bailey Springs, 80, 81, 82, 83, 136
Bailey, Frances, 81, 83
Bailey, James J., 83
Bailey, Jonathan, 63, 80, 81, 82, 83, 136
Bailey, Margaret, 80
Bainbridge, 12, 81, 123
Bainbridge Ferry, 12, 81

Baker, Elijah Adam, 84
Baker, James, 84
Baker, Mary Jane, 84
Baylor, Jacob, 63
Bear Creek, 30, 31
Beckwith, Ann, 78, 91
Beckwith, Jonathan, 90
Bee Tree Shoals, 40
Berlin, 6
Bibb, Thomas, 156
Bibb, William W., 81
Big Lick, 25
Big Muscle Shoals, 1, 7, 12, 40, 148
Big Nance, 7, 12, 20
Big Spring, 2, 47
Binford, Hugh, 95, 96, 97, 98
Binford, James A., 95
Binford, James Robert, 99
Binford, John, 95, 96, 97
Binford, John Henry, 95, 97, 98, 99
Binford, L. H., 97
Binford, Mary Susan, 98
Binford, Thomas, 96, 146
Binford, Thomas Albert, 95, 97, 99
Binford, William Cook, 96, 97, 98
Bird Doublehead, 8, 13, 19, 20, 22, 27
black slaves, 74, 75
Black, James, 19, 20
Blood Law, 27
Bloody Fellow, 24
Blount Conspiracy, 46
Blount, William, 42, 43, 46, 47, 54, 56, 108
Bluewater Creek, 4, 5, 7, 9, 10, 12, 13, 14, 15, 20, 25, 27, 56, 67, 148

Bluewater Ferry, 12
Bluewater Oldfields, 15, 25
Boddie, James, 102
Boddie, James Smith, 100
Boddie, Mary Eliza, 100
Boddie, Nathan, 99
Booth, George W., 169
Boudinot, Elias, 27
Bradford, John, 148
Brahan, John, 188, 189, 191, 195
Brandy Station, 76
Brantley, John Harrison, 98
Brantley, Saleta Amanda Penelope, 98
Brickhouse Ford, 126
Broadfoot, Thomas S., 79
Brown, John, 47, 51
Brown, Patsy, 47, 51
Brown, Richard, 47
Brown's Ferry, 10, 47
Brown's Village, 47
Browns Ferry, 2, 7
Buck Key Plantation, 172, 174, 175, 176
Bullen, Joseph, 31
Burwell, William Bell, 98
Bush, George W., 84
Butler, Eliza Eleanor, 61
Butler, Gabriel, 148
Butler, Thomas F., 146
Byler Road, 81
Byler, John, 81
Bynum, Oakley, 179
Cannon Cemetery, 215, 216
Carmack, Cornelius, 63
Carroll, Addison, 84
Carroll, John S., 84
Carroll, Wilson, 84
Casey, Elisabeth Duckett, 104
Casey, Jacob Duckett, 106
Casey, John A., 106
Casey, Levi, 104, 105, 106
Casey, Samuel Otterson, 106
Cassety, Julia Turner, 102
Celtic, 6
Center Star, 14
Chake Thlocko, 40
Charles Town, 28
Chattanooga, 3, 67, 97, 148, 193
Cheatham, Christopher, 205
Cherokee, 6
Cherokees West, 25, 26, 27, 50
Cherry Plantation, 151
Chickamauga, 1, 2, 3, 4, 5, 9, 10, 12, 23,
    24, 25, 26, 32, 34, 40, 45, 47, 48, 53,
    56, 57, 58, 74, 126, 135, 147, 154
Chickasaw, 74
Chisholm Tavern, 43
Chisholm, Dennis, 51, 52
Chisholm, Ignatius, 51, 52
Chisholm, James, 52
Chisholm, Jesse, 51, 52, 56
Chisholm, John D., 5, 19, 20, 22, 23, 42,
    43, 44, 45, 46, 47, 48, 49, 50, 51, 52,
    53, 54, 55, 56
Chisholm, Joseph McHenry, 52, 53, 54
Civil War, 41, 63, 75, 83, 87, 88, 89, 94,
    95, 101, 102, 115, 123, 132, 139, 141,
    142, 145, 149, 151, 152, 153, 166,
    174, 175, 176, 181, 182, 183, 187,
    190, 191, 192, 194, 196, 199, 200,
    201, 207, 209, 215, 221
Clark, Thomas Norris, 19, 20, 22, 23
Clarksville, 4
Cleere, Velma Moore, 182
Clinch River, 74

Cloverdale, 65, 129, 133
Cobb, Jabez, 84
Cockran, John, 134
Coffee, Alexander, 112
Coffee, Alexander Donelson, 108, 115, 131
Coffee, John, 56, 61, 62, 64, 106, 107, 108, 109, 110, 111, 112, 113, 131, 156, 201, 217, 222, 224
Coffee, John R., 106, 107, 112
Coffee, Joshua, 108, 114
Coffee, Mary, 107, 108, 112, 113, 114, 115, 116, 201
Coffee, Virginia Malone, 113
Coffee, William Donelson, 108
Colbert County, 2, 5, 9, 28, 31, 33, 34, 35, 125, 127, 156, 165, 171, 178, 179, 224
Colbert Shoals, 40
Colbert, James Logan, 28, 29, 30
Colbert, Levi, 38
Colbert, William, 32
Colbert's Ferry, 1, 28, 34, 35, 37
Colbert's Old Reserve, 100, 101
Colbert's Reserve, 1, 37, 93, 99, 102, 116, 201, 202, 204
Colberts Island, 35
Colby Hall, 122, 209
Coldwater, 2, 109
Collier, Alice Walker, 119
Collier, Henry W., 117
Collier, James, 117
Collier, Wyatt, 116, 117, 118, 119, 120, 145
Conner, Joseph Cable, 173
Cotton Gin Port, 38
Cotton Gin Treaty, 17

Coulter, George, 63, 122
Courtland, 47, 62, 126, 194
Cox Creek, 66, 110
Cox, Laura E., 131
Craig, John, 63
Craig, Samuel, 63, 81
Creek Indian War, 47, 109
Crittenden, William H., 147
Croft, Samuel, 84
Cumberland Settlements, 3
Cunningham, Mattie Moore, 182
Cypress Cotton Mill, 102, 184
Cypress Creek, 1, 5, 6, 22, 23, 48, 65, 66, 67, 76, 106, 154, 157, 168
Cypress Land Company, 110, 156, 222
Cypress Mill, 65, 168
Darby, Josephus, 116
Dardanelle Rock, 26
Davis, Thomas Culver, 106
Deaf and Dumb Institute of Hartford, 99
Dearborn, Henry, 11, 48, 50
Deford, Risden, 65, 183
DePriest, Barney, 201, 202
Devils Backbone, 33
Dinsmoore, Silas, 16
Donegan, Ellen M., 217
Donegan, James H., 219, 220
Donelson, John, 56, 57, 59, 60, 61, 62, 108, 113
Donelson, Mary, 108, 113
Doublehead, 3, 1, 2, 3, 4, 5, 6, 7, 8, 9, 10, 11, 12, 13, 14, 15, 16, 17, 18, 19, 20, 21, 22, 23, 24, 25, 26, 27, 28, 32, 33, 34, 35, 40, 42, 45, 47, 48, 49, 51, 52, 53, 54, 56, 57, 58, 81, 127, 135, 147, 148, 154, 163

Doublehead's Reserve, 1, 5, 6, 13, 22, 48
Dowdy, Rufus B., 164
Dragging Canoe, 24, 58
Driskell, Boyce, 172
Duckett, John, 106
Dugan, Thomas, 105
Durett, Francis, 63
Duwali, 24, 58
Eagle Cotton Mill, 67
Elgin, 14, 149, 150
Elk River, 1, 2, 5, 6, 22, 23, 40, 48, 57, 178
Elk River Shoals, 1, 40
Ellis, A. G., 83
Finley, Bird Moore, 182
Florence, 10, 16, 31, 32, 42, 51, 53, 54, 55, 56, 61, 62, 63, 65, 66, 67, 76, 77, 78, 79, 84, 85, 87, 90, 99, 100, 101, 102, 104, 109, 110, 112, 113, 115, 116, 117, 118, 119, 120, 121, 122, 123, 124, 125, 126, 127, 128, 129, 130, 131, 132, 136, 138, 139, 149, 151, 152, 153, 157, 159, 161, 162, 170, 171, 172, 173, 174, 176, 183, 184, 185, 187, 189, 190, 191, 193, 194, 195, 196, 197, 198, 199, 200, 201, 202, 203, 204, 206, 207, 209, 213, 214, 216, 217, 218, 219, 220, 221, 222, 224, 225
Florence Canal, 195
Florence Guards, 189
Forks of Cypress, 5, 99, 116, 150, 151, 153, 154, 156, 157, 158, 159, 161, 162, 163, 164, 200
Fort Donelson, 152
Fort Henry, 127
Fort Towson, 1, 35, 38
Foster, George, 126
Foster, George W., 41, 122, 209
Foster, George Washington, 122
Foster, James, 126
Foster, Robert Coleman, 126
Foster, Thomas Jefferson, 126
Foster's Mill, 127
Foutch, Ina, 66
Fox's Creek, 2, 40, 57
Franklin, Jesse, 36
French Lick, 25, 56
Fuqua, John, 146
Fuqua, Julia A., 146
Garrard, Thomas, 63
George Colbert, 3, 1, 2, 5, 28, 30, 31, 32, 33, 34, 35, 36, 37, 38, 40, 99, 116, 165, 171
Georgia Road, 9
Glen Ella, 76, 79
Glenco, 177, 179
Glenco Plantation, 179
Glencoe, 158, 159, 160, 161
Globe Cotton Factory, 65
Gourd's Settlement, 47
Gravelly Springs, 84, 85, 87, 92, 93, 138, 139, 140, 143, 144, 145, 202, 214, 215
Gray, Young A., 78
Green Bluff, 12, 13
Green Onion Plantation, 126
Gulustiyu, 9
Gunwaleford Road, 67, 171, 200
Hale, Joshua S., 133
Haley, Queen Jackson, 151
Hannah, Alex, 129, 132

Hannah, Alexander John William, 130, 133
Hannah, Malcolm H., 131
Hannah, Sarah, 130
Hannah, William Cox, 131
Haraway, Susan, 95, 97
Haraway, Walter, 146
Harkins, Samuel, 63
Harlan, John Marshall, 123, 124
Harris, Cyrus, 30
Harris, Peter, 64
Harvey, James, 64
Henderson, Martha, 64
Hendrix, Larkin, 133
Henley, David, 7
Herald, Frances, 80
Herman, Alexander, 64
Hickory Hill Plantation, 62, 106, 110, 115
Hicks, Robert, 64
High Town Path, 28
Hightower, Harriett, 85
Hightower, Jane S., 85
Hiwassee Garrison, 8, 11, 20, 25, 48
Hodges, Henry, 64
Holland, Thomas, 64
Holleman, William M., 135
Hollingsworth, David Wills, 129
Holmes, Martha, 51
Hood, John Bell, 123, 152, 195
Horseshoe Bend, 67, 108, 109
Hostler's Mill, 67
Hough, Allen J., 133
Hough, David, 134
Hough, John, 133, 135, 136
Hough, John Reeves, 134, 137
Hough, Joseph, 64, 82, 133, 134, 135, 136, 137
Hough, Pleasant James, 134
Hough, William, 133, 135, 136
Houston, David, 138, 141, 142, 144
Houston, David Ross, 138, 140, 142, 144
Houston, George S., 63, 143, 144
Houston, George Smith, 141
Houston, Gray Jones, 141, 212
Houston, John Pugh, 140
Houston, Russell, 141, 143
Houston, William Ross, 140
Howell, Levi, 64
Hunt, James, 64
Huntsville, 47, 67, 81, 84, 85, 86, 97, 109, 148, 171, 189, 190, 194, 197, 198, 199, 205, 217
Hutchings, John, 64
Indian, 6
Ingram, Benjamin, 146, 147
Ingram, George, 148
Ingram, George M., 146
Ingram, Moses, 146, 147, 148, 149
Ingram, Sarah, 147
Ingrams Crossroads, 149
Ireland, 114, 120, 124, 140, 154, 155, 156, 166, 167, 168, 170, 172, 189, 206, 208, 217, 218
Irion, Phillip Jacob, 140
Irions, Jane Houston, 144
Irvine Place, 209
Irvine, James B., 122, 209
Irvine, James Bennington, 122, 124
Jackson, Andrew, 32, 36, 47, 56, 61, 85, 107, 108, 112, 115, 151, 152, 157, 178, 195

Jackson, George Moore, 152, 157
Jackson, James, 5, 63, 99, 116, 145, 150, 151, 152, 153, 154, 155, 156, 157, 158, 159, 160, 161, 162, 163, 164, 200
Jackson, James Kirkman, 151, 153
Jackson, Rachel, 61, 108, 113
Jackson, Robert, 148
Jackson, Sarah, 41, 115, 155, 162
Jackson, William B., 151
Jackson, William Moore, 152, 157
Jackson's Military Road, 12, 96
Jackson's Old Military Road, 81
Jefferson, Thomas, 25, 27, 48, 126, 127
Jones, Albert H., 100, 102
Jones, Emmitt Lee, 102
Jones, Francis F., 166
Jones, James, 172
Jones, James Carey, 166
Jones, Lulie, 101, 102
Jones, Mary Philippa, 102
Jones, Percy Rivers, 102
Jones, Rebecca Boddie, 100, 102
Jones, William, 171
Jubilee Day, 197
Kattygisky, 24, 126
Kattygisky's Spring, 127
Keller, David, 178, 179
Keller, Helen, 178, 179
Kennedy, Hiram, 96
Kennedy, John, 64
Kernachan Plantation, 165
Kernachan, Abraham, 165, 166, 167, 168, 172
Kernachan, Robert, 171
Kernachan, Robert Thomas, 166, 167, 168, 170
Kernachan, William J., 171
Key, William, 172
Key, William H., 41, 172, 173, 174, 175, 176
Key, William Henry, 172, 173, 176
Kirk, Allen, 142
Kirkman, Thomas, 160
Knoxville, 7, 22, 42, 43, 45, 125, 179
Labadie, Silbestre, 29
Lacy, Theophilus, 96
Lamb, James, 141
Lamb, John, 142
Lauderdale County, 3, 1, 2, 4, 5, 6, 7, 10, 12, 14, 15, 25, 27, 28, 36, 37, 40, 41, 42, 48, 51, 52, 53, 54, 56, 57, 61, 62, 63, 64, 65, 66, 67, 75, 76, 77, 78, 79, 81, 82, 83, 84, 85, 86, 88, 89, 91, 92, 93, 94, 95, 96, 97, 99, 100, 101, 102, 103, 104, 106, 110, 112, 113, 114, 115, 116, 118, 119, 120, 122, 123, 126, 127, 129, 130, 131, 133, 134, 135, 136, 137, 138, 140, 141, 142, 143, 144, 145, 147, 150, 151, 153, 154, 156, 157, 158, 160, 161, 162, 165, 166, 167, 168, 170, 171, 172, 173, 174, 175, 176, 180, 181, 183, 184, 186, 187, 188, 190, 191, 192, 193, 200, 201, 202, 204, 205, 207, 208, 209, 210, 211, 213, 214, 216, 217, 218, 219, 221, 223, 225
Lawson, Rachel, 106
Leftwich, Lelia Elizabeth, 221
Little Cypress, 66, 67, 154, 157
Little Muscle Shoals, 40
Loretta, 12
Lower Cherokees, 2, 3, 24, 26, 40, 48, 57

Lucas, Jane Moore, 182
Madison Rifles, 97
Major Ridge, 24, 25, 27
Malone House, 126, 128
Malone, John Nicholas, 167
Mapleton, 121, 122, 123, 124, 131
Maplewood Cemetery, 126
Mars Hill, 180, 181, 182, 183
Mars Hill Plantation, 180, 181
Mason, Almon H., 85
Maud Lindsay Free Kindergarten, 101
McArthur, Douglas, 185
McCleish, John, 38
McDonald, James, 178, 179
McDonald, John, 3
McFarland Bottoms, 124
McFarland Park, 124
McFarland, Kate Armistead, 125
McFarland, Robert, 124
McGee, Malcolm, 28
McGillivray, Alexander, 29, 44
McHenry, James, 7, 43, 54
McKight, William, 66
McKinley, John, 63, 64, 122, 156
McLaren, James, 135
McNutt Cemetery, 23
McVay, Atlantic Pacific, 181
McVay, Hugh, 63, 158, 180, 181, 182
Meigs, Return J., 11, 12, 16, 26, 31, 47, 49, 50
Melrose, 77
Melton, John, 1, 4, 17, 23
Melton's Bluff, 2, 4, 17, 23, 57, 109
Merchant Prince of Cotton, 202
Meriwether, David, 36
Mississippi River, 1, 25, 26, 27, 29, 35, 48, 50, 52, 53, 109

Mitchell, William H., 123
Moody, Henry A., 83
Moore, Albert Howe, 182
Moore, Claude Lillard, 182
Moore, Hugh McVay, 181
Moore, James K. Polk, 181
Moore, James Thomas, 182
Moore, John E., 64
Moore, Lewis Capit, 181, 182, 183
Moore, Samuel H., 182
Morgan, John Hunt, 125
Morgan's Raiders, 124
Mouse Town, 2
Murdock, James, 173, 176, 177
Muscle Shoals, 2, 5, 6, 9, 10, 11, 12, 17, 19, 20, 21, 22, 25, 32, 40, 41, 45, 47, 48, 51, 52, 56, 57, 59, 60, 61, 62, 67, 75, 84, 88, 92, 128, 129, 131, 165, 178, 183, 194, 195, 222, 224, 225
Natchez District, 74
Natchez Trace, 1, 9, 10, 16, 28, 31, 34, 108, 116, 134, 138
New Orleans, 8, 62, 108, 109, 193, 203
Nichols Hill, 184, 185
Nichols, John Martin, 184
Nichols, Reeder, 184, 185
Nichols, William Thomas, 184
Nigodigeyu, 9
Noel, James, 186
Noel, James Alexander, 186
Noel, Samuel, 186
North Carolina, 74
North River Road, 15, 16, 148
Nutt, Rush, 30
O'Neal, Edward Asbury, 115
Oakland Community, 37
Old Settlers, 25, 26, 27, 50

Old Tassel, 3, 52
O'Neal, William, 151
Oppenheimer, Louise Lacy Binford, 99
Otali, 47
Page, James, 134
Park, Wiley, 66
Patton Island, 184, 187, 194, 195, 199
Patton, Charles Hays, 189
Patton, Robert, 187
Patton, Robert Miller, 124, 188, 189, 190, 191, 192, 193, 194
Perry, Frank M., 176
Peters, John, 41, 200, 201
Philadelphia, 3, 12, 34, 44, 45, 155, 166, 168, 193, 218
Phillips, Joseph, 19, 20, 22
Plumbtree Island, 28
Pope, John, 63, 192
Pope, LeRoy, 156
Pope's Tavern, 159
Priber, Christian G., 34
Price, Susan, 101
Probasco, Catherine Hightower, 85
Probasco, Samuel, 85
Prosser, Loulie Moore, 182
Pumpkin Boy, 3, 13, 17, 18
Purnell, Mary, 61, 108
Rapier, Jim, 204
Rapier, John, 204
Rapier, Richard, 202, 203
Rawhide, 65
Red River, 1
Redding, William James, 66
Reese, Washington, 133
Rhodes, Jacob, 106
Rhodesville, 85, 87, 215
Richard Rapier Company, 203

Ridge, John, 27
Riley, John, 23
Riley, Samuel, 9, 19, 20, 22, 23
Riverton, 67
Robertson, James, 2, 59, 60
Rogers Hall, 122
Rogers, John, 24, 25
Rogers' Ville, 2, 16
Rosemont Plantation, 126
Rowell, Neal, 41, 204, 205, 206
Royall, Anne, 17
Saleechie, 2, 33, 35
Saunders, Alex, 24, 25
Scots Irish, 6
Second Creek, 67
Sevier, John, 3, 42, 44
Sevier, Joseph, 4
Sevier, Valentine, 3
Sharp's Mill, 67
Sherrod, Benjamin, 194
Shoal Creek, 123, 136
Shoal Town, 2, 7, 8, 10, 11, 12, 14, 16, 25, 27, 127, 148
Shoals Creek, 66, 67, 81, 134, 135, 136
Simmons, William, 45
Simpson, Hugh, 207, 208
Simpson, Isaac P., 206
Simpson, James, 32, 126, 208
Simpson, James Patton, 207
Simpson, John, 41, 118, 189, 204, 206, 208, 209
Simpson, Margaret Patton, 206, 209
Simpson, Robert Tennent, 118, 208
Simpson, William, 118, 119, 120, 207, 208
Skipworth Mill, 168
Sloss, Ann Eliza, 115

Sloss, Joseph H., 131
Smith, Henry, 63, 91, 93, 210, 211
Smith, Henry D., 41, 64, 210, 211, 212
Smith, John A., 220
Smith, Jonathan, 78
Smith, Mary Thomas, 99
Smithsonia, 166, 205
Snyder, Charles, 4
Soldier's Wife, 6
South River Road, 9
Southwest Point, 9, 20, 22, 23, 74
Spencer, Catherine, 13, 14, 17, 22
Stanton, Martha L., 95
Starr, Caleb, 13, 20, 22
Stewart, Bettie, 177
Stewart, Elizabeth, 173
Stockley, Rachel, 60
Stribling, T. S., 213, 214, 216, 217
Swaney, John, 33
Sweetwater, 93, 124, 187, 188, 190, 192, 195, 196, 197, 198, 199
Sweetwater Plantation, 124, 187, 188, 199
Tahlontuskee, 26
Tate Springs, 81
Tate, John S., 81, 135
Tate, Milly, 81
Tellico Block House Treaty, 6
Tennessee Militia, 108
Tennessee River, 1, 2, 5, 6, 7, 9, 10, 11, 12, 13, 14, 20, 22, 23, 25, 28, 30, 31, 34, 35, 36, 37, 38, 40, 47, 48, 53, 57, 58, 62, 63, 67, 74, 81, 86, 116, 118, 121, 123, 127, 136, 138, 148, 149, 165, 172, 187, 194, 195, 201, 202, 205
Tennessee Valley Authority, 66

The Glass, 24
The Oaks Plantation, 116, 118, 120
The Sinks Plantation, 150, 151, 153
Thompson, Joseph, 212
Todd's Hill, 123
Tombigby River, 38
Tootemastubbe, 30
Town Creek, 2, 7, 12, 126, 127
Treaty of Sycamore Shoals, 74
Tripoli, 6
Truitt, Ann Eliza Binford, 99
Turkey Town, 74, 75
Turkey Town Treaty, 37, 40, 52, 63, 74, 157, 165
Tuscumbia, 2, 31, 56, 62, 101, 109, 128, 178, 179
Tuskiahooto, 2, 33, 34, 35
Twickenham Hotel, 205
Uncle Champ, 195, 196, 197, 199
Upper Creeks, 3
Vann, James, 24, 33
Virginia, 74
Waits, James, 214, 215
Walker, James, 118
Walker, Janet, 117, 118, 119, 120
Walker, Joel, 50
Walker, Richard Wile, 207
Walker, Rickey Butch, 6
Warrior Mountains, 6
Washington, George, 3, 4, 34, 38, 44, 45, 60, 77, 117, 126, 169, 207
Waterloo, 40, 57, 63, 67, 79, 87, 92, 138, 139, 214
Waterloo Shoals, 40
Watkins, Robert H., 41, 126
Watkins, Virginia Prudence, 126
Watson, Charles McAlpin, 174

Watts, John, 24
Weakley, Ellen M., 218, 219, 220
Weakley, James H., 109, 217, 219, 220
Weakley, James Harvey, 217
Weakley, Samuel, 195
Webb, John L., 201, 202
Weeden Mountain Plantation, 199
Weeden, Howard, 197, 198, 199
Weeden, John, 189
Weeden, John D., 198
Wesson, Harry John, 183
Wheeler, Joseph, 194
White Horse Cavalry, 152, 200
White, Daniel, 16, 148
Wildwood Plantation, 138, 139, 141, 142, 144
Wilkinson, James, 108
Williams, Henry, 141
Williams, Isaac B., 166, 171
Wilson, James Harrison, 139
Wilson, Kateeyeah, 21
Wilson, Patrick, 9, 10
Winston, Isaac, 76, 92
Winston, Martha Henry, 75, 78, 92
Wolf Creek, 35
Wood, Alex, 221
Wood, Alexander, 220
Wood, Alexander Hamilton, 220, 221
Wood, Henry Clay, 221
Wood, S. A. M., 64
Wood, S.A.M., 221
Wood, Sterling A. M., 66
Wood, Sterling Alexander Martin, 221
Wood, William Basil, 203, 220, 221
Young, Samuel, 63

www.ingramcontent.com/pod-product-compliance
Lightning Source LLC
Chambersburg PA
CBHW050458110426
42742CB00018B/3302